Rethinking the North American Long Poem

Recencies Series: Research and Recovery in Twentieth-Century American Poetics
Matthew Hofer, Series Editor

This series stands at the intersection of critical investigation, historical documentation, and the preservation of cultural heritage. The series exists to illuminate the innovative poetics achievements of the recent past that remain relevant to the present. In addition to publishing monographs and edited volumes, it is also a venue for previously unpublished manuscripts, expanded reprints, and collections of major essays, letters, and interviews.

Also available in the Recencies Series:

Thinking with the Poem: Essays on the Poetry and Poetics of Rachel Blau DuPlessis edited by Andrew R. Mossin

"A Serpentine Gesture": John Ashbery's Poetry and Phenomenology by Elisabeth W. Joyce

Amiri Baraka and Edward Dorn: The Collected Letters edited by Claudia Moreno Pisano

Yours Presently: The Selected Letters of John Wieners edited by Michael Seth Stewart

All This Thinking: The Correspondence of Bernadette Mayer and Clark Coolidge edited by Stephanie Anderson and Kristen Tapson

Geopoetry: Geology, Materiality, Ecopoetics by Dale Enggass

Ingenious Pleasures: An Anthology of Punk, Trash, and Camp in Twentieth-Century Poetry edited by Drew Gardner

A Description of Acquaintance: The Letters of Laura Riding and Gertrude Stein, 1927–1930 edited by Jane Malcolm and Logan Esdale

Evaluations of US Poetry since 1950, Volume 1: Language, Form, and Music edited by Robert von Hallberg and Robert Faggen

Evaluations of US Poetry since 1950, Volume 2: Mind, Nation, and Power edited by Robert von Hallberg and Robert Faggen

For additional titles in the Recencies Series, please visit unmpress.com.

Rethinking the North American Long Poem

Form, Matter, Experiment

Edited by **RIDVAN ASKIN**
and **JULIUS GREVE**

University of New Mexico Press — Albuquerque

© 2024 by the University of New Mexico Press
All rights reserved. Published 2024
Printed in the United States of America

ISBN 978-0-8263-6710-5 (cloth)
ISBN 978-0-8263-6711-2 (paper)
ISBN 978-0-8263-6712-9 (ePub)
ISBN 978-0-8263-6713-6 (pdf)

Library of Congress Control Number: 2024946016

Founded in 1889, the University of New Mexico sits on the traditional homelands of the Pueblo of Sandia. The original peoples of New Mexico—Pueblo, Navajo, and Apache—since time immemorial have deep connections to the land and have made significant contributions to the broader community statewide. We honor the land itself and those who remain stewards of this land throughout the generations and also acknowledge our committed relationship to Indigenous peoples. We gratefully recognize our history.

Cover image and design by Isaac Morris
Composed in Garamond Premier Pro

Contents

Acknowledgments   vii

Introduction.
    Form, Matter, Experiment, and the North American Long Poem   1
      Ridvan Askin and Julius Greve

PART I.   **FORM**

Chapter One.
    Assemblage as a Genre of the Long Poem   39
      Rachel Blau DuPlessis

Chapter Two.
    Incompleteness: The Project of the Long Poem   56
      Nathan Brown

Chapter Three.
    "A Restless Surface": Everyday Phenomenology in James Schuyler's Long Poems   79
      Matthew Carbery

PART II.   **MATTER**

Chapter Four.
    Matter, Rhetoric, and Ambient Form in Susan Howe's Poetic Space   107
      Brian J. McAllister

Chapter Five.
    Paterson's Analogies: Iteration, Recursion, and Contingency   130
      Paul Jaussen

Chapter Six.
    Against Spectatorship: "Being with" in Claudia Rankine's Long Poems   149
      Kathy Lou Schultz

PART III.   **EXPERIMENT**

Chapter Seven.
   The Paradise of *Rock-Drill*: Far-Right Politics in the Late Cantos
   of Ezra Pound   181
      Josephine Nock-Hee Park
Chapter Eight.
   Petitionary Long Poems: Layli Long Soldier, Juliana Spahr,
   and Srikanth Reddy   201
      Peter Middleton
Chapter Nine.
   Whitman's Long, Long Poem   232
      Sascha Pöhlmann

Contributors   259

Acknowledgments

The editors would like to thank all contributors for their commitment, patience, and intellectual generosity: Nathan Brown, Matthew Carbery, Rachel Blau DuPlessis, Paul Jaussen, Brian J. McAllister, Peter Middleton, Josephine Nock-Hee Park, Sascha Pöhlmann, and Kathy Lou Schultz. We would also like to thank the following individuals without whom this volume would not be what it is: Kathrin Eckerth, Michaela Frey, Joana Gut, Melanie Küng, Thomas Manson, Sofie Sabbioni, and Philipp Schweighauser. Thanks are also due to the two reviewers of the manuscript for their thoughtful and engaging comments: Michael Leong and a second reader who preferred to remain anonymous. Hanna Riggert, Stella Marleen Greve, and Jonah Henri Greve: thank you for your support and inspiration, your patience and trust. Finally, we would like to thank Drew Bryan for the lightning fast and careful copy editing and Matthew Hofer, Elise McHugh, and the editorial staff at the University of New Mexico Press for their encouragement, guidance, and professional diligence.

Rachel Blau DuPlessis's chapter has been previously published in different form in her book *A Long Essay on the Long Poem: Modern and Contemporary Poetics and Practices* (2023). We are grateful to Rachel and the University of Alabama Press for granting permission to use this content for the present volume. Permission gratefully acknowledged, © Rachel Blau DuPlessis and the University of Alabama Press.

Introduction

Form, Matter, Experiment, and the North American Long Poem

Ridvan Askin and Julius Greve

> The United States themselves are essentially the greatest poem.
> —Walt Whitman, *Leaves of Grass*

> You might want more poem the same way you might want more time.
> —Rachel Blau DuPlessis, "After the Long Poem"

Given that both the variegated literary-historical trajectory and the typically incoherent character of the North American long poem are marked by detours and digressions, let these two neatly epigraphical statements sit for a while. Instead, let us begin with a different but related topic and consider how French philosopher Gilles Deleuze conceives of the reciprocal influence of literature and life in the eponymous short essay that opens his *Essays Critical and Clinical*. Going beyond any straightforwardly psychoanalytical or phenomenological reading of this relation, Deleuze begins his essay with the following observation: "To write is certainly not to impose a form (of expression) on the matter of lived experience. Literature rather moves in the direction of the ill-informed or the incomplete [. . .]. Writing," he maintains, "is a question of becoming, always incomplete, always in the midst of being formed, and goes beyond the matter of any livable or lived experience."[1] Even though Deleuze does not discuss the long poem per se in "Literature and Life," nor anywhere else in his *Essays* (although there are unique remarks on Walt Whitman's work as a whole), these initial statements quite neatly describe, we feel, the key aspects of this equally chided and appraised phenomenon in literary history: Hijacking

Deleuze for our purposes, we want to suggest that his remarks encapsulate the irreducible entanglement of form, matter, and experiment that define the North American long poem from the mid-nineteenth century onward.

For centuries, critics, poets, poet-scholars, and philosophers have either openly proclaimed or tacitly assumed the long poem as the highest expression of literary ambition and excellence, particularly in its epic guise. Following in the footsteps of recently reawakened scholarly interest, this volume focuses on the North American variant of this notorious poetological form, notorious because of its often forbidding and difficult character, particularly with respect to the dialectics of content and form, of aesthetics and politics, and of matter and genre. The authors featured in this book aim to scrutinize questions such as the following: Does the "long" in long poem refer to the temporality of composition, the duration of reading, or simply the length of form irrespective of compositional and perceptual duration? Is there a specific aesthetics entailed by the length of the long poem? If so, what are its affordances? Does it tend to correlate with a specific genre? In other words, "When does a poem become long? What does length do, and how does it go about doing it?"[2] What constitutes a long poem apart from its sheer length? Which themes and issues are discussed both in seminal long poems by North American writers—such as Whitman's "Song of Myself," Ezra Pound's *The Cantos*, Muriel Rukeyser's *The Book of the Dead*, and Charles Olson's *The Maximus Poems*—and in more recent efforts that have redefined or, better still, reopened the case of the long poem, such as Rachel Blau DuPlessis's *Drafts*, M. NourbeSe Philip's *Zong!*, and Nathaniel Mackey's *Double Trio*? Has the once crucial opposition between mythology and history waned as a conceptual backdrop in recent long poems, or have contemporary writers merely reframed its contours in light of pressing social, political, and media-technological issues?

Genealogies of this peculiar literary form that focus on the North American context tend to adhere to the American "origin story" of the emergence of free verse, which, again and again, has been located (problematically, for many reasons) in Whitman's 1855 edition of *Leaves of Grass*. In this account, following on from Whitman, the North American long poem comes into its own in the twentieth century. Yet there are, of course, North American long poems before *Leaves of Grass*. If we loosely define this form as a unit of verse—metered or not—that extends over the space of a given number of pages, then eminent pre-Whitmanian examples would include poetry by the Transcendentalists and the Fireside Poets, to mention just the most obvious practitioners. But if we take the long poem, with Deleuze, as a poem in which literature and life are correlated in and through the interplay of form, matter, and experiment, then it is arguably indeed a (post-)Whitmanian phenomenon. This is also why the majority of the efforts to rethink the North American long poem in this volume focus on twentieth- and twenty-first-century authors. Coincidentally, Deleuze too, in his short essay on Whitman, seems to suggest the adequacy of such a privileging as his description of the American bard's poetics very much reads like a poetics of the North American long poem after 1900, or better still, 1922: "The world as a collection of heterogeneous parts: an infinite patchwork, or an endless wall of dry stones (a cemented wall, or the pieces of a puzzle, would reconstitute a totality). The world as a *sampling:* the samples ('specimens') are singularities, remarkable and nontotalizable parts extracted from a series of ordinary parts. Samples of days, *specimen days.*"[3]

In this perspective, the long poem after Whitman is a nontotalizable, essentially incomplete, infinite patchwork of heterogeneous parts. Apart from singling out Whitman as the proper point of departure and model for a form of poetry that comes to fruition in the twentieth century (although it must be conceded that seminal figures like T. S. Eliot and Pound repeatedly tried to dismiss Whitman's influence on and importance for their work), extant genealogies of the North American long poem also emphasize its gendered nature: According to Susan Stanford Friedman, for example, "as a descendant of the epic and the autobiographical long poems of William Wordsworth and Walt Whitman, the twentieth-century long poem has been a defining genre for male poets—from the modernists through the 'confessionals' and the postmodernists."[4] The apparent masculinism of the long poem is a recurrent theme in the scholarship, and it already shines through in Whitman's own, oft-cited conception of America as "essentially the greatest poem,"[5] in its claim to unsurpassable greatness, its muscularity, and its desire for ineffable expansiveness. While traditionally, the long poem qua descendant of the epic has been conceived as the mode supposedly reserved for male poets, women writers have been primarily linked, ever since Sappho, to the lyric. And yet, as Friedman, DuPlessis, and others have observed, the history of the North American long poem since Whitman is also a history of revision and rewriting.[6] If the long poem is uniquely suited to exploring the correlations of literature and life, then such rewriting essentially amounts to exposing and foregrounding certain relations that otherwise tend to be obscured in masculinist grandstanding.

In this sense, the title of H.D.'s *The Walls Do Not Fall* can well be read as a comment on the male-centered "infinite patchwork" of the "endless wall" constituted by the major tradition of long form poetics.[7] By extension, the same holds true for contributions by other marginalized communities, as recent recovery work has made eminently clear.[8]

Lynn Keller, too, notes the long poem's relation to "traditional epic" poetry, but she also importantly mentions the near-paragonic relationship of this form to the cultural dominance of narrative fiction: "Particularly in the aftermath of World War I, the Modernists' desire to reclaim for poetry the range and significance it had ceded to the novel—a breadth of subject and discursive scope that would insure poetry's social relevance—led them to invent extended forms, usually with some qualities of traditional epic in mind."

According to her, there are "three sometimes overlapping chronological divisions" of the twentieth-century long poem in the United States: "The first, in which collage-based texts dominate, extends from the first flowering of the Modernist long poem in the early 1920s through the late long poems of the High Modernists published after World War II," namely, from Eliot's *The Waste Land* to *The Walls Do Not Fall* and the subsequent two volumes of H.D.'s *Trilogy*. The second division comprises "works published from the late fifties through the early seventies as part of the widespread reaction among younger poets against the standards of the 'well-wrought' lyric that dominated American poetry in the forties and fifties." According to Keller, these include the publications of writers from Black Mountain College, the Beats, the confessional poets, and the New York school. The third chronological section that Keller posits comprises "long poems of the seventies and especially the eighties, an era in which poetic decentralization and pluralization render text selection particularly difficult," given postmodernism's bending of genre and gender in equal measure. "Currently," Keller can still write in 1993, "identity politics surrounding ethnicity or sexual preference often are more important determinants of poetic groupings than shared ideas about form and language,"[9] a characterization that arguably rings less true today, both with respect to ethnic inscription and formal experimentation, after the publication of long poems as diverse as Claudia Rankine's highly acclaimed *Citizen: An American Lyric* and Craig Dworkin's major postconceptual achievement *The Pine-Woods Notebook*. That is to say, ethnic difference and literary form are themes that by now pertain in equal measure to what is being explored in contemporary long poems.

Furthermore, long poems are also in agreement with the thematic scope of the epic as they "handle long events: the collapse of civilizations and civility, war, revolution, pogrom, refugee migration and displacement, and other sundry occasions of violence and trauma."[10] The North American long poem in the twentieth century, it seems, almost voraciously devours, digests, and regurgitates the epic tradition, including its mythographic impetus, its heroism, didacticism, nationalism, and narrative digressiveness.[11]

But focusing on the epic at the expense of the lyric would be misguided, as J. Mark Smith shows. "Until the early eighteenth century," he concedes, "a long poem was as a matter of course epic, or for a time mock-epic—but, in any case, narrative. In the decades following, lyric (or some combination of the lyric and the prophetic) swallowed epic whole. Things came to such a pass that Poe could speak for most in declaring that the long poem was 'simply a flat contradiction in terms.'" No major attempts, including *Leaves of Grass*, changed that status quo, according to Smith, until the publication of *The Cantos*, "admitted by all, even Pound, to be a failure, somehow did—with the improbable consequence that Pound has dominated mid-twentieth through early twenty-first century poetry as John Milton did mid-eighteenth through early nineteenth." In particular, it is the self-diagnosis of inescapable finitude, the near-lyric "self-conscious announcement of failure [that] is in effect a convention of the long poem after Pound."[12]

Pound's "major poem sequence torn between utopianism and bestiality," "at once lyrical and polemical, visionary and demonic," as Cary Nelson fittingly describes *The Cantos*,[13] thus comes to serve as a second model next to Whitman's *Leaves of Grass*. Hence Cohen and Golston can write that "long poems deal with issues of human failure, and in doing so, they court failure themselves."[14] This courting of failure is further amplified through the simple fact that by the end of their life's work, writers of the long poem often face incoherence or pass away before being able to prepare the final parts of their lifelong endeavor for publication. Ever provisional and incomplete, the long poem is antithetical to the idea of the well-wrought urn. There is, then, unmistakably a shattered, postromantic relation between the concepts of transience and finitude on the one hand and permanence and infinity on the other, epitomized by the dialectic of epic and lyric as the generic polarities of the long poem, which has consequently also been labeled, for lack of a better term, "the epic lyric."[15]

With respect to the other side of the dialectic, then, the "lyric sequence," which Jonathan Culler in his *Theory of the Lyric* defines as "a series of related poems in which a broad narrative is discernable,"[16] has come to pass as an alternative term for the long poem, particularly for those scholars who would like to downplay its epic heritage but still acknowledge a narrative dimension. Yet while one might, along the lines of Smith's pendulum logic, trace a return of the lyric in recent decades analogous to the return of the epic in the first half of the twentieth century, the long poem, generally speaking, has not swung back in the second half of the twentieth century toward lyricism so much as doubled down on the inclination to write poetry via prose instead of verse, to write poetry by writing sentences.[17] This inclination is by no means a late-twentieth-century invention but goes back to Gertrude Stein and her *Tender Buttons* with its equally and magisterially antiepic and antilyric experimentalism.[18] In any case, it seems impossible to capture the North American long poem in terms of genre, be it epic, lyric, or prose poetry.

Prefiguring our conviction that it is misleading to conceive of the North American long poem as either a kind of (modern) epic, lyric sequence, or anything in between, Margaret Dickie, too, suggests that this generic terminology "obfuscates more than it clarifies," and instead focuses on the one characteristic that all long poems share, namely length: "Bare and simple as it is, *the long poem* as a term identifies [. . .] the single feature that most attracted the poet and made his [*sic*] work most problematic. Long in the time of composition, in the initial intention, and in the final form, the Modernist long poem is concerned first and last with its own length." In this impetus, "the Modernist long poem is not a genre but an aspiration to form."[19] Sometimes called by the name of its conceptual sibling—"life-poem"[20]—the long poem is a testament to the given poet's "aspiration to form," with "form" being understood, crucially, both as a verb (to form as in: to make, that is, *poiein*) and a noun (a form as in: a shape, that is, *morphē*). As our discussion of the notion of form in the next section will make clear, the long poem is a particularly salient form for emphasizing the production of the new, making and "remaking it new,"[21] precisely because it is an enterprise in ongoing morphogenesis; that is, a perpetual generation of form. This is why, ultimately, as Dickie aptly puts it, "every long poem will defeat its creator"[22]: As a literary form that emphasizes the generation of form, that is, creation as process, and thus doubles as a "life poem," it eventually takes on a life of its own, while pointing toward the finitude, not merely of things in the world, but of the one who writes.

This, finally, is where DuPlessis's take on the long poem and its ambition to form comes into play. For her, there is a fundamental distinction to be made between one type of long poem that "is book-length, generally ending, taking months or a few years to complete, relatively contained if also thematically rich. The second kind takes decades to write, has multiple-book construction, possibly does not end, and is often excessive: a life's work."[23] In terms of this distinction, therefore, the statement that we used as the second epigraph to this introduction testifies to a feature of the long poem as form that is not exhausted by mere page space and poetic design, with all the culturally inscribed problematics of gender- and genre-specific connotations related to expansion, enlargement, mastery, containment, and failure. For the long-poem form always necessarily amounts to a negotiation of time and process, becoming and being. After all, there is a reason that the long poem is called thus rather than sequence, cycle, epic, or any other term. In the context of the long poem, length primarily denotes temporality. For the writer, "length itself is like a symptom without being the germ of the enterprise. It's not even how many years it takes," as DuPlessis writes. "Rather, it is a way of stating that the necessity doesn't end. It's the writer's relationship in time, with time, via the poem. You might want more poem the same way you might want more time."[24] We would like to suggest that the interplay of the three categories of form, matter, and experiment constitutes the arena in which this "relationship in time, with time, via the poem" plays out. The long poem does not merely amount to an expansion of the possibilities of page space for *poiesis*. It is the prime poetic expression of how poiesis essentially remains "always incomplete, always in the midst of being formed" and thus "goes beyond the matter of any livable or lived experience."[25] It is a "groping experimentation" with all kinds of materials in the generation of form.[26] But what, exactly, is form? And how does the long poem provide a unique occasion to address this question?

FORM

Anyone writing on form today needs to contend with Caroline Levine's highly influential book on the topic. While one might not agree with Levine's conceptual apparatus and overall argument, her characterization of the discourse on form is certainly shared by most critics:

Over many centuries *form* has gestured to a series of conflicting, sometimes even paradoxical meanings. Form can mean immaterial idea, as in Plato, or material shape, as in Aristotle. It can indicate essence, but it can also mean superficial trappings, such as conventions—*mere forms*. Form can be generalizing and abstract, or highly particular [...]. Form can be cast as historical, emerging out of particular cultural and political circumstances, or it can be understood as ahistorical, transcending the specificities of history. In disciplinary terms, form can point us to visual art, music, and literature, but it belongs equally to philosophy, law, mathematics, military science, and crystallography. Even within literary studies, the vocabulary of formalism has always been a surprising kind of hodge-podge, put together from rhetoric, prosody, genre theory, structural anthropology, philology, linguistics, folklore, narratology, and semiotics.[27]

Form seems to be a particularly polyvalent, elusive, and unruly concept. But this is only due to a misapprehension. The apparent discursive hodge-podge becomes much less daunting, unwieldy, and "chaotic"[28] once one understands that form is inherently a matter of *aisthesis*, that it is a purely aesthetic term, regardless of the context in which it is employed. In this sense, the widespread distinction between "aesthetic and social forms"[29] that Levine also subscribes to and which fundamentally structures the argument in her book is not just arbitrary but skewed: To juxtapose the social and the aesthetic with respect to form amounts to a category mistake. The social is one realm of many in which forms emerge, occur, intersect, collide—to use one of Levine's favorite terms—and dissolve. But they invariably do so as *aisthetika*. Put differently: The very moment we speak of social forms we speak of certain aesthetic qualities, forces, assemblages, and occurrences of the social. These can well be immaterial ideas (in both a Platonic and a more mundane sense) as much as material shapes. For what the term "form" designates in these expressions does not necessarily impinge on the distinction between the material and the immaterial, only on the modality of their perception.[30]

Form always and invariably relates to questions of aisthesis. And these questions arise in all those instances and situations in which perception and sensation (that is, sensibility) are involved, never mind whether the questions pertain to the social or the artistic, the essential or the superficial, conventionality or novelty, the general or the particular, the abstract or the concrete, the historical or the timeless. Disciplinarity, too, is irrelevant to the question of form. It is a mere trivial observation and not perplexing at all to note that, for example, mathematical formulas, crystals, artworks, and philosophical ideas all assume or come in certain forms. The same holds for subdisciplines within disciplines: Against Levine's allegation, it is not at all surprising that the vocabulary of formalism avails itself of a range of subdisciplines of literary studies as they engage with particular and specific formal, that is aesthetic, aspects of a diverse array of literary expressions such as linguistic rhythm, relations between signs, narrative structure, and figures of speech. For all we do when we speak about the form of something—whether material or immaterial—is to say that it has a certain aesthetic makeup. Sometimes these things are even nothing but this aesthetic makeup. Indeed, the Greek notion of the *idea*, which precisely translates as *form* or *pattern*, is fundamentally aesthetic in the above sense, deriving from Greek *idein*, to see. An idea is that which can only be seen or, by extension, grasped (that to see and to grasp also function as synonyms of "to know" has its roots in the Greek concept of the idea). To put it bluntly: The concept of form entails aisthesis, and nothing else. To say that form "has never belonged only to the discourse of aesthetics" and to speak of a "heterogeneity at the heart of form's conceptual history" is to misread that history.[31] Arguably, this misreading is due to an unnecessarily narrow understanding of aesthetics as synonymous with theory of art.[32]

Already Alexander Gottlieb Baumgarten, the founder of the modern discipline of aesthetics, understood aesthetics only secondarily as theory of art when he defined it as "the science of sensuous cognition."[33] Aesthetics is thus the discipline concerned with cognition by means of sensibility. It is this understanding of aesthetics that informs one of Russian formalism's foundational documents, Viktor Shklovsky's "Art as Device," when it famously posits art as the tool "to make us feel objects, to make a stone feel stony." Importantly, art achieves this feat precisely by means of "complicating form" as such complication "makes perception long and 'laborious.'" In other words, art manipulates form in such a way as to prolong the state or process of perception. It is by means of the prolongation and saturation of perception that art affords "knowledge of a thing through the organ of sight instead of recognition."[34] In a nutshell: Art manipulates form for the sake of aisthetic (rather than conceptual) knowledge. As Ewan James Jones puts it in a memorable phrase in his discussion of Samuel Taylor

Coleridge's poetics, "Forming always is feeling."[35] Russian formalism, at least in Shklovsky's formulation, is thus a direct descendant of Baumgarten. Shklovky's text also helps us to circumscribe more precisely the role of art in the discourse on form. If art can claim any privileged relation to form, it is this: Art emphasizes form, puts it front and center. It makes us dwell on form, on color, texture, contour, pitch, rhythm, cadence, idea, and so on.

Seen this way, even if we disagree with the way she sets up the problem, Levine's focus on the question of affordance is spot on. We ourselves just wrote about how according to Shklovsky art affords knowledge by means of sensibility. What, exactly, is a given form "capable of doing?"[36] This, indeed, becomes the central question.[37] What are the affordances of color, texture, contour, pitch, rhythm, cadence, idea, and so on the way they are employed in a given context and situation? For the purposes of this introduction and the volume as a whole, this question translates as follows: What are the affordances of the long poem as it occurs in North America in a period that stretches from the second half of the nineteenth to the early twenty-first century?

We would like to highlight three such affordances. Undoubtedly there are more, but we take these three to constitute the hallmarks of the North American long poem since the romantic period when conceived in terms of form. First, the long poem is characterized by what Paul Jaussen calls emergence, Denise Gigante calls epigenesis, and what in more general philosophical parlance can be called becoming. This means that the long poem affords a particularly acute experience of formation or morphogenesis, that is, literally, the genesis of form or, more generally, the process of creation. Second, the long poem is the paradigm case of what Gigante calls polymorphous prolificity. It affords a particularly apposite testing ground for the intersection, collision, fusion, and propagation of all kinds of forms.[38] Third, the long poem thus becomes at least a fierce contender for "the form that best captures the experience of colliding forms,"[39] a title Levine reserves for narrative. The long poem then affords not just the testing ground for but a particularly pronounced experience of the collision or intersection of forms.

Gigante and Jaussen focus on different literary periods—late eighteenth to mid-nineteenth century in Gigante's case, mid-nineteenth to early twenty-first in Jaussen's—and employ different theoretical frameworks—romantic organicism and modern systems theory, respectively. Still, they end up advocating for a strikingly similar poetics to the point where

Gigante's "epigenetic poetics" and Jaussen's "emergent poetics" become almost indistinguishable (Gigante repeatedly uses the qualifier emergent to explain what she means by epigenetic).[40] Employing the conceptual apparatus of systems theory, Jaussen characterizes long poems as emergent insofar as they "develop through the ongoing activity of writing in real time. Poetic form, far from being determined in advance, arises as a dynamic second-order pattern out of first-order activities, prompting the poem to further evolution."[41] Similarly, Gigante glosses organic epigenesis in terms of an "innate tendency [. . .] toward form, otherwise known as teleology, entelechy, or emergence"[42] and a process in which "parts are bound to the whole through the voluntary activity of an internal drive toward unity."[43] According to Gigante, whereas "neoclassical theories of poetry [. . .] emphasize structure," romantic poetics is based on "emergent, self-expressive power."[44]

Thus, what Jaussen claims as characteristic of a certain literary form, Gigante singles out as specific to a particular literary period. Interestingly, Gigante's prime examples are invariably long poems: Christopher Smart's *Jubilate Agno*, William Blake's *Jerusalem*, Percy Bysshe Shelley's "The Witch of Atlas," and John Keats's *Lamia*. As poems that feature their "own generative processes," according to Gigante, they all exhibit "a polymorphous prolificity that is sympathetic to epigenesis."[45] The following passage on Blake's "Jerusalem" gives us a brief account of how the polymorphous prolificity of romantic epigenetic poetics may manifest itself:

> Formal experimentation allows for the poem's minute particulars, or *simple* parts (words or visual bits like spirals, arches, and squiggly lines), to combine into *stuck-together* or *interdependent* parts, such as individual lines of poetry and fictional characters. These, in turn, form *self-standing* parts (prefaces, passages of verse, composite designs), which combine into the various forms the poem as a whole can take. The force driving this combination is imaginative power, which works analogously to essential power and which Blake models for the reader.[46]

For both Gigante and Jaussen, the respective poems they are concerned with emphasize and actively flaunt their processual, morphogenetic character, the very act of poiesis, their "aspiration to form."[47] In other words, they adhere to an aesthetics of the processual. It is in this sense that in his chapter for this volume, "'A Restless Surface': Everyday Phenomenology in James Schuyler's Long Poems," Matthew Carbery emphasizes how Schuyler's poetry "bear[s] witness to, for example, the day or the month as 'spontaneous organization' rather than as an objective totality."[48] Long poems are fundamentally poems of becoming, a characteristic further enhanced by the long poem's "*constitutive* incompleteness in the first and last instance,"[49] as Nathan Brown makes clear in "Incompleteness: The Project of the Long Poem," his contribution to this volume. This nontotalizable processuality is precisely due to polymorphous prolificity, to use Gigante's term.[50] The question that remains to be answered is whether polymorphous prolificity is specific to romanticism or the long poem. Or maybe the long poem is an essentially romantic form of literature. In a sense, this is what we actually believe to be the case: We do think that Gigante is right in claiming polymorphous prolificity as a hallmark of romantic poetics. But we also think that it has manifested itself most fervently in the long-poem form ever since. In this vein, it is not at all a coincidence that in his contribution to this volume, Brown reverts to the romantic conceptualization of the project in order to theorize twentieth-century long-form poetry's essential incompletion.

In any case, as Jaussen points out, "the modern long poem has always been treated as a formal misfit."[51] In "Assemblage as a Genre of the Long Poem," the opening essay to part 1 of this volume, Rachel Blau DuPlessis presents a similar diagnosis when she maintains that "genre polysemy is a perpetually discovered characteristic of long poems."[52] Indeed, as we have seen, the long poem easily assumes, accommodates, and incorporates many different genres from the epic to the lyric sequence, from narrative to the verse novel, to name but a few, but it does not constitute a genre in and by itself. This is precisely due to its condition of polymorphous prolificity. This condition, in turn, has something to do with length. In her reading of Charles Dickens's *Bleak House* as an example of what she terms the network form, Levine emphasizes "sheer length" as the formal feature that allows for "an especially loose and baggy narrative form" thus "afford[ing] not individual agency, not the primacy of families, and not the wholeness of the nation, but a kind of narratively networked sublime."[53] But does not the long poem with its even fewer strictures and greater looseness (no logical coherence, no plot, not even characters are required) outperform narrative in this respect? We could then say that the long poem affords a kind of poetically networked sublime.[54] Seen this way, Edgar Allan Poe was not wrong in his judgment that "the long poem does not exist," given that he defined poetry in terms of his famous unity of effect.[55] Unity of effect cannot be achieved through length.[56] On the contrary, length combined with polymorphic prolificity actively works to de-emphasize unity in favor of process, emergence, creation, that is, becoming. In other words, the long poem testifies to form as the very process of formation. What, then, is being formed in, and by, the long poem? What is the material of this process of formation?

MATTER

At the beginning of section 23 of "Song of Myself"—precisely in the middle of the fourth sequence, which Malcolm Cowley simply names "the poet in person"—the speaker of the American bard's best-known poem announces: "Endlessly unfolding words of ages! / And mine a word of the modern . . . a word en masse."[57] Whitman's "word en masse" is a key phrase, arguably, insofar as it points to the immediacy his poetic stance seems to promote. This stance, "grounded in the American poet's Adamic self-reliance," according to Mark Bauerlein, seeks to express in the pages of *Leaves of Grass* what cannot be expressed, namely the immediacy of natural feeling, an ostensibly unfiltered transmission of affect: "Whitman begins to compose a writing against itself, a writing that promotes the unwritten, what cannot be written. In other words, Whitman initiates in *Leaves of Grass* a poetic project whose goal is, paradoxically, to nullify language, whose various affirmations and celebrations of self and nature are, in fact, antithetical reactions to linguistic effects."[58]

The centrality of the concept of matter here becomes apparent when the questions of form and of poiesis are linked to the question of what it is that is being formed and made in the literary unit called long poem. For even in Bauerlein's Whitman, in which writing seeks to undo itself, this undoing needs something, some material that is undone. Unsurprisingly, this material is language, and unsurprisingly, too, language subsequently became the prime material of literary investigations from the early avant-gardes to concrete and visual poetry to the language poets.

But in the context of modernism and postmodernism the question of materiality or of the material is also pertinent insofar as what authors such as Eliot, Pound, Louis Zukofsky, and, later on, proponents of projective verse, language writing, and even conceptual poetry based their practice on was, simply put, a reliance on other texts and traditions into which the poet could dig. From these textual traditions, they would—often literally—take content in order to "merely" rearrange it and subsequently frame it according to a poetics formerly foreign to the source text. From *The Waste Land*, *The Cantos*, and *"A,"* to *Lip Service* and all the way to *Zong!*, the history of the North American long poem since Whitman is a history of shaping and reshaping extant materials. Otherwise, there are no China and Adams Cantos, no "Voyage of the Sable Venus" by Robin Coste Lewis, no *Ark* by Ronald Johnson. Therefore, to foreground matter qua material with respect to the long poem is to acknowledge that modern, postmodern, and contemporary long poems are, for the most part, either samplings and reconstructions of, or, at the very least, responses to their specific source materials. In other words, the North American long poem's self-reflection as form and formation and, in the majority of cases, as a necessarily failed form due to either incoherence or incompleteness or both, depends on and operates through the explicit (mis)appropriation of—often unpoetic—source materials. *Cantos LII–LXXI*, for example, relies heavily on such sources (namely, a Jesuit's reiteration of Chinese history and *The Works of John Adams*): "No other series in Pound's epic opens with a table of contents, and as we examine the table we can't help remarking upon how unpoetic it seems—even in the context of *The Cantos*,"[59] Josephine Park notes. Her remark about the seeming unpoeticity projected by the table of contents preceding the China and Adams Cantos says a lot about the reliance of long-poem writers on their material. The long poem afforded writers of verse a more polymorphous form to compete with the novel. This form could, however, become thus only by way of incorporating more and more material formerly deemed unpoetic, similar to the inclusion of newspaper announcements, for instance, in the fiction of modernists like John Dos Passos. Thus, Rukeyser in *The Book of the Dead* "interweaves dramatic monologues with documentary materials and reflective or lyric passages in her own voice, to create a full picture of a horrendous industrial crime."[60] The long-poem form is always already an attempt at panoramic literature that necessarily depends on the declarative strength of its source materials.

That these source materials in Rukeyser's work were class-specific—and *The Book of the Dead* is part of a tradition to give workers of the industrial age a voice that nobody else would grant them—brings us to another crucial aspect that concerns the notion of matter or materiality, namely the racial or ethnic body. In its co-optation of source materials, modernism often used and misused the forms of expression of the ethnically other, thus embodying speech that came from outside of the given (white) writer's own environments, amounting to what Michael North, in *The Dialect of Modernism*, terms "racial ventriloquism." He specifies that "the real attraction of the black voice to writers like Stein and Eliot was its technical distinction, its insurrectionary opposition to the known and familiar in language. For them the artist occupied the role of racial outsider because he or she spoke a language opposed to the standard. Modernism, that is to say, mimicked the strategies of dialect and aspired to become a dialect itself."[61]

That is to say, the materials the North American long poem worked with in its inclusion of a whole array of dialects reflected back on the cultural heritage of the nineteenth century as a century in the course of which philosophical and literary idealism waned and was eventually replaced by the grimness of realism, naturalism, and materialism. From Ralph Waldo Emerson's "transparent eye-ball" to Whitman's *Drum-Taps*, the vexed issue of a nation built on slavery bled into the conception and composition of the North American long poem from its inception and is, unsurprisingly, still at work, as Kathy Lou Schultz makes clear in "Against Spectatorship: 'Being with' in Claudia Rankine's Long Poems," her contribution to this volume. According to Schultz, Rankine "demonstrates in *Citizen* that enduring [. . .] daily aggression and structural racism is not a fleeting experience, but is 'stored' in the body."[62] Given its history of appropriations and reworkings, the long poem, too, may be somatically understood as just such a storage system.

In any case, morphogenesis always entails the shaping of some material, linguistic or otherwise, creation and formation out of a formless *chora*, a Platonic concept that Julia Kristeva famously reconceptualized in terms of "the maternal body," and which Friedman has, in turn, employed for her discussion of the revisionary work of women's twentieth-century long poetry.[63] In particular, scholarship on H.D. has shown that the etymology of matter, in the third volume of *Trilogy*, is linked unmistakably to the Virgin Mary and the sexualized connotations of the myrrh, which the sage Kaspar carries with him in the nativity scene and which he supposedly gives to Mary Magdalene on another occasion. Materiality qua maternity: In H.D.'s work, mythography and the politics of gender intersect by way of a modernist revision of what matter signifies.[64] Furthermore, "myrrh, like the Magdalene, is strongly aligned with the sexual body, both in that it adorns and in that it expresses that body, or rather the body's forbidden sexuality, its pleasurable odors,"[65] as Susan Edmunds writes. What form and genre mean for the long poem ought thus to be unshackled from its masculinist heritage, acknowledging the conceptual vicinity of *matter* to *mater* that inheres even in the most abrasively patriarchal of Pound's, Eliot's, Williams's, or Olson's pages.[66]

Finally, given that "media determine our situation,"[67] as Friedrich Kittler once wrote, and given that the North American long poem from the nineteenth century onwards keenly appropriates new and emergent media for its own purposes, one cannot talk about materiality without also speaking about mediality. Already Whitman's fascination with the body, with human and nonhuman materialities, correlates with his obsession with photography and the book qua material entity; H.D. loved the cinema and even acted in the avant-garde film *Borderline*; and Pound is infamous for his radio speeches that led to his indictment as a traitor to the United States. More recently, and more to the point, Rankine's multimodal *American* project not only incorporates visual material as part of the text but also includes proper video poems and essays as extensively discussed in Schultz's chapter. In his contribution on "Matter, Rhetoric, and Ambient Form in Susan Howe's Poetic Space," Brian McAllister shows how the New England poet Susan Howe, in turn, has collaborated with sound artist David Grubbs to forge a poetics and aesthetics that is to be regarded in relation to both ambient music and the theorizations of ambience that can be traced from Brian Eno all the way to today's new realisms and materialisms. "Ambient poetics are particularly fruitful when looking at works by poets like Howe, who foreground material conditions of poetry and embrace intermedial collaboration,"[68] as McAllister puts it.

Matter, materiality, maternity, mediality: The North American long poem thrives in the engagement with and the appropriation, shaping, and modulation of the material ecologies of cultural history; or, in the words of Jaussen's contribution on "*Paterson*'s Analogies: Iteration, Recursion, and Contingency," in "tapping local archives and experiences in order to construct dynamic poetic forms adequate for contingent encounters with a changing, material present."[69] But how, exactly, does this shaping and modulation take place? How is it effectuated? It is effectuated by means of "groping experimentation,"[70] as we would like to suggest. What, then, is a literary experiment? And why should we think of the long poem as inherently experimental?

EXPERIMENT

Whenever scholars speak of experimentalism in literature, they usually emphasize keywords like innovation, creativity, and difficulty, and they insist on the scientific legacy of the term. Literary experiments are said to import the scientific hallmarks of autonomy, objectivity, and reduction and precision. In this vein, autonomy is taken to translate to (often hermetic) self-containment and self-rule, objectivity to the primacy of description and abstraction resulting in a pronounced distance instead of immersion, and reduction and precision to linguistic condensation, terseness, exactness, rigor of expression, and sureness of execution, often achieved and emphasized through a focus on minute detail, technicality of expression, and a penchant for parataxis. In addition, a decidedly materialist poetics is said to provide the overall framework that holds these disparate elements together: Like in the sciences, to conduct experiments, one needs some kind of material they can be conducted with and on. Thus Joe Bray, Alison Gibbons, and Brian McHale understand the term experimentation in the context of literature as "describing literary innovation," Andreas Hägler singles out literary experimentalism's "eschewal of conventions" and its emphasis on "materiality" as the means to achieve "objective autonomy," and Natalia Cecire points out that experimental literature borrows science's "coherency-making tactics, drawing on epistemic virtues to make wildly varying practices theoretically consistent."[71]

Unsurprisingly, most of the textual examples discussed in the scholarship pertain to the twentieth-century canons of modernism, postmodernism, and the literary avant-gardes. In his useful genealogy of experimental writing, Paul Stephens explicitly mentions some of the more science-oriented strands of modernism and the historical avant-gardes as well as "'Pataphysics and the OULIPO tradition."[72] In the North American context, frequently discussed writers include modernists like Stein, Marianne Moore, Williams, and the objectivist poets, postmodernists like John Barth and Donald Barthelme, and the language poets, the majority of which, importantly, have produced long poems at specific moments of their respective careers.

Indeed, many modernists and writers in the modernist lineage embraced the sciences, particularly physics, for their materialist poetics and even as an outright methodological model to emulate, "claim[ing] their own right of experiment and inquiry as scientific Americans"[73]: Eliot famously compared the function of the poet to that of a "catalyst" and the poet's mind to the "shred of platinum" in chemical catalysis; Williams embraced "the new physics" and "Einstein's theory of relativity," employed the terms "field" and "action" for his poetics, and went so far as to claim poetry as a kind of "chemistry: Or better, physics"; and Olson further amplified Williams's borrowings with his own take on poetry's "energy" and "kinetics."[74] These writers both apprehended and employed language, particularly written language, as a material entity in its own right, seeking to arrange its constituents—from syllables to phonemes, from visual patterns to page space—in such ways as to produce and elicit material effects, affects, and, indeed, objects rather than their "mere" linguistic representations. In this sense, literary experimentation always means material and formal experimentation.

But Stephens also mentions another, different tradition, which is arguably more specifically American and less invested in formal and material innovation, namely the American pragmatist tradition, with its insistence on the correlation of experiment and experience.[75] This tradition stretches back to the American Transcendentalists and includes thinkers and writers such as John Dewey, Henry and William James, John Cage, Stanley Cavell, and neopragmatists like Robert Brandom. It avails itself of the "double-sense of experiment and experience,"[76] of an understanding of "experience as experiment."[77] Stephens points to Cage's understanding of "the experimental as that work which is indeterminate in its outcomes" and, drawing on Cavell, Paul Grimstad glosses literary experimentation as "an activity taking the form of a search; one which does not know where it is going ahead of time, fashions provisional goals as part of the unfolding of the process, and remains open to the surprises that emerge from an attention to work as it is being made."[78] As Hägler makes clear, with such an understanding of experimentation, "even if a literary work remains largely embedded in traditional forms of writing, it can still qualify as an experimental work."[79] Indeed, Grimstad is primarily interested in the process of composition, in how "experience and composition can be thought to form a continuity,"[80] and in how writers in the pragmatist vein transpose and rework journal entries into lectures into essays into books, in "poetry and prose" that display and trace "a move from experience understood as a squaring of inner with outer matters to experience understood as a search for the conditions by which a work becomes shareable." It is this open-ended, hazardous, uncertain movement that he terms "'experimental writing.'"⁸¹ Hägler sympathetically maintains that while such an understanding "might dilute the notion of experimental writing, [. . .] it just as well dilates it."⁸² Of course, the problem with this concept of experimental writing, which includes authors such as, for example, Emerson, Poe, Herman Melville, and Henry James (the four authors at the heart of Grimstad's book), is that it dilutes the notion of literary experimentalism precisely *because* it dilates it.⁸³ Such a wide-ranging notion of experimental writing runs the danger of rendering it indistinct and thus virtually useless.

This does not mean, however, that the emphasis on experience should have no place in discussions of literary experimentalism. While we would insist on a predominantly formal and material determination of the notion of experimentalism in literature, we do think that such a notion cannot do without a recourse to the question of experience as highlighted in the pragmatist tradition. Indeed, we advocate a synthesis of the two seemingly incompatible approaches. Harking back to Deleuze and Guattari's insistence on the necessity of experimentation in creation quoted above, we hold fast to the idea that "experimentation is always that which is in the process of coming about—the new, remarkable, and interesting" and defend the notion that because experience is fundamentally experimental in this sense, experimental literature can be said to be more fully in tune with lived experience, within and without the latter concept's phenomenological horizon.⁸⁴ After all, was this not also, at least in part, the very argument of Virginia Woolf's "Mr. Bennett and Mrs. Brown," in which she famously pronounced the unreality of realist characters and defended modernist storytelling on the grounds that it is realer than realism, that it is much more in tune with lived experience?⁸⁵

This is where the long poem enters the picture: For the pragmatist insistence on the double sense of experience and experiment and its conceptualization in terms of process and search neatly aligns with Jaussen's account of the long poem in terms of emergence and Gigante's epigenetic poetics as discussed above. It also resonates with Carbery's insistence on the long poem form as particularly attuned to extended phenomenological meditations on lived experience. For are long poems not particularly acute renderings of "processual, developmental *Erfahrung* rather than episodic, self-intimating *Erlebnis*"⁸⁶ precisely because they tend to be emergent, epigenetic, and extended material and formal experiments? Put differently, perhaps the long-poem form is particularly attuned to providing certain kinds of experience by means of extending its formal and material experiments over a long stretch of time. That is, its prolonged formal and material experimentations correlate with the otherwise unexperienceable processes of experience, or, alternatively, in Sascha Pöhlmann's admittedly playful conceptualization in "Whitman's Long, Long Poem," his contribution to this volume, by giving us a poetry that "projects a sufficient temporal scope from the present into the future (and in doing so may well incorporate the past as well)."[87] In Deleuzian terms, long poems would then constitute particularly acute examples of the correlation of literature and life. Perhaps long poems are indeed exceptionally well suited to make "perception long and 'laborious,'" to speak once more with Shklovsky.[88] At least the practitioners of long poetry seem to think so: As Charles Altieri and Nicholas D. Nace point out, "for many poets [...] difficulty takes place less in short lyric or anti-lyric forms than in longer book-length works."[89]

But what exactly do these formal and material experiments and difficulties consist of? Zeller's essay comes in handy for answering this question, as he conveniently provides a list of characteristics. According to Zeller, texts can be said to be experimental if they:

- thematize language and writing and thus explicitly flaunt their materiality and mediality;
- combine different aspects of media;
- display their theoretical preconditions;
- accentuate print layout and sound patterns;
- are composed in accordance with methodological or procedural principles (reduction, variation, combination, permutation);
- are based on randomness, statistics, and probability;
- are produced with the help of machines, without regard to individual talent and subjective world view;
- are composed in collaboration;
- question narrativity;
- provoke doubt about the referentiality of language and thus, by extension, reality;
- refer to their own process of production;
- take their impact into account;
- reference or are composed according to the tradition of visual poetry;
- do not simply *represent* or *register* but actually *are* experiments.[90]

This is a fairly exhaustive list. The employment of a combination of (some of) these characteristics results in an experimental text that, by dint of its experimentalism, is apt to provide an exceptional, otherwise unattainable experience. The long poem, through its length, its polymorphous prolificity, and its openness toward the incorporation of all kinds of external materials, is particularly attuned to this kind of work.

Importantly, none of these formal and material characteristics are historically specific (though obviously they manifest themselves differently in and throughout literary history, hence, for example, Middleton's suggestion in his contribution to this volume, "Petitionary Long Poems: Layli Long Soldier, Juliana Spahr, and Srikanth Reddy," that if we want "to understand the innovative strategies of these poets we should think about the communicative ontology of the internet itself"[91]). Something similar also holds for their political ramifications, despite Zeller's insistence on their inherent "resistance to ideologically directed language" and their adherence to the values of "enlightenment and critique."[92] It might well be true that, historically, most practitioners of experimental literature adhered to these values. It might even be true that they believed in experimental literature's inherent anti-ideological and critical potential. But that in itself does not rest the case; it remains but a historical contingency. As Ben Lerner asks, "Who among us still believes, if any of us ever really did, that writing disjunctive prose poems counts as a legitimately subversive political practice?"[93] There are, in fact, quite a few counterexamples when it comes to political allegiances and convictions, many of them from the anglophone world: Italian futurism, Eliot, Wyndham Lewis, and, perhaps most prominently, Pound. In her contribution to this volume, "The Paradise of *Rock-Drill*: Far-Right Politics in the Late Cantos of Ezra Pound," Park shows that Pound pursued "interlocking aesthetic and political visions,"[94] that it was precisely his experimental aesthetic and poetic leanings that most prominently carried, subtended, and emphasized his abhorrent politics. In other words, experimental literature cannot be determined either on historical or on political grounds. Like form, experimentation in literature is a purely aesthetic affair; any politics resulting from such experimentation only supervenes on the aesthetic.

We thus also emphatically reject Cecire's focus on epistemic virtue: "Experimental writing as we now understand it," she writes, "does not *do experiments* (follow a method) but rather *performs epistemic virtues*."[95] Against Cecire's claim, we hold fast to the idea that experimental literature actually does do experiments. It might well perform epistemic virtues—and Cecire's account of the language poets is not unconvincing in this respect—but it only performs them through and by means of experimentation. And the experimentations it undertakes are on and with experience by means of language and other writerly materials and media (e.g., ink, paper, digital screen, and so on).

That we disagree with Cecire on this point does not preclude us from agreeing with her that "experimental writing [...] make[s] a claim to material efficacy via form." We also agree with her that experimental writing is "far from the first writing" to do so and that "what sets it apart is the intensity of its claim to do so secularly, as technology rather than as magic."[96] We would just suggest that the material efficacy in question is primarily ontological rather than political: It concerns the production of specific aesthetic objects and of affects, not changes in the material conditions of social life. Along with Lerner, we take the latter claim to be vastly overblown and untenable.[97]

Of course, the production of particular aesthetic objects (poems, novels, plays) and of affects is the purview of literature in general, not just experimental literature in particular. Seen this way, the notion of experimental literature is in danger of becoming a pleonasm, with "experiment" simply marking the literariness of literature, as Grizelj correctly points out.[98] This is not necessarily the case, however, if with Cecire one takes the modifier "experimental" to signify a certain "intensity." Experimental literature then becomes a particularly emphatic expression of what literature can do.[99] Rather than to "*hide the joint*," as William Dean Howells glossed the formal and aesthetic impetus of literary realism,[100] it actively and emphatically displays it. It becomes "literature's way of reinventing itself," as Bray, Gibbons, and McHale put it.[101] Such an understanding of experimental literature "suggests that it is a particularly fundamental form of literature."[102]

If, then, the long poem is to literary experimentalism as literary experimentalism is to literature, then the long-poem form—in alignment with our hunch regarding its exceptional malleability and inclusiveness, not only, but also, in terms of genre—is, at least *in potentia*, the epitome of literariness. And it is so precisely because, due to its length and its polymorphous prolificity, it tracks the emergence of form as the experimental shaping of a diverse array of materials. This is also why the long poem is such a great example of the Deleuzian correlation of literature and life. "Life alone," Deleuze and Guattari once wrote, "creates such zones where living beings whirl around, and only art can reach and penetrate them in its enterprise of co-creation."[103] The long poem, we would like to suggest, is the literary paragon of this enterprise in cocreation.

NOTES

1. Gilles Deleuze, *Essays Critical and Clinical*, trans. Dvaniel W. Smith and Michael A. Greco (Minneapolis: University of Minnesota Press, 1997), 1.
2. Uri S. Cohen and Michael Golston, "Rereading the Long Poem: Introduction," *Dibur Literary Journal* 4 (2017): n.p. https://arcade.stanford.edu/dibur/rereading-long-poem-introduction. In some ways, Uri S. Cohen and Michael Golston's special issue on the long poem prefigures the present volume, and we appreciate their thinking concerning this literary form. The special issue's conceptual framing and thematic focus, however, differ from ours in multiple respects, as will become clear in this introduction and the individual chapters that follow.
3. Deleuze, *Essays Critical and Clinical*, 57.
4. Susan Stanford Friedman, "Craving Stories: Narrative and Lyric in Contemporary Theory and Women's Long Poems," in *Feminist Measures: Soundings in Poetry and Theory*, ed. Lynn Keller and Cristanne Miller (Ann Arbor: University of Michigan Press, 1994), 15.
5. Walt Whitman, *Leaves of Grass: The First (1855) Edition*, ed. Malcolm Cowley (London: Penguin Books, 1986), 5.
6. See, in particular, Lynn Keller, *Forms of Expansion: Recent Long Poems by Women* (Chicago: University of Chicago Press, 1997) and DuPlessis's trilogy of feminist poetic criticism, *The Pink Guitar: Writing as Feminist Practice*, 2nd ed. (Tuscaloosa: University of Alabama Press, 2006 [1990]), *Blue Studios: Poetry and Its Cultural Work* (Tuscaloosa: University of Alabama Press, 2006), and *Purple Passages: Pound, Eliot, Zukofsky, Olson, Creeley, and the Ends of Patriarchal Poetry* (Iowa City: University of Iowa Press, 2012).
7. Deleuze, *Essays Critical and Clinical*, 57.
8. See, for example, Kathy Lou Schultz, *The Afro-Modernist Epic and Literary History: Tolson, Hughes, Baraka* (New York: Palgrave Macmillan, 2013).
9. Lynn Keller, "The Twentieth-Century Long Poem," in *The Columbia History of American Poetry*, ed. Jay Parini (New York: Columbia University Press, 1993), 534, 536–37.

10. Cohen and Golston, "Rereading the Long Poem," 2.
11. Klaus Heinrich Köhring, *Die Formen des „long poem" in der modernen amerikanischen Literatur* (Heidelberg: Winter, 1967), 125, 179; see also Michael André Bernstein's classic *The Tale of the Tribe: Ezra Pound and the Modern Verse Epic* (Princeton, NJ: Princeton University Press, 1980).
12. J. Mark Smith, "Introduction: Poetic Form and the Rhetoric of North American Avant-Gardism, 1963–2008," in *Time in Time: Short Poems, Long Poems, and the Rhetoric of North American Avant-Gardism, 1963–2008*, ed. J. Mark Smith (Montreal: McGill-Queen's University Press, 2013), 6.
13. Cary Nelson, "Modern American Poetry," in *The Cambridge Companion to American Modernism*, ed. Walter Kalaidjian (Cambridge: Cambridge University Press, 2005), 81, 82.
14. Cohen and Golston, "Rereading the Long Poem," 2.
15. Edward Proffitt, "The Epic Lyric: The Long Poem in the Twentieth Century," *Research Studies* 46 (1978): 20–27.
16. Jonathan Culler, *Theory of the Lyric* (Cambridge, MA: Harvard University Press, 2015), 123.
17. Ron Silliman, "I Wanted to Write Sentences: Decision Making in the American Longpoem," *Sagetrieb* 11, no. 1–2 (1992): 12–13.
18. Robert Grotjohn, "Gertrude Stein and the Prose Long Poem," *Genre* 24, no. 2 (1991): 173–75. While Stein might be the direct forebear of this particular tradition, there are of course earlier manifestations of long prose poems, most notably during the romantic period, such as, for example, some of William Blake's and Novalis's works.
19. Margaret Dickie, *On the Modernist Long Poem* (Iowa City: University of Iowa Press, 1986), 6, 148.
20. Rachel Blau DuPlessis, "After the Long Poem," *Dibur Literary Journal* 4 (2017): n.p. https://arcade.stanford.edu/dibur/after-long-poem.
21. See Lynn Keller, *Re-making It New: Contemporary American Poetry and the Modernist Tradition* (Cambridge: Cambridge University Press, 2009).
22. Dickie, *On the Modernist Long Poem*, 15.
23. DuPlessis, "After the Long Poem," 6. DuPlessis is in good company: Peter Middleton and Ron Silliman, both of whom she quotes, make a similar case when they distinguish, respectively, between "the long poem and the Very Long Poem (VLP)" (Middleton) and "the long poem and the 'longpoem' (one word)" (Silliman). Peter Middleton, "The Longing of the Long Poem," *Jacket* 40 (2010): n.p. jacketmagazine.com/40/middleton-long-poem.shtml;

Ron Silliman, "'As to Violin Music': Time in the Longpoem," *Jacket* 27 (2005): n.p. jacketmagazine.com/27/silliman.html.
24. DuPlessis, "After the Long Poem," 12.
25. Gilles Deleuze, *Essays Critical and Clinical*, 1.
26. Gilles Deleuze and Félix Guattari, *What Is Philosophy?*, trans. Hugh Tomlinson and Graham Burchell (New York: Columbia University Press, 1994), 41.
27. Caroline Levine, *Forms: Whole, Rhythm, Hierarchy, Networks* (Princeton, NJ: Princeton University Press, 2015), 2. Levine's characterization echoes Angela Leighton's in *On Form: Poetry, Aestheticism, and the Legacy of a Word* (Oxford: Oxford University Press, 2007), 1–3.
28. Levine, *Forms*, 2.
29. Levine, *Forms*, 3.
30. It might be hard to imagine how something immaterial could ever be perceived. But there is a venerable tradition of philosophy stretching precisely back to Plato that argues the case, usually in terms of intuition—the English equivalent of German *Anschauung*, which more obviously flaunts its essential aesthetic character—intellectual intuition, intuitive understanding, or contemplation. German idealism and romanticism constitute a crucial moment in this history. The go-to source on these matters is still Xavier Tilliette, *Recherches sur l'intuition intellectuelle de Kant à Hegel* (Paris: Vrin, 1995). For a more recent discussion see Eckart Förster, *The Twenty-Five Years of Philosophy: A Systematic Reconstruction*, trans. Brady Bowman (Cambridge, MA: Harvard University Press, 2012), particularly chapters 6, 7, and 11, and an edited collection devoted to Förster's book, Johannes Haag and Markus Wild, eds., *Übergänge—diskursiv oder intuitiv? Essays zu Eckart Försters* Die 25 Jahre der Philosophie (Frankfurt am Main: Vittorio Klostermann, 2013).
31. Levine, *Forms*, 2, 3. Just to be clear, the point in question is conceptual: We are not denying the social or political import of form. Yet form becomes political or social as an aesthetic category. It is one way in which the aesthetic manifests itself in the social or political.
32. While in her book Levine never explicitly subscribes to such an understanding, a passage like the following that short-circuits aesthetics with art certainly implies it: "It [form] does not originate in the aesthetic, and the arts cannot lay claim to either the longest or the most far-reaching history of the term." Levine, *Forms*, 3.

33. Alexander Gottlieb Baumgarten, *Ästhetik [Aesthetica]*, 2 vols., trans. Dagmar Mirbach (Hamburg: Meiner, 2007), §1, I:10. In the original Latin, the full definition reads as follows: "AESTHETICA (theoria liberalium artium, gnoseologia inferior, ars pulchre cogitandi, ars analogi rationis) est scientia cognitionis sensitivae." Theory of art only features parenthetically next to lower-level epistemology, the art of thinking finely, and the art of the analogy of reason. We here adopt the translation of Jeffrey Barnouw, "Feeling in Enlightenment Aesthetics," *Studies in Eighteenth-Century Culture* 18 (1988): 324.
34. Viktor Shklovsky, "Art as Device," in *Theory of Prose*, trans. Benjamin Sher (Champaign, IL: Dalkey Archive, 2009 [1991]), 6.
35. Ewan James Jones, *Coleridge and the Philosophy of Poetic Form* (Cambridge: Cambridge University Press, 2017 [2014]), 63.
36. Levine, *Forms*, 6.
37. We duly note that this way of interrogating form was already the focus of discussion in the fields of psychology and music sociology long before Levine's publication. See, for example, Tia DeNora, *Music in Everyday Life* (Cambridge: Cambridge University Press, 2004 [2000]), 39–41.
38. Coincidentally, this might well be the reason why next to the novel the long poem of roughly the past two hundred years constitutes one of the preferred arenas for literary experimentation.
39. Levine, *Forms*, 19.
40. Jones, too, emphasizes that Coleridgean organicism is "govern[ed]" by "*autopoiesis.*" Jones, *Coleridge*, 92. That romantic organicism and modern systems theory chime well is not particularly surprising given that the latter is a twentieth-century scientific spin-off of eighteenth- and nineteenth-century idealism. For the details concerning this legacy see Jeremy Dunham, Iain Hamilton Grant, and Sean Watson, *Idealism: The History of a Philosophy* (London: Routledge, 2014 [2011]), 223–55.
41. Paul Jaussen, *Writing in Real Time: Emergent Poetics from Whitman to the Digital* (Cambridge: Cambridge University Press, 2017), 3.
42. Denise Gigante, *Life: Organic Form and Romanticism* (New Haven, CT: Yale University Press, 2009), 22.
43. Gigante, *Life*, 26.
44. Gigante, *Life*, 62.
45. Gigante, *Life*, 168, 133.
46. Gigante, *Life*, 133–34.
47. Dickie, *On the Modernist Long Poem*, 148.

48. Matthew Carbery, this volume. Carbery is quoting Maurice Merleau-Ponty here.
49. Nathan Brown, this volume.
50. We already note here in passing that Gigante's passage on Blake quoted above short-circuits polymorphous prolificity with experimentation. Poiesis is thus correlated with experiment. Indeed, Deleuze and Félix Guattari once boldly declared that "there is no creation without experiment," a point we will come back to. Deleuze and Guattari, *What Is Philosophy?*, 127.
51. Jaussen, *Writing in Real Time*, 6.
52. Rachel Blau DuPlessis, this volume.
53. Levine, *Forms*, 127, 130.
54. Coincidentally, such a reading also chimes with Keller's diagnosis of the modernist rivalry between the novel and the long poem referenced above.
55. Edgar Allan Poe, "The Poetic Principle," *Critical Theory: The Major Documents*, ed. Stuart Levine and Susan F. Levine (Urbana: University of Illinois Press, 2009), 178.
56. This explains why Poe was not just a champion of shorter lyric poetry but also of short stories.
57. Malcolm Cowley, "Editor's Introduction," in *Leaves of Grass: The First (1855) Edition*, ed. Malcolm Cowley (London: Penguin Books, 1986), xviii; Whitman, *Leaves of Grass*, 47.
58. Mark Bauerlein, *Whitman and the American Idiom* (Baton Rouge: Louisiana State University Press, 1991), 12.
59. Josephine Nock-Hee Park, *Apparitions of Asia: Modernist Form and Asian American Poetics* (Oxford: Oxford University Press, 2008), 40. The monograph charts orientalist modernisms and their obsessions with and, importantly in our context, pilfering of Asian culture, including the work of Whitman, Pound, and the Beats, among others.
60. Burton Hatlen, "The Long Poem," in *The Oxford Encyclopedia of American Literature*, ed. Jay Parini and Philipp W. Leininger (Oxford: Oxford University Press, 2004), n.p. https://www.oxfordreference.com/view/10.1093/acref/9780195156539.001.0001/acref-9780195156539-e-0167.
61. Michael North, *The Dialect of Modernism: Race, Language, and Twentieth-Century Literature* (Oxford: Oxford University Press, 1994), i.
62. Kathy Lou Schultz, this volume.
63. Friedman, "Craving Stories," 19.

64. Sandra M. Gilbert and Susan Gubar, *No Man's Land: The Place of the Woman Writer in the Twentieth Century, Volume 3 – Letters from the Front* (New Haven, CT: Yale University Press, 1994), 172, 198; Eileen Gregory, *H.D. and Hellenism: Classic Lines* (Cambridge: Cambridge University Press, 1997), 4.
65. Susan Edmunds, *Out of Line: History, Psychoanalysis, and Montage in H.D.'s Long Poems* (Stanford, CA: Stanford University Press, 1994), 74. Consider, in this regard, Fred Moten's assertion in terms of not just the gendered body, but the racialized one, "that enslavement—and the resistance to enslavement that is the performative essence of blackness (or, perhaps less controversially, the essence of black performance) is a *being maternal* that is indistinguishable from a *being material*," in a discussion of Frederick Douglass's work. Fred Moten, *In the Break: The Aesthetics of the Black Radical Tradition* (Minneapolis: University of Minnesota Press, 2003), 16.
66. In this context, see also Susan McCabe, *Cinematic Modernism: Modernist Poetry and Film* (Cambridge: Cambridge University Press, 2009 [2005]) on the mechanics and aesthetics of "male hysteria" in Eliot, Williams, and others.
67. Friedrich Kittler, *Gramophone, Film, Typewriter*, trans. Geoffrey Winthrop-Young and Michael Wutz (Stanford, CA: Stanford University Press, 1999), xxxix.
68. Brian J. McAllister, this volume.
69. Paul Jaussen, this volume.
70. Deleuze and Guattari, *What Is Philosophy?*, 41.
71. Joe Bray, Alison Gibbons, and Brian McHale, "Introduction," in *The Routledge Companion to Experimental Literature*, ed. Joe Bray, Alison Gibbons, and Brian McHale (London: Routledge, 2012), 2; Andreas Hägler, "History, Critique, Utopia: Experimental Writing in the Context of Contemporary Anglophone Literature" (PhD diss., University of Basel, 2015), 38, 26; Natalia Cecire, *Experimental: American Literature and the Aesthetics of Knowledge* (Baltimore: Johns Hopkins University Press, 2019), xi. On how the discourse on experimentation in literature was indebted to and often affirmatively appropriated scientific discourse, particularly with respect to categories like abstraction, precision, and reduction, see also Christoph Zeller, "Literarische Experimente: Theorie und Geschichte – Eine Einleitung," *Literarische Experimente: Medien, Kunst, Texte seit 1950*, ed. Christoph Zeller (Heidelberg: Winter, 2012), 11–54; and Mario Grizelj, *"Ich habe Angst vor dem Erzählen": Eine Systemtheorie experimenteller*

Prosa (Würzburg: Ergon, 2008), 283–84. Zeller's and Grizelj's studies focus primarily on the literature of the German-speaking countries.

72. Paul Stephens, "What Do We Mean by 'Literary Experimentalism'?: Notes Toward a History of the Term," *Arizona Quarterly* 68, no. 1 (2012): 149–54.
73. Peter Middleton, *Physics Envy: American Poetry and Science in the Cold War and After* (Chicago: University of Chicago Press, 2015), 18. Middleton's book provides a particularly illuminating account of the importance of physics in the context of twentieth-century poetry. Brown even asserts that poetry is "a practice of material construction" and "a branch of materials research and fabrication." Nathan Brown, *The Limits of Fabrication: Materials Science, Materialist Poetics* (New York: Fordham University Press, 2017), 11.
74. T. S. Eliot, "Tradition and the Individual Talent," in *The Sacred Wood: Essays on Poetry and Criticism* (London: Methuen, 1957 [1920]), 54; William Carlos Williams, "The Poem as a Field of Action," *Selected Essays of William Carlos Williams* (New York: New Directions, 1969), 282, 283, 287; Charles Olson, "Projective Verse," in *Collected Prose*, ed. Donald Allen and Benjamin Friedlander (Berkeley: University of California Press, 1997), 240.
75. Stephens, "What Do We Mean by Literary Experimentalism?," 150–52.
76. Hägler, "History, Critique, Utopia," 31.
77. Paul Grimstad, *Experience and Experimental Writing: Literary Pragmatism from Emerson to the Jameses* (New York: Oxford University Press, 2013), 7. This conflation of experience and experiment is traced to the Latin root of both words, *experiri*: to test, to try out. On this conundrum, see also Zeller, "Literarische Experimente," 20.
78. Stephens, "What Do We Mean by 'Literary Experimentalism'?," 150; Grimstad, *Experience and Experimental Writing*, 7.
79. Hägler, "History, Critique, Utopia," 178.
80. Grimstad, *Experience and Experimental Writing*, 93.
81. Grimstad, *Experience and Experimental Writing*, 120.
82. Hägler, "History, Critique, Utopia," 191.
83. Broader notions of experimental writing are not without historical precedent: In Émile Zola's famous essay on "The Experimental Novel," for example, experimentation is not at all understood in formal and aesthetic terms but in those of a scientific, realist-naturalist experiment concerning social relations. Émile Zola, "The Experimental Novel," in *The Experimental Novel and Other Essays*, trans. Belle M. Sherman (New York: Cassell Publishing, 1893), 1–54; see also Zeller, "Literarische Experimente," 24.

84. Deleuze and Guattari, *What Is Philosophy?*, 111.
85. As Woolf points out toward the end of her essay, "in the course of your daily life this past week you have had far stranger and more interesting experiences than the one I have tried to describe. You have overheard scraps of talk that filled you with amazement. You have gone to bed at night bewildered by the complexity of your feelings. In one day thousands of ideas have coursed through your brains; thousands of emotions have met, collided, and disappeared in astonishing disorder." For Woolf, it is in the capturing and relaying of this disorder of lived experience that modernism's literary procedures are far superior to those of realism. Virginia Woolf, "Mr. Bennett and Mrs. Brown," in *Collected Essays: Volume One* (London: Hogarth Press, 1966 [1924]), 336.
86. Robert Brandom, *Between Saying and Doing: Toward an Analytic Pragmatism* (New York: Oxford University Press, 2008), 87; qtd. in Grimstad, *Experience and Experimental Writing*, 9.
87. Sascha Pöhlmann, this volume.
88. Shklovsky, "Art as Device," 6.
89. Charles Altieri and Nicholas D. Nace, "Introduction," in *The Fate of Difficulty in the Poetry of Our Time*, ed. Charles Altieri and Nicholas D. Nace (Evanston, IL: Northwestern University Press, 2018), 3.
90. Zeller, "Literarische Experimente," 44, our translation. This list also roughly aligns with Grizelj's discussion of the criteria of literary experimentalism, though we should note that Grizelj's systems theoretical constructivism ultimately leads him to proclaim "experimental literature" a purely discursive, theoretical, and observational category rather than any inherent formal or material feature of the object of observation. Grizelj, *"Ich habe Angst vor dem Erzählen,"* 282–98.
91. Peter Middleton, this volume.
92. Zeller, "Literarische Experimente," 50. As the title of his thesis suggests, Hägler, too, upholds experimental literature's critical and even utopian thrust, calling it "a fundamentally democratic form of writing." Hägler, "History, Critique, Utopia," 247.
93. Ben Lerner, "After Difficulty," in *The Fate of Difficulty in the Poetry of Our Time*, ed. Charles Altieri and Nicholas D. Nace (Evanston, IL: Northwestern University Press, 2018), 136.
94. Josephine Nock-Hee Park, this volume.
95. Cecire, *Experimental*, 23.
96. Cecire, *Experimental*, 188.

97. In this context we should also note that it may well be true that "experimentalist discourses have had a distinct and singular allergy to writers of color," as Cecire maintains—though we note a slate of recent publications that seem to indicate otherwise—we just do not think it has anything to do with literary form and everything with the sociology and politics of what could be termed the literary scene, including writers, publishers, newspapers and magazines, funding agencies, public events, and readers. Cecire, *Experimental*, 33. For accounts of literary experimentalisms of color, see, for example, Anthony Reed, *Freedom Time: The Poetics and Politics of Black Experimental Writing* (Baltimore: Johns Hopkins University Press, 2014), Schultz, *The Afro-Modernist Epic and Literary History*, and Schultz's contribution on Rankine in this volume.
98. Grizelj, *"Ich habe Angst vor dem Erzählen,"* 285.
99. This is of course a point that has already and repeatedly been made; see Grizelj, *"Ich habe Angst vor dem Erzählen,"* 292–94.
100. William Dean Howells, "Novel-Writing and Novel-Reading: An Impersonal Explanation," *Selected Literary Criticism, Volume III: 1898–1920* (Bloomington: Indiana University Press, 1993), 222.
101. Bray, Gibbons, and McHale, "Introduction," 1.
102. Hägler, "History, Critique, Utopia," 30.
103. Deleuze and Guattari, *What Is Philosophy?*, 173.

BIBLIOGRAPHY

Altieri, Charles, and Nicholas D. Nace. "Introduction." In *The Fate of Difficulty in the Poetry of Our Time*, edited by Charles Altieri and Nicholas D. Nace, 1–26. Evanston, IL: Northwestern University Press, 2018.

Barnouw, Jeffrey. "Feeling in Enlightenment Aesthetics." *Studies in Eighteenth-Century Culture* 18 (1988): 323–42.

Bauerlein, Mark. *Whitman and the American Idiom*. Baton Rouge: Louisiana State University Press, 1991.

Baumgarten, Alexander Gottlieb. *Ästhetik [Aesthetica]*. 2 vols. Translated by Dagmar Mirbach. Hamburg: Meiner, 2007.

Bernstein, Michael André. *The Tale of the Tribe: Ezra Pound and the Modern Verse Epic*. Princeton, NJ: Princeton University Press, 1980.

Brandom, Robert. *Between Saying and Doing: Toward an Analytic Pragmatism*. New York: Oxford University Press, 2008.

Bray, Joe, Alison Gibbons, and Brian McHale. "Introduction." In *The Routledge Companion to Experimental Literature*, edited by Joe Bray, Alison Gibbons, and Brian McHale, 1–18. London: Routledge, 2012.

Brown, Nathan. *The Limits of Fabrication: Materials Science, Materialist Poetics*. New York: Fordham University Press, 2017.

Cecire, Natalia. *Experimental: American Literature and the Aesthetics of Knowledge*. Baltimore: Johns Hopkins University Press, 2019.

Cohen, Uri S., and Michael Golston. "Rereading the Long Poem: Introduction." *Dibur Literary Journal* 4 (2017): n.p. https://arcade.stanford.edu/dibur/rereading-long-poem-introduction.

Cowley, Malcolm. "Editor's Introduction." In *Leaves of Grass: The First (1855) Edition*, edited by Malcolm Cowley, vii–xxxvii. London: Penguin Books, 1986.

Culler, Jonathan. *Theory of the Lyric*. Cambridge, MA: Harvard University Press, 2015.

Deleuze, Gilles. *Essays Critical and Clinical*. Translated by Daniel W. Smith and Michael A. Greco. Minneapolis: University of Minnesota Press, 1997.

Deleuze, Gilles, and Félix Guattari. *What Is Philosophy?* Translated by Hugh Tomlinson and Graham Burchell. New York: Columbia University Press, 1994.

DeNora, Tia. *Music in Everyday Life*. Cambridge: Cambridge University Press, 2004 [2000].

Dickie, Margaret. *On the Modernist Long Poem*. Iowa City: University of Iowa Press, 1986.

Dunham, Jeremy, Iain Hamilton Grant, and Sean Watson. *Idealism: The History of a Philosophy*. London: Routledge, 2014 [2011].

DuPlessis, Rachel Blau. "After the Long Poem." *Dibur Literary Journal* 4 (2017): n.p. https://arcade.stanford.edu/dibur/after-long-poem.

DuPlessis, Rachel Blau. *Blue Studios: Poetry and Its Cultural Work*. Tuscaloosa: University of Alabama Press, 2006.

DuPlessis, Rachel Blau. *The Pink Guitar: Writing as Feminist Practice*, 2nd ed. Tuscaloosa: University of Alabama Press, 2006 [1990].

DuPlessis, Rachel Blau. *Purple Passages: Pound, Eliot, Zukofsky, Olson, Creeley, and the Ends of Patriarchal Poetry*. Iowa City: University of Iowa Press, 2012.

Edmunds, Susan. *Out of Line: History, Psychoanalysis, and Montage in H.D.'s Long Poems*. Stanford, CA: Stanford University Press, 1994.

Eliot, T. S. "Tradition and the Individual Talent." In *The Sacred Wood: Essays on Poetry and Criticism*, 47–59. London: Methuen, 1957 [1920, 1916].

Förster, Eckart. *The Twenty-Five Years of Philosophy: A Systematic Reconstruction*. Translated by Brady Bowman. Cambridge, MA: Harvard University Press, 2012.

Friedman, Susan Stanford. "Craving Stories: Narrative and Lyric in Contemporary Theory and Women's Long Poems." In *Feminist Measures: Soundings in Poetry and Theory*, edited by Lynn Keller and Cristanne Miller, 15–42. Ann Arbor: University of Michigan Press, 1994.

Gigante, Denise. *Life: Organic Form and Romanticism*. New Haven, CT: Yale University Press, 2009.

Gilbert, Sandra M., and Susan Gubar. *No Man's Land: The Place of the Woman Writer in the Twentieth Century, Volume 3 – Letters from the Front*. New Haven, CT: Yale University Press, 1994.

Gregory, Eileen. *H.D. and Hellenism: Classic Lines*. Cambridge: Cambridge University Press, 1997.

Grimstad, Paul. *Experience and Experimental Writing: Literary Pragmatism from Emerson to the Jameses*. New York: Oxford University Press, 2013.

Grizelj, Mario. *"Ich habe Angst vor dem Erzählen": Eine Systemtheorie experimenteller Prosa*. Würzburg: Ergon, 2008.

Grotjohn, Robert. "Gertrude Stein and the Prose Long Poem." *Genre* 24, no. 2 (1991): 173–89.

Haag, Johannes, and Markus Wild, eds. *Übergänge—diskursiv oder intuitiv? Essays zu Eckart Försters* Die 25 Jahre der Philosophie. Frankfurt am Main: Vittorio Klostermann, 2013.

Hägler, Andreas. "History, Critique, Utopia: Experimental Writing in the Context of Contemporary Anglophone Literature." PhD dissertation, University of Basel, 2015.

Hatlen, Burton. "The Long Poem." In *The Oxford Encyclopedia of American Literature*, edited by Jay Parini and Philipp W. Leininger, n.p. Oxford: Oxford University Press, 2004. https://www.oxfordreference.com/view/10.1093/acref/9780195156539.001.0001/acref-9780195156539-e-0167.

Howells, William Dean. "Novel-Writing and Novel-Reading: An Impersonal Explanation." In *Selected Literary Criticism, Volume III: 1898–1920*, 215–31. Bloomington: Indiana University Press, 1993.

Jaussen, Paul. *Writing in Real Time: Emergent Poetics from Whitman to the Digital*. Cambridge: Cambridge University Press, 2017.

Jones, Ewan James. *Coleridge and the Philosophy of Poetic Form*. Cambridge: Cambridge University Press, 2017 [2014].

Keller, Lynn. *Forms of Expansion: Recent Long Poems by Women*. Chicago: University of Chicago Press, 1997.
Keller, Lynn. *Re-making It New: Contemporary American Poetry and the Modernist Tradition*. Cambridge: Cambridge University Press, 2009.
Keller, Lynn. "The Twentieth-Century Long Poem." In *The Columbia History of American Poetry*, edited by Jay Parini, 534–63. New York: Columbia University Press, 1993.
Kittler, Friedrich. *Gramophone, Film, Typewriter*. Translated by Geoffrey Winthrop-Young and Michael Wutz. Stanford, CA: Stanford University Press, 1999.
Köhring, Klaus Heinrich. *Die Formen des „long poem" in der modernen amerikanischen Literatur*. Heidelberg: Winter, 1967.
Leighton, Angela. *On Form: Poetry, Aestheticism, and the Legacy of a Word*. Oxford: Oxford University Press, 2007.
Lerner, Ben. "After Difficulty." In *The Fate of Difficulty in the Poetry of Our Time*, edited by Charles Altieri and Nicholas D. Nace, 135–41. Evanston, IL: Northwestern University Press, 2018.
Levine, Caroline. *Forms: Whole, Rhythm, Hierarchy, Networks*. Princeton, NJ: Princeton University Press, 2015.
McCabe, Susan. *Cinematic Modernism: Modernist Poetry and Film*. Cambridge: Cambridge University Press, 2009 [2005].
Middleton, Peter. "The Longing of the Long Poem." *Jacket* 40 (2010): n.p. jacketmagazine.com/40/middleton-long-poem.shtml.
Middleton, Peter. *Physics Envy: American Poetry and Science in the Cold War and After*. Chicago: University of Chicago Press, 2015.
Moten, Fred. *In the Break: The Aesthetics of the Black Radical Tradition*. Minneapolis: University of Minnesota Press, 2003.
Nelson, Cary. "Modern American Poetry." In *The Cambridge Companion to American Modernism*, edited by Walter Kalaidjian, 68–101. Cambridge: Cambridge University Press, 2005.
North, Michael. *The Dialect of Modernism Race, Language, and Twentieth-Century Literature*. Oxford: Oxford University Press, 1994.
Olson, Charles. "Projective Verse." In *Collected Prose*, edited by Donald Allen and Benjamin Friedlander, 239–49. Berkeley: University of California Press, 1997.
Park, Josephine Nock-Hee. *Apparitions of Asia: Modernist Form and Asian American Poetics*. Oxford: Oxford University Press, 2008.

Poe, Edgar Allan. "The Poetic Principle." In *Critical Theory: The Major Documents*, edited by Stuart Levine and Susan F. Levine, 175–99. Urbana: University of Illinois Press, 2009.

Proffitt, Edward. "The Epic Lyric: The Long Poem in the Twentieth Century." *Research Studies* 46 (1978): 20–27.

Reed, Anthony. *Freedom Time: The Poetics and Politics of Black Experimental Writing*. Baltimore: Johns Hopkins University Press, 2014.

Schultz, Kathy Lou. *The Afro-Modernist Epic and Literary History: Tolson, Hughes, Baraka*. New York: Palgrave Macmillan, 2013.

Shklovsky, Viktor. "Art as Device." In *Theory of Prose*, translated by Benjamin Sher, 1–14. Champaign, IL: Dalkey Archive, 2009 [1991].

Silliman, Ron. "'As to Violin Music': Time in the Longpoem." *Jacket* 27 (2005): n.p. jacketmagazine.com/27/silliman.html.

Silliman, Ron. "I Wanted to Write Sentences: Decision Making in the American Longpoem." *Sagetrieb* 11, no. 1–2 (1992): 12–13.

Smith, J. Mark. "Introduction: Poetic Form and the Rhetoric of North American Avant-Gardism, 1963–2008." In *Time in Time: Short Poems, Long Poems, and the Rhetoric of North American Avant-Gardism, 1963–2008*, edited by J. Mark Smith, 3–21. Montreal: McGill-Queen's University Press, 2013.

Stephens, Paul. "What Do We Mean by 'Literary Experimentalism'?: Notes Toward a History of the Term." *Arizona Quarterly* 68, no. 1 (2012): 143–73.

Tilliette, Xavier. *Recherches sur l'intuition intellectuelle de Kant à Hegel*. Paris: Vrin, 1995.

Whitman, Walt. *Leaves of Grass: The First (1855) Edition*, edited by Malcolm Cowley. London: Penguin Books, 1986.

Williams, William Carlos. "The Poem as a Field of Action." In *Selected Essays of William Carlos Williams*, 280–91. New York: New Directions, 1969.

Woolf, Virginia. "Mr. Bennett and Mrs. Brown." In *Collected Essays: Volume One*, 319–37. London: Hogarth Press, 1966 [1924].

Zeller, Christoph. "Literarische Experimente: Theorie und Geschichte – Eine Einleitung." In *Literarische Experimente: Medien, Kunst, Texte seit 1950*, edited by Christoph Zeller, 11–54. Heidelberg: Winter, 2012.

Zola, Émile. "The Experimental Novel." In *The Experimental Novel and Other Essays*, translated by Belle M. Sherman, 1–54. New York: Cassell Publishing, 1893.

PART I

Form

Chapter One

Assemblage as a Genre of the Long Poem

Rachel Blau DuPlessis

Genre polysemy is a perpetually discovered characteristic of long poems, and traces of epic, quest, and assemblage, sometimes mixed and always interpreted in their contemporary critical uses, characterize the long poems of the twentieth and twenty-first centuries. The long poems I address are extensive and synoptic, and many poets visibly articulate a challenging and theoretically questionable goal for their work: They want their long poem to encompass "everything."[1]

This goal of including everything suffuses our contemporary version of the genre of the "epic" (claimed by Charles Olson and Anne Waldman) and of the genre of the "quest" (often signaled, even in our centuries, by the appropriation and repurposing of Dante as in, say, James Merrill and John Ashbery). "Assemblage" as a third descriptor for achieving this goal of an expanding, "world"-encompassing genre also addresses the shared poetic desire for an overarching long-poem work encompassing "everything" necessary for negotiating social, political, cultural, aesthetic, and metaphysical concerns. As in the other long-poem genres, the assemblage poem is the work of a poet acting as public intellectual. In "assemblage," the general issue faced is "the numerous," a term inflected by George Oppen: peoples, the array, the many, and their bonds in the relative absence of any teleology (or cosmological conclusions, as in the traditional quest) and any particular social struggles of a hero or notable protagonist (as in the epic). In this generally secular (or more accurately, antiteleological) assemblage, a poet depicts a general social panoply and its ethical, existential, and other problematic arrangements.

ASSEMBLAGE

Assemblage, array, accumulation, album, and compendium are related, flexible terms that characterize this genre of long poems. Some long poems construct a large-scale cultural and social address, making a portrait of the force of a varied "many": many peoples, many voices, many observations interacting. These are set in an album, with the potential for additions to that accumulation. Walt Whitman's *Leaves of Grass* is arguably the most canonical case in point. Here are some further examples: listings, transformed but also set in an endless report of specific tragedies as in Charles Reznikoff; careful modules of peoples' portraits saturated in their social space as presented by Hart Crane in his vignettes; or Oppen and Langston Hughes in serial modes examining some fundamental social situations in their multiple facets. In assemblage, one also sees collections of varied but specific units of description, as in Kamau Brathwaite. Then, in a quite different use of the potential of assemblage as a loose genre concept, one sees a poet's deploying widely various genres in an album collected together, as in Louis Zukofsky. Accumulation based on individual tallying statements is itself propelled by specific procedures of structural counting, as in Ron Silliman. All these structured accumulations are baselines for the overwhelming and implacable feelings of a peopled "such-ness" and "many-ness" and their evident social being, in some historical specificity, set out in the poem. Most of these assemblages are a narrative, without plot, but assembling many bits or suggestions of ongoing stories. These commitments characterize the loose genre of assemblage in long poems.

Assemblage comes through at least two historical strands; one is from Whitman for US poetries. It led him to an endless additive set of works about peoples, their presences, beauties, and skills, celebrated as present and fused in one nation. *Leaves of Grass* has an affirmative furor, channeled into a catalog of political uplift and social joy in vignettes and odes, that offer a sense of array, the many, all present and all particular in a vast general scheme. The grouped poems in *Leaves of Grass* depict a nation by describing various citizens in their typical specificities, affirming them as bound together in a spiritual-political community as one adhesive body, made by and sung through the poet's inclusive, polymorphous voice. This Whitmanic array has both social scope and the aesthetic potential for adding more poems in paratactic formal units (as the poet did throughout his life with different editions of *Leaves of Grass*).

Assemblage poems also confront doctrinal ideas like "one" hegemonic goal for our world in its universal context, a goal congruent with the shape of the poem. This brings the problematic of ending into play for long poems, with their ceaseless toggling between potential closure and the endlessness of trying to capture and include "everything." And further, for works I have grouped in this genre, a point that I do not want overread: It seems as if sections—the large middle of a work of assemblage—could be read or arranged in almost any order.[2]

The triumph and drama of this structural theological-existential assurance were given their fullest and richest exfoliation in the *Commedia* of Dante; its dilemmas were examined, repeatedly and in various facets, by the genre of quest poems. Many, even in our centuries, were often directly affected by Dante's magisterial depiction of a teleological quest. A resistant examination of these spiritual findings, however, was staged by Mallarmé, for whom any institutionalized religion or nationalism with their mythological trimmings were distasteful and inadequate.

Mallarmé postulated that a substitute formation, based on his complex version of the genre of assemblage, was aesthetically crucial to depict a gathered plurality. Poetry, a concept and practice intellectually and ideologically empowered in Mallarmé's thought, was the key enterprise charged with providing this formation. Mallarmé's recognition of the necessity for a cosmological sense in the secular world led to his influential (and obscure) proposal of a generally civic but ritualized genre—assemblage—whose vague yet suggestive outlines had consequential impact on the modern long poem. In Mallarmé's critical perceptions, assemblage has two related aspects: the *Gesamtkunstwerk* (the total artwork, here interpreted as, and in, a heteroglossic long poem) and the Book with a capital B, an endless Book that (like a total artwork) allows the claim of capturing "everything" to be advanced.

He proposed (in private notes toward a poetics) an influential civic and ritualized book/event, an assemblage constructed of a set of ceremonial performances written (apparently) in a variety of aleatoric scripts. These ideas emerge in Mallarmé's essays and in his sketchy notes called "Le Livre." These helixed senses of a great and additive Book, and of its public performance at punctual, seasonal moments (like a year's worth of secular ritual) have the added interest (and frustration) of being a mix of theoretical, literary, and practical notes (a sketch in poetics) that was never completed for a work never written and thus never performed. Therefore, this virtually missing work of Mallarmé is like an ultimate conceptual postulate or supposition. Yet what can be discerned from these notes and some essays are the related benchmark ideas of Book and Gesamtkunstwerk, each suggestive, both intertwined, and, further, having serious resonance in the world of the anglophone long poem.

Both the Whitmanic album and the Mallarméan Book and Gesamtkunstwerk are interlocked, continuous, and intersecting manifestations of the genre I am calling assemblage: presentations of many-ness, much-ness, and their problematics. A secular ceremonial performance, a page space work, interlinked with, or as, an essayistic long poem with social and spiritual meanings might also be exemplified in aspects of *Un Coup de Dés*, posited by some critics as one blueprint for such a great synoptic work. This fascinating poem is a syntactic assemblage of nested hypotheticals concerning social-mythic figures and nonteleological cosmological forces. Instead of evoking any version of the Dantean teleology, Mallarmé presents the force of the universe as ever-fascinating Chance, throwing the dice of possibility into a fairly unconsoling void. So be it. But my issue here is neither theologies nor their interesting absences, nor French literary history, but rather the anglophone long poem.

I propose that anglophone writers of the long poem articulate a similar desire as "Le Livre" for an ideal synthesis of the arts and a celebration of civic coherence and/or enactment of critique. Heteroglossic dictions, citations, polyvocal languages, and the dynamic juxtaposed page space of these long poems are among anglophone poets' ways of creating the socially universalizing sound of their Gesamtkunstwerk and their Book. Hence particular, individual combinations of Whitmanic and of Mallarméan versions of assemblage—Book and Gesamtkunstwerk—characterize many modern and contemporary long poems. Such particular versions of the poetics of assemblage operate in authorial choices of method and in formal/thematic materials in Zukofsky, Ezra Pound, Nathaniel Mackey, Philip, and Brathwaite. None of these poets needs to be narrowly "influenced" by either Mallarmé or Whitman; I am positing another type of argument by placing them in the nexus of the long poem concerns identified above. None of these poets expresses these concerns similarly.

Briefly, a first interesting case: Zukofsky was experiencing difficulty facing the completion of his lifelong long poem called *"A."* To help with his 24th section (a number always posited as the ending), his family as helper figures produced a weird Gesamtkunstwerk, a recitative theater piece for four voices. The actual effect of its few performances literalizes a Gesamt-kunstwerk, making it like that imagined final exam written, with superior élan, on one line by the examinee. This total artwork is the book's final section, collected/collated by his wife Celia from Zukofsky's own writings (essays, plays, poems, stories) and scored by his son (the late violinist Paul Zukofsky) from Handel. The four speakers in *"A"*-24 speak a collage of words (all written by Zukofsky), mostly at the same time; this aural simultaneity creates the difficult effect of simultaneous voices, often obscuring each other. Despite Zukofsky's evident general knowledge of Mallarmé and Celia's serious and proud homage, this performative section is not really in the spirit of Mallarmé's social goals for a civic event; it is more like an homage to Zukofsky's career and its scope. Nonetheless, *"A"*-24 is an idiosyncratic version of a total artwork (Gesamtkunstwerk), a background source that I posit here for the poetics of the North American long poem.

EZRA POUND

Turning to Pound, let me examine one distinctive and telling way he redefined or homed in on his vocation in *The Cantos*, from before the Italian period to the end of his career. Pound can be said to evoke Mallarmé, if allusively, for his poetics, by repeating a phrase that Pound *said* was said by Yeats: "new sacred book of the arts," a phrase consonant with a Mallarméan poetics. Pound evoked this notion in 1932, in one of his several recastings of the question of *The Cantos'* structure and purpose.[3] Pound fused, into his (Yeats's?) complex phrase, the two aspects of Mallarmé's project. One is a book "of [all] the arts" (the Gesamtkunstwerk) and the other is a new "sacred" Book, a book that can bear that capital B for its purpose of transforming "everything," including politics.

This sense of the Book as further defined in Pound's Italian period resembles an urgent manifesto, calling people into political action. The telegraphic style of his essays, and even more so of his long poem, evoke the agreeable electricities of group credibility or gullibility supposedly present in occult communication along with the brisk persuasions of slogans in advertising and politics. Speed was of the essence; instantaneity led to conviction. Signage, sloganizing, and stereotypes in dialect gave readers the sense of stepping into a significant ongoing event without any analytic context. These traits contribute to the scintillating texture and bemusing tone of the *Cantos*. In his Italian (fascist) and intense conspiracy-theory period, his model of his heteroglossic long-poem texture was to provide encoded information for those with eyes to see. If, as Pound seriously postulated, the historical world now was the work of a conspiracy, then his undertaking (and continuing) *The Cantos* became his desperate, heroic attempt singlehandedly to throw enough real "facts" and historical information into play to befuddle and paralyze this conspiracy and to construct new cultural and social benchmarks for his readers. The Pound character in his poem is a warrior-griot; his war is waged with repressed information, and his battlefield is the archive. His version of "true fact" guarantees that the "one enemy" has been defeated, at least temporarily, when Pound unburies what he calls history (signal flares from cited documents). Pound *did* probably feel he was a self-elected savior of modernity from itself; he would, in *The Cantos*, thwart the work of the conspiracy by giving access to rectifying information. The poem thereby assumes a fiercely polemical task, an instrumental purpose, and—in his mind—a historical role.

In 1933, as a signal of this renewed purpose, he brought *The Cantos* as a Book to Mussolini to show its potential importance as a catalog of excellent leadership and to suggest he was the man for a high-level cultural appointment to help the regime. (This was the culmination of a desire to be at the center of a Renaissance about which Pound repeatedly spoke, from the teens on.) That Mussolini had a tepid polite response to Pound's claims did not daunt the poet, who chose to become a lower-level polemicist for fascist Italy, in several explicit ways publicly voicing his opinions and support.

Beyond his political activity (his citizen's rights to do so unprotected in wartime), Pound continued to use *The Cantos* as an assemblage, organizing the work in such a way as to claim the status of a synthesizing Book, a collection point for necessary documents, and a suggested replacement archive, library, research midden to embolden a new Italian Renaissance in fascism. *The Cantos* were built by Pound selecting from, retelling, glossing, and juxtaposing documents and materials that he presented as the unvarnished truth to show the bad or good of history, his goal being to construct an evaluative—not an interpretive—summary Book of his ideas of society and culture. The long-term goal of this assemblage got specifically redefined in this later period of Pound's career as a new sacred Book of Mussolini's regime in Italy, its answer, and Pound's, to failed modernity.[4]

Pound had wanted *The Cantos* to become a version of some all-encompassing Book with a special sociocosmological status insofar as it diagnosed, in Pound's terms, a politically and culturally bankrupt world and summed up a new or renewed world system that *The Cantos* celebrated and perpetuated. Is this exactly Mallarméan? Probably not. But it is a version of the Book as goal. Pound's use of *The Cantos* generally participates in the desire for the long poem to construct a great summary work, an assemblage of social knowledge and cultural meaning. It appears that Mallarmé, for his version of this goal, wanted to invoke a sense of cosmology, chance, contingency, the void, a mixing of narrative elements, not a political certainty. *The Cantos* is Pound's version of a summary, a "sacred Book" of secular histories. At the very end, in the image of the book as light and crystal ball, Pound thus positions the book as a "sacred" enterprise, with himself as prime mover of that crystal ball/book. Both, he thinks, have seen the future.

NATHANIEL MACKEY

Mackey's version of the assemblage-Book and Gesamtkunstwerk is a kaleidoscopic album of a recurrent quest narrative in which orphaned, wounded subjectivities struggle to change "Andoumboulou" incompleteness to human possibility. This proper noun comes from a Dogon myth—appropriated as a Mackey allegory—of incomplete humans trying to evolve and consolidate human traits. Mackey's work is infused with a sociocosmological poetics involving gnosis, myth, and music worked through "creative incorporation" of the "disruptive or even catastrophic" elements in both general and African diasporic social and historical experiences.[5] The work to date, including *Double Trio* (2021), is a heightened example of a contemporary "gathered" or assemblage work with a Gesamtkunstwerk flair, alluding to song and performances as its main "arts." Its heft (at about two thousand pages of resonant poetry to date) increasingly emphasizes the total work as an assembled Book. With conscious and repeated allusions to music as theme and event, and to dialogic encounters among travelers on this pilgrimage, the total artwork motif is strong; poem becomes performance as well as a summary Book.

This whole work, meditative and recursive, has a loose narrative trajectory. It stages multiple encounters, journeys through various landscapes and relationships, and then crashes into disappointment and compromise, often caused by outside forces. Then come passages and cantos reassembling the self and others via song and sexuality and via the cumulative thematic force of this Afro-diasporic historical story of a passage to social justice and community, all in order to begin again. A single meditative figure is set in relation to many other richly depicted figures encountered on these recurrent travels/quests of a "band." This is a musical and an "earthical" group, with a pun on ethical, perpetually undertaking quests that frustrate and fascinate by never quite achieving their goal: full humanity, a goal repeatedly thwarted by social/political/internal forces barely in their control, despite the aesthetic celebrations and social striving. The mixture of longing, struggle, and hope is characteristic, and the yearning for a "Soon-Come" social and aesthetic equality is the goal of pilgrimage after pilgrimage. When this "Soon-Come" hope is rebuffed, lost, broken, compromised, the trip perpetually uphill, nonetheless some band slowly regathers, affirms the sense of its longing through memories and cultural knowledge, and reclaims its metamorphic community through shared music, yearning eros, and a battered idealism. After another failure (often a "crash"), sometimes after crab-like side-steps, another beginning is again painfully and hopefully affirmed, and the pilgrimage renews and begins once more. The band reboards "box, book, break, boat, bus" for a continuing quest.[6] The boat materials evoke the Middle Passage, among other journeys.

Two other modes of transport designated by Mackey (box and break) allude to the music that inspires and uplifts; the book is this whole poem, a sacred-secular journey and assemblage of its own history. The current work (in *Double Trio*) intermingles the examination of quest with an exacting, sometimes bitter political commentary on the United States as the flat, intransigent, and belligerent "Nub."

In an early moment of this major work, Mackey evokes a vision of the vocation of the long-poem writer. This is a moment in which the book is a goal, a theme, and an actual item: "So I wake up handed a book / by an angel," with this book "announcing the / end of time" and the project of the Book itself as the poem to come.[7] Thereupon emerges a thrilling and daunting multiplication of potential books set forth in the Udhra "school": "Book of / sound, book of sand, book of / water [...] Book of glint, book / of glimmer, book of then [...]"; and a "Mute / book we read from," setting up the hope that this book will be actualized (if not finalized) in the works to come.[8]

This long work of several books has become, in an extension of the Mallarméan and Whitmanic nexus proposed here, a secular-spiritual Book. In Mackey, the making of the work becomes the theme of the work; the product or object of all this work is the career-culminating "boxed set" of musical performances, in keeping with the genre of assemblage and the ceremonial mixture of Book and Gesamtkunstwerk. For the Book in Mackey is not the only goal, as it is always intertwined with music and community, as in a passage at the end of *Nerve Church* that proposes "an imaginal sound no sound could / equal" and "the sound of words / on a page." Mackey evokes both assemblage as book and the Gesamtkunstwerk within the ultimate Book: "syn-aesthetic the best we could do trying to speak / of it, the sound we were driven by."[9]

This dilemma of making the Book is articulated in a passage in the first volume of *Double Trio*. "*All my life I plotted the one book of so, no / clue there'd be others, the book of a better / life 'like so' such the one I drafted.*"[10] A performed or enacted Book is what Mackey increasingly proposes as the desideratum of his poem. As Mackey's *Double Trio* unrolls, *The Book of So* may be the title postulated in the future and is always available to read against Nub's book of US politics and society. At root, Mackey declares and performs a spiritual and a political long poem with a multifaceted Book as its goal. Mackey pursues *The Book* and at the same time plural *Books of So* as assemblages of performative quests.

M. NOURBESE PHILIP

Many long poems ground themselves in their Book-ness as a material concept, in heteroglossia and page-space uses (as already noted), and in the physicality of the poem as an extended site, to make a large-scale cultural address. *Zong!* by Philip and *Ancestors* by Brathwaite (plus his *ConVERSations*) both claim the zone of the material text itself. The ethical-aesthetic goals of speaking to a culture by means of the total artwork as Book are visible in the works of Brathwaite and Philip. For these two authors' explorations of the textual visuality and the embodied materiality of the book have a particular status, in one case as a major revision of authorial attitudes toward poetry's purposes and audiences, and in the other a notable critical-poetic exploration and the making of a ceremony of mourning for an unassimilable historical tragedy. The design of the page and of typography and syntax along with diction and construction of the performative books create material texts that embody their contents. And this content constantly expresses a critical resistance to the uses and abuses of Africans and their descendants in the settler and slave-built societies of the New World.

In *Zong!* Philip claims the ethical import of page space and both political and spiritual purposes for the material shape of her book. Philip states this explicitly in her poetic paratext (the "Notanda") when posing the question of "how to write a story that must be told" yet "can only be told by not telling."[11] The story in question concerns the failure of a historically significant slave ship voyage: a drastic lack of adequate water that resulted in the death of many Africans and a few crew members from thirst, failures of navigation, and the throwing overboard of live Africans treated as cargo to be offloaded, in order eventually to make an insurance claim about losses (the subsequent historic trial is not about murder). The ship's fate is known from the trial records that Philip uses and transforms in her mid-length long poem. The paradox of authorship and responsibility facing this episode is "resolved" by having the story tell itself by breaking up the words that were originally used to frame it: a legal brief, inadequate words with significant silence at the core. The garbled irrational speech, the sound of people being tortured and drowned, the silencing of the Africans, and the silence of the law granting no personhood to enslaved people are all evoked by the rhetoric of Philip's writing. This kind of "not telling" proceeds by way of multiple paratexts of explanatory and semiexplanatory materials arranged around the core of the book. This core consists in telling the untellable, an expressive visual and aurally freighted text that makes *Zong!* into a Gesamtkunstwerk-Book in the mode of assemblage.

The textual center of this book can only be partly read. It must be seen, mouthed, felt in its brokenness. It consists of bits and pieces of language dissolved into phonemes and syllables in which bits of words and stories can occasionally be picked out, but that otherwise float unjoined in white space, disperse, disappear without having been fully "grasped." Readers witness this textual fragmentation and dissolution as an approximation of the victims' drowning conveyed as the long, "unreadable" center of the work. It is also a haptic embodiment of gasping. The page space is open to this floating of phonemes, arranged in such a way that none is placed on top of another; all are accorded a space for themselves, to honor their being. The linguistic and formal presentation thus creates an ethical meaning within the page space.

These fragmented, suggestive, half- or barely readable phonemes constitute the central section and the bulk of the book, a critical representation of the great inhumane commerce and trade in the Atlantic basin. On these central pages (the largest section of *Zong!*),[12] in a mix of European and African languages, phonemes split and untoward spaces challenge the reader, whose meaning-making capacities are more and more "at sea" or face unpalatable information. The entire middle section of the book makes use of the alphabetic letters from *Gregson v. Gilbert*'s words (and the entries from the "Manifest" list and other sections),[13] then has repeatedly broken them to shards, sometimes forming words accidentally, recombining, undoing, slipping like the understory or the ghosts of the words that were used in the law document and on the voyage.[14] The words have come apart and the story barely exists except in bits and fragments, often suggesting outcries or visually and syntactically enacted drownings or visually and phonetically rendered vestiges of bone. The pages include, for example, the shamed (possibly posthumous, underwater) confession by a sailor to his fiancée of having raped one of the African women. The middle part of *Zong!* enacts a Middle Passage and serves as a monument for the drowned by means of language, approximating the state of water itself, ungraspable and fluid. This is the Book of the dissolution of what a regular book might undertake. To say this is uncanny hardly begins to acknowledge the impact of this use of page space and of the dissolving monument of the book itself, as if a set of words and cries writ on water. The mechanisms of the Book are thus used against the reason, argument, and rationality that documents and legal accounts are thought to chart. The book, by being turned inside out and by disclaiming its possibility ever to be "written," becomes a Book, a total artwork as a sociocultural summary, a compendium of the values and histories that the poet shapes in order to make a serious, confrontative statement about the society to which the work is addressed.

Rather than giving "poetry readings" of this work, Philip has organized events (group performances) that turn *Zong!* into a civic ritual or ceremony of mourning.[15] This book thereby passes from a secular judgment on the past (and the self-judgment on the present that has benefited from societies built on past enslavements) to a ritualistic Gesamtkunstwerk, Philip's own "Ceremony of Souls" analogous to Caribbean spiritual practices.

KAMAU BRATHWAITE

The ethical-aesthetic goals of speaking to a culture with a total artwork in the form of a Book are visible in different fashion in a career-arching revisionary project undertaken by Brathwaite. Originally published by Oxford University Press (1977, 1982, and 1987) as *Mother Poem, Sun Poem*, and *X/Self*, Brathwaite's trilogy was at the time understood as a significant contribution to postcolonial writing. Years later, in a major act of self-assessment and historical intervention, Brathwaite transformed these initial interventions into a long-poem Book (a "reinvention" called *Ancestors*, a conceptual and visual remaking of the poems) and in a further extension into a poetics of the Book-in-society in *ConVERSations*.[16]

That is, Brathwaite fully alters these three original poem sequences with major textual and conceptual bibliographic shifts into the retitled *Ancestors* (2001). His refabricated poetic design makes use of the "'Sycorax video style' type[face] as developed by the Author,"[17] taking the normative typography of most books as colonizing of the social meanings of these works, and positing Sycorax (mother of Caliban in Shakespeare's *The Tempest* and a symbol of Indigenous peoples) as a new compositor. When the trilogy is drastically remade and reimagined, it is not only as a verbal revisioning or a refreshing, but as "A Reinvention."[18] Brathwaite not only changes specific granular elements of his poetry (line break, certain words, orthographies, punctuation, additions and cuts, with some spaces altered, and all poems centered a-normatively), but he also changes the whole visual design and compositional presentation: page space, font size and mode, particularly boldface and typefaces that thicken blackness, new margins, with additions of glyphs and illustrations, and allusions to newspapers, posters, and manifesto stylizations. The whole bearing and address of the work *Ancestors* makes his trilogy of poems into a confrontative visual work.

The former sequence of poems is thereby transformed into a long-poem Book of Caribbean culture. It is a Book as a social and spiritual instrument. The changed typography with its fleshy thickness of boldface (sometimes with jagged pixelation like early video game fonts) amounts to a textually bold presence embodying alternative Bookness, vernacular diction, and affirmative Blackness. This heft is newly set on the page with visual drama, evoking such temporal art metaphors as sculpture and dance and thus expressing the goal of the total artwork.

Brathwaite's changes make the thrust of my argument particularly clear: that the use of heteroglossic language, strong allusions to the other arts, and a unique and emphatic page space all combined into an *engagé* mode of the Gesamtkunstwerk propel these long poems and underwrite their cultural-social stance as Books with a capital B. With Brathwaite, not only his own personal autobiography, but a syncretic mythography and dynamic presentation of a Caribbean ethos are manifested as a poetics. This change is further discussed and analyzed in his meta-book of Caribbean poetics, *ConVERSations* (first published in 1999). The new presentation, he argues, has "liberated" him from "the School" of British and European modes of writing.[19]

ConVERSations is structured as an assemblage-album, primarily a dialogue-interview, including poems by others, some surveying of Caribbean literary history, a memoir in Q & A form, a self-study of the motives and contexts of the poems in *Ancestors*, and more. Brathwaite presents a poetics, an apologia, a research-based elaboration of scholarship, brief highlights of anticolonial resistance in Barbados, and political cautionary tales of realignments post-Emancipation, when historical forces of further oppression come into play. The book presents family memories (framing *Ancestors*) so that his "personal" life is taken to exemplify the political and economic forces that work on and around life choices of individuals in a colonized society, limiting them, modifying them, twisting possibility. The book cites news reports of often merciless events. It includes audience participation, extending the dialogue outward in a "call-and-re/sponse kinesis."[20] And this list is by no means exhaustive.

ConVERSations is a polygeneric scrapbook-assemblage (the book's format is a large 8 1/2 x 11 inches or 21 1/2 x 28 centimeters), about one-third poetry, two-thirds prose. It formulates a poetics in which Brathwaite explores his major redesign of the visual elements of a book, a statement concerning a Book made, in its material texture of presentation, to summarize Caribbean cultures, their sea-inflected aesthetic and struggles. As the "VERS" of the title indicates, the turning of verse—toward (*vers*)—not only involves the dialogism of conversation—turning toward others—but also indicates a radical turning of the Book itself.[21] The text is focused and purposeful, but visually jumpy in its attempts to synthesize many separate "fields"—autobiography, social history, reportage, scholarship on the Caribbean, poetry, and more—with presentational panache, resulting in a Book of multiplicity in the form of assemblage. This work is close to an artist's book, a major text of "writing the visual," and it evokes "intermedia" work, for Brathwaite cites numerous visual genres: "video-poetry," "a mural," "cinema-painting," even "graffiti," the whole functioning as a "wall of memory."[22] In his Book, then, a Gesamtkunstwerk is postulated, again within the logic of such projects, emphasizing a social and ethical dimension and articulating a poetics of multiple arts, presented by means of typography and page space.[23]

CONCLUSION

The long poems of assemblage discussed in this chapter tend to mix the album and Book/Gesamtkunstwerk forms, and all are engaged in some sort of fundamental critical act as social understanding and intervention by means of the medium of language and, variously, that of visuality and (non-linguistic) sound. The context from which much long poem assemblage work emerges critically reflects on the uses and affordances of narrative, poetry, and literature in general, of official history and its occlusions.

That is why the literary is never only literary in many of these long poems. These works are not only at the service of literature; indeed, they are sometimes invested precisely and exactly in a turn away from the felt limits of that institution and constitute a rejection of it. These poems, by the accumulation of (often) repeated evidence, by virtue of their length, and by their visual presentation make striking interventions into poetic form and what it can achieve, choosing a particular literary mode, the long-poem form, as the site of struggles for knowledge and perception. Writers of contemporary long poems often enter this practice with a sense of historical crisis that they can and must address. The crises differ, their observations differ, the means to address them differ; some crises may be more urgent than others. To propose a Book as assemblage aims to sum up the crisis; the Book as conceptual work can mark it, annotate it, with visual and auditory flair, sometimes resulting in entire Gesamtkunstwerk-style visual, musical, and page-space dramas of enactment, ritual, and ceremony.

NOTES

1. This article is a revised and condensed version of chapter 4 of *A Long Essay on the Long Poem* published by the University of Alabama Press in 2023. The Press has helpfully and generously given permission for this summary of some of its arguments to be published here. This permission is gratefully acknowledged. © Rachel Blau DuPlessis and the University of Alabama Press.
2. This is less true of M. NourbeSe Philip's *Zong!* than of the other works noted here. And Stéphane Mallarmé's *Un Coup de Dés*'s structuring cannot be summarized in a brief discussion such as this one.
3. Ezra Pound, "To John Drummond, 18 February, 1932," in *The Letters of Ezra Pound 1907–1941*, ed. D. D. Paige (New York: Harcourt, Brace, 1950), 240.
4. For a discussion of Pound's influence on and repercussions for the contemporary alt-right's agenda, see Josephine Park's contribution to this volume.
5. The preface to *Blue Fasa* identifies the "unending" claim of these poems beyond ego: "To pull the long song, the long poem, particularly the serial poem, the extended lyric, is to be taken over and to be taken afar." Nathaniel Mackey, *Blue Fasa* (New York: New Directions, 2015), xv, xiv, xiii.
6. Nathaniel Mackey, *Tej Bet*, vol. 1 of *Double Trio* (New York: New Directions, 2021), 324.
7. Nathaniel Mackey, *Eroding Witness* (Urbana: University of Illinois Press, 1985), 91–92, evoking Olivier Messiaen's title "Quatuor pour la Fin du Temps."
8. Nathaniel Mackey, *School of Udhra* (San Francisco: City Lights Books, 1993), 67, 85.
9. Nathaniel Mackey, *Nerve Church*, vol. 3 of *Double Trio* (New York: New Directions, 2021), 338, 339.
10. Mackey, *Tej Bet*, 282.
11. M. NourbeSe Philip, *Zong! As Told to the Author by Setaey Adamu Boateng* (Middletown, CT: Wesleyan University Press, 2008), 194.
12. Philip, *Zong!*, 57–182.
13. Philip, *Zong!*, 185–86.
14. This is Philip's stated goal in *Zong!* about her procedure of dissolution: to decode "a story locked in this text." She thus offers a survey of the ethical

rationale for rhetorical tactics that also critically negate sense and the rational uses of language. Philip, *Zong!*, 191–201.

15. Her website mentions "more than 60 readings / performances of *Zong!* that NourbeSe has presented in nine countries." "*Zong!*," M. NourbeSe Philip, n.p., nourbese.com/poetry/zong-3/.
16. Kamau Brathwaite, *Ancestors: A Reinvention of Mother Poem, Sun Poem and X/Self* (New York: New Directions, 2001); Kamau Brathwaite, *ConVERSations with Nathaniel Mackey* (We Press, 1999).
17. Brathwaite, *Ancestors*, copyright page.
18. Brathwaite, *Ancestors*, title page.
19. Brathwaite, *ConVERSations*, 35. Mackey's role in the event in which Brathwaite first performs this essay in poetics is quite important. I am aware that *ConVERSations* (1999) was published before *Ancestors* (2001), but clearly not before the latter was written; sheer vagaries of book production might explain this reverse chronology.
20. Brathwaite, *ConVERSations*, 222.
21. As a preposition, *vers* is pluralist, meaning to, toward, about, around. As a noun it is mainly verse, poetry, line, but also an icy frost (rime in English).
22. The phrase "writing the visual" is from Johanna Drucker's elegant typology of artists' books, books that have a special fascination for the emotional energy invested in them. Although neither Philip nor Brathwaite had their books produced as small-batch rarities (like artists' books), both bring the psychological—and political—commitment of the artists' books' aura into their long poem Books. Johanna Drucker, *The Century of Artists' Books* (New York: Granary Books, 2004), 139; Brathwaite, *ConVERSations*, 207, 208.
23. Even though they do not necessarily use the terms assemblage, Gesamtkunstwerk, and Book (with a capital B), most contributions to this volume operate under the assumption of the very characteristics of the assemblage form I have been discussing in my contribution (I am particularly thinking of the chapters by Nathan Brown, Brian McAllister, Peter Middleton, and Kathy Lou Schultz).

BIBLIOGRAPHY

Brathwaite, Kamau. *Ancestors: A Reinvention of Mother Poem, Sun Poem and X/Self*. New York: New Directions, 2001.
Brathwaite, Kamau. *ConVERSations with Nathaniel Mackey*. We Press, 1999.
Drucker, Johanna. *The Century of Artists' Books*. New York: Granary Books, 2004 [1994].
DuPlessis, Rachel Blau. *A Long Essay on the Long Poem: Modern and Contemporary Poetics and Practices*. Tuscaloosa: University of Alabama Press, 2023.
Mackey, Nathaniel. *Blue Fasa*. New York: New Directions, 2015.
Mackey, Nathaniel. *Double Trio: Tej Bet, So's Notice, Nerve Church*. New York: New Directions, 2021.
Mackey, Nathaniel. *Eroding Witness*. Urbana: University of Illinois Press, 1985.
Mackey, Nathaniel. *School of Udhra*. San Francisco: City Lights Books, 1993.
Mallarmé, Stéphane. *Divigations*. Translated by Barbara Johnson. Cambridge, MA: Belknap Press of Harvard University Press, 2007.
Mallarmé, Stéphane. *The Book*. Translated by Sylvia Gorelick. Cambridge, MA: Exact Change, 2018.
Mallarmé, Stéphane. *Mallarmé*. Translated by Anthony Hartley. Harmondsworth: Penguin Books, 1965.
Mallarmé, Stéphane. *Selected Poetry and Prose*. Edited by Mary Ann Caws. New York: New Directions, 1982.
Philip, M. NourbeSe. *Zong! As Told to the Author by Setaey Adamu Boateng*. Middletown, CT: Wesleyan University Press, 2008.
Pound, Ezra. *The Cantos*. New York: New Directions, 1996.
Pound, Ezra. *The Letters of Ezra Pound 1907–1941*. Edited by D. D. Paige. New York: Harcourt, Brace, 1950.
Whitman, Walt. *Leaves of Grass: Authoritative Texts, Prefaces*. Edited by Sculley Bradley and Harold W. Blodgett. New York: W. W. Norton, 1973.
"*Zong!*," M. NourbeSe Philip, n. d., n. p. nourbese.com/poetry/zong-3/.
Zukofsky, Louis. *"A."* Berkeley: University of California Press, 1978.

Chapter Two

Incompleteness

The Project of the Long Poem

Nathan Brown

I will begin with an untitled poem from the third volume of Charles Olson's *The Maximus Poems*, a short poem within a long poem, dated Sunday, January 9, 1966.

> The whole thing has run so fast away it breaks my heart
> Winter's brilliance with the sun new-made from living south
> I also re-arisen another numbered year from December's
> threat. Love all new within me ready too to go abroad. Ice
> snow my car as hidden as a hut beneath it children pass-
> ing without even notice, every house so likewise in-
> teresting because of snow upon each roof. Lamps, and day,
> nothing not new and equally forever upon this earth. All
> but me, damned as each man in death itself the evil
> which throws a dart of dirt and shadow on my soul and on
> this Sunday when in this light, and on this point, no
> conceivable hindrance would seem imaginable to darken
> or in fact any difficulty of any sort except to keep
> my eyes out of the sun-blaze on the sea and careful also
> not to notice too directly the street, frozen and slippery as
> the light
>   Sunday January 9 1966[1]

This is a poem of sixteen lines, or perhaps fifteen, with the last full line passing over through enjambment into a truncated beginning or surplus ending that does not quite amount to a unit of its own. Indeed, enjambment is the primary formal device of the poem, with at least eleven of its lines running over into the next and with two of those strongly marking this device by ending with hyphenated words. The meter orbits around heptameter, but with most of the lines at either fifteen or thirteen syllables, again marking formally a concern with deficit and surplus, abbreviation and excess. "The whole thing has run so fast away it breaks my heart," the poem begins, and it ends with a description of the street as "frozen and slippery as the light." So the poem is formally slippery, mimicking the problem of keeping one's balance and of holding one's gaze in the middle distance, not too far out over "the sun-blaze on the sea" and "careful also / not to notice too directly the street." The lyric speaker—for it is a lyric—is brokenhearted at what has already run so fast away, at what has already happened and cannot be recovered, and he tries to keep his balance amid the brilliance of a winter day, the freshness of its snow, and in which there is "nothing not new and equally forever upon this earth" except the speaker himself:

> All
> but me, damned as each man in death itself the evil
> which throws a dart of dirt and shadow on my soul and on
> this Sunday

Death enters the poem through the damnation of the speaker, who shares the evil of that anticipation with "each man" yet who is also isolated by it, his soul picked out amid the children and amid all that is "equally forever" by the "dart of dirt and shadow" thrown by knowledge of mortality, of finitude, of passing away between the already of what has happened and the not yet of what is to come. It is a poem whose elegiac tone and biblical rhetoric evokes the age of William Shakespeare, or John Donne, or John Milton:

> In me thou seest the glowing of such fire
> That on the ashes of his youth doth lie,
> As the deathbed whereon it must expire,
> Consumed with that which it was nourished by.[2]

"I also re-arisen another numbered year," writes Olson, counting the concatenated continuum of an existence already run away like a hyphenated line break, whose sense can only be registered after it has passed by.

Olson's wife, Betty Kaiser, died in a car accident in March 1964, after which he fell into the state of aching, riven solitude evident in this poem and so many others in the incomplete final volume of *The Maximus Poems*. He would die on January 10, 1970, one calendar day, in a later numbered year, after the date of this poem. The fragmentary, yearning, disordered incompleteness of the end of the *Maximus* unfolds between two deaths, Kaiser's and Olson's own, in moods oscillating between persistent ambition (carrying on the mythic and historical projects of the poem) and the melancholic dissolution of broken craving. One poem ends:

>   [after this snow not a jot of food left
> in this silly benighted house   all night long sleep
> all day, when activity, & food, And persons]
> 5:30 AM hungry for every thing[3]

And another written two months later:

> & it is now again as it was last night a
> Smokey Moon of Dog-day Summer
> Time   Sweet Love Time   Natural Crazy.   Time
> Human Dogs stay out in the
> Natural Time
> (of Night
>   I again am
>   Up
>
>   O
>
>   & wobbly again from
>   etc and
>   <u>solid pure hunger</u>
>
>   Charles Olson alone
>   still Saturday–Sunday night
>   June 1969[4]

Much of the beauty of the final volume of *The Maximus Poems* inheres in the drift and tension between what might be considered programmatic contributions to the overarching project of the long poem and these jotted lyric fragments rife with longing and nostalgia. Often these two registers intersect or entwine in longer, titled poems weaving together contingencies of mood and happenstance with gleanings from research and the construction of an epic framework, and of course this happens throughout *The Maximus Poems*. But the final volume is different not only due to its incompleteness and its posthumous assembly by editors from notes and scraps in Olson's papers and around his house, but also due to the sheer pressure of death and loneliness upon the poetic sensibility of its author. A deeper vulnerability enters the fabric of the poem, which one can retrospectively recognize as accreting throughout the work and now manifest in what I would call *the fragmentation of a project*, the falling of a project into fragments such that it becomes a fragmentary project perhaps best encapsulated by the simple lyric statement concluding the first line of the poem with which I began: "it breaks my heart." The formal resonance of the brokenheartedness of the second half of volume III of *The Maximus Poems* inscribes with particular clarity and pathos a major feature of the modernist long poem: its formal relation to death. That the composition of such a poem is structured by the possibility of continuing to accrue and incorporate unanticipated materials until the death of the poet—that the death of the poet will determine the end of the poem—is a peculiarity differentiating this kind of long poem from the epic. I want to consider how this peculiarity is bound up with the relation between *the project* and *the fragment*, a link that binds the modernist long poem, as well, to the project of early German romanticism.

.   .   .   .

The incompleteness of modernist poems like *The Cantos* or *Paterson* or *The Maximus Poems* is frequently described in negative or even pejorative terms, as a collapse that compromises their epic project. Discussing Ronald Johnson's *ARK*, Mark Scroggins notes that he

> must have begun his work with a worried backward glance at Pound's *Cantos*, Williams's *Paterson*, and Olson's *Maximus*. These were the looming achievements of the American non-narrative long poem in the twentieth century, and all three of them had petered out into incompletion. Pound sank into depression and silence before he could figure out how to end his *Cantos*; Williams thought he'd finished *Paterson* with its fourth book, only to tack on a fifth seven years later and leave a handful of notes for a sixth at his death;

and while Olson specified the one-line poem with which he wanted *The Maximus Poems* to end, the last volume of that work was largely reconstructed by editors after his death.[5]

Johnson himself strikes a posture of heroic resolution: "To spend twenty odd years writing a poem, undeterred by risks and shipwrecks of those before, would seem sheer folly. They stand before me, great obstacles."[6] For Johnson the unfinished long poems of his predecessors are "shipwrecks," while he has proven the successful helmsman, able to navigate the "great obstacles" of their ruins. Likewise, Ron Silliman notes that Olson's *Maximus* is "the first of the longpoems to attempt to proceed without anything like a firm numbering system. Like *The Cantos*, however, it's a text that starts strong & ends wispy, unraveling as it goes, dissolving into palimpsests, ending, as someone once predicted, not with a bang but a whimper."[7] Reducing the formal particularity of such endings to an opposition between the strong and the wispy, the bang and the whimper, for Silliman the fragmentary dispersal of these poems undermines their achievement, though he sympathizes with the descent of their authors into mental illness and alcoholism. He finds that "Zukofsky, on the other hand, who is never taken seriously by Olson, who is treated condescendingly (at best) by Ezra Pound, accomplishes what they cannot. He lives to see *'A'* complete, and in fact the first published edition of the work as a whole appears in 1978, the year he dies."[8] This orientation toward the long poem, shared by Johnson and Silliman, equates completion with accomplishment and incompleteness with failure. To die *after* the completion of the poem amounts to a successful voyage; to die *as* the poem dissolves into palimpsests is to suffer shipwreck.

But what George Oppen calls "the bright light of shipwreck"[9] might illuminate another approach. A poem like Rachel Blau DuPlessis's *Drafts* dissolves into palimpsests right from the beginning; she describes it as "a palimpsest of encounters and stacked timelines, necessities, drives, and stubbornness."[10] And although the poem is indeed finished, the final section of its final "Draft" begins as follows:

> That this began
> that this ends
> that this refused to begin
> (though it started)

that it refuses to end
(though it is folding itself up)[11]

The ending of *Drafts* enters "'*into an imagined endlessness*' / endlessly overwritten," such that "it is / finished but it is / not complete."[12] This insistence on the long poem's *constitutive* incompleteness in the first and last instance is shared by Nathaniel Mackey's ongoing serial poems *Song of the Andoumboulou* and "*Mu*." The Andoumboulou, he explains, "are a failed, earlier form of the human being in Dogon cosmogony," and he elaborates further: "I couldn't help thinking of the Andoumboulou as not simply a failed, or flawed, earlier form of the human being but a rough draft of human being, the work-in-progress we continue to be."[13] Not only the ongoing serial poem, "the long song," but also we ourselves are a rough draft or work in progress. The poem and those who write or read it are not yet what they are in the process of becoming, or they are the becoming of an incompletion in process. The long poem is the form of this incompleteness, of the incompleteness we *are*. It is the *not yet* of form itself, the *lag* of a form that never coincides with itself insofar as it can only be what it is by being what it is not yet.

This dimension of the long poem, which we could call its ongoing *projection*, its constitutive incompleteness as a project, is compellingly foregrounded by those projects interrupted by death and also fractured, prior to death, by the finitude and contingency of "form"; that is, by the fragmentation of form, by the dissolution of planned structure, by the shipwreck of authorial intention itself. This is indeed what we witness in the final book of *The Maximus Poems*, where the epic intentions of its author come apart at the seams, making these visible and opening rifts and fractures within which we find the lyric yearning of parts that will not come together as a whole. The *anticipation* not only of death, but of the eventual and permanent incompleteness of the poem, is precisely what seems to produce those fragmentations of form that cannot be anticipated: The incipient finitude of mortality *already* involves a finitude of intention, an interruption of authorship that actually constitutes an orientation toward authorship itself, the unraveling wispiness that endows volume III with its singularity of tone and its disorganization of sense.

This is to say that the event of death is not merely something exterior to the long poem, which breaks its composition and thereby ends it. When Johnson refers to the "risks and shipwrecks of those before" he recognizes that the long poem is constitutively exposed—precisely through the ongoing magnitude of its project—to the sheer contingency of what can happen and therefore to a certain default of intention. Death is the limit case of that default—the irrevocable insistence of finitude—but it is far from the only case of that default. Death is specific insofar as it is the *necessary* case of a general contingency, of that finitude that is endemic to all projects. The long poem is an exemplary inscription of such finitude in literature, the adequate form of that exposure. Despite the grandiose posture by which it is often accompanied—as in the cases of Pound and Olson—it is the most fragile of forms. It is this fragility against which Johnson braces himself when he declares that he is "undeterred." But through this compensatory gesture, which is indeed an overcompensation, we perhaps lose something of what makes the long poem so singular a form. The curiosity of *The Cantos* and *The Maximus Poems* is that these projects make manifest the fragility of the long poem despite or at least regardless of the intention of their authors: And this default of intention, the finitude of authorial will, becomes an element of their form—the formal process of their dissolution—which somehow strangely resists the disaster of masculine authority with which it is bound up precisely through that *unintentional* illumination that is the bright light of shipwreck.

Is this not the bright light at which Olson is careful not to look too directly? The sun-blaze of the sea and the frozen, slippery street—points of focus too far off and too proximate—are the only imaginable hindrance comparable to the dart of dirt and shadow cast by death over a fresh winter day in which there is otherwise "nothing not new and equally forever upon this earth." Death is the exception to all that is new; finitude is a contingent fall amid the equally forever. Olson's lyric becomes a site of formal reckoning—through enjambment—with the fragility of epic, its fragmentation, and here we could recognize a distinction between the long poem and the epic: In the openness of its project, the potential ongoingness of that project beyond any narrative or structural frame, it exposes the epic to that fragmentary *instance* of experience that is the purview of the lyric, while it also exposes the closed form of the lyric to the contingencies of history and of narrative duration that are the purview of the epic. This double exposure fractures both lyric and epic. It is intrinsic to the modernist long poem, at the scale of *The Cantos*, that the formal closure and narrative cohesion of both lyric and epic are at least potentially undone, and this is the *drama* of the form's historical contingency, of the way in which it "includes history."

Even the capacious scope of Goethe's *Faust* or Milton's *Paradise Lost* or the personal/political narrative and multiple editions of Wordsworth's *Prelude* are too unified in their project to encompass the strange contingencies we encounter in the progress of the modernist long poem, refracting lyric events through ungainly epic ambitions while undoing the narrative or structural determinacy of the latter through contingencies unbound from the discrete unity of lyric closure.

We could locate a romantic anticipation of this modernist form in Friedrich Schlegel's contributions to the *Athenaeum*, wherein he sketches an inchoate theory of the relation between *project* and *fragment*. According to Schlegel, "a project is the subjective embryo of a developing object," and "the feeling for projects—which one might call fragments of the future—is distinguishable from the feeling for fragments of the past only by its direction: progressive in the former, regressive in the latter."[14] A poem including history draws fragments of the past into its form as fragments of the future: a project grasped as the subjective embryo of a developing object. The "subjective," here, designates not so much the identity of an author or lyric speaker, but rather an activity of research, assemblage, and formation mediated by the *feeling* for a project, the particular sense of poetic particulars brought to bear upon every single decision, tendency, or indeed contingent error in the course of composition. The developing object is the poem or perhaps the book that will come to be printed as *The Cantos* or *The Maximus Poems*, which we can hold in our hands, but the peculiarity of the modernist long poem is that this object bears within its apparently finished form its status as a project, folding fragments of the past into what remain fragments of the future.

Schlegel characterizes this kind of poetry as "romantic": "The romantic kind of poetry is still in the state of becoming; that, in fact, is its real essence: that it should forever be becoming and never be perfected."[15] Schlegel then states that such poetry "can be exhausted by no theory and only a divinatory criticism would dare try to characterize its ideal." It makes sense, then, that this romantic ideal would be retroactively realized by a modernist poetic form that itself remains a fragment of the form it projects. In *History of a Shiver: The Sublime Impudence of Modernism*, Jed Rasula points out that the adjective *romantisch*, for the Athenaeum group, connoted the novel or *Roman* as a still indeterminate modern genre, which they imagined might "absorb all previous modes and genres."[16] Rasula notes that the romantic book, "freely drawing on aspects of existing genres and combining them in unforeseeable ways," was "envisioned as a *Mischgedicht* (or "mixed composition"), itself generally subsumed under the visionary role of "universal progressive poetry."[17] Thus, for Schlegel and the Jena Romantics, *romantische Poesie* was a concept denoting their aspiration to displace classical genres, along with distinctions between forms of knowledge and activity undergoing new separations amid the social, economic, and institutional conditions of modernity. From this perspective, experimental contexts of artistic production like the Bauhaus or Black Mountain College might be considered "romantic" as much as "modernist" institutions, and Rasula makes a compelling case that if modernism might be "succinctly understood in broad historical terms as the self-overcoming of genres in all the arts," then "the first *modernism* was Romanticism."[18]

But it is doubtful whether the Jena Romantics actually did develop forms of writing adequate to the *actual* instantiation of their project, rather than the articulation of it as an *ideal*, though Novalis's so-called romantic encyclopaedia—his open-ended, unfinished *Allgemeine Brouillon*—is perhaps the closest they came. Wordsworth's projected long poem, *The Recluse*, is another example of a romantic approach to this ideal. But in my view, it is only the advent of two distinctively modernist techniques—free verse and collage composition—that constitute the formal ground for the sort of generic openness, topical agility, thematic range, and historical permeability characteristic of works like *The Cantos* and *The Maximus Poems*. The unbinding of the poem from metrical regularity and the treatment of the page as a compositional field untether the construction of poetic content from narrative continuity and make possible the constellation of luminous details as fragmentary particulars whose associative logic becomes increasingly visual or punctual and grammatically fractured as the poems unfold. Moreover, I would argue that these formal affordances enable poets (and readers) to *feel* the relationship between historical circumstance and poetic composition in radically new ways. Relationships between research, personal life, historical determination, and poetic logic seem to become more contingent as the poems proceed, such that the materials they include are sutured more tenuously but also—through a dialectic pressing toward the very limits of poetic form or compositional unity—more *necessarily*, insofar as these relationships are allowed to impinge upon the making of the poem with a harrowing immediacy particularly evident in the final volume of *Maximus*. Insofar as they are held together by the relatively open approaches to the organization of poetic language Olson theorizes as "composition by field" or that Pound describes through figures of the vortex or the ideogram, these poems have a particularly felicitous formal relationship to the codetermining tension between project and fragment theorized by Schlegel. The modernist long poem develops compositional methods adequate to the attunement of the Jena Romantics toward the contingency of poetic genres, the fragmentary possibilities of poetic thinking, and the open-ended nature of projects. That is, they find forms adequate to making "poetry" the name of a practice of writing open to a radical fracturing of generic or disciplinary traditions and regularities.

The second volume of Olson's *Maximus Poems* is emblematic in this respect, at the level of both form and content. The formal fragmentation of the work into short passages cast across the expanse of otherwise blank pages is accompanied by a radical expansion of the poem's project onto the scope of geomorphic transformation and geological history, at once including and exceeding the localism of Olson's dominant concern with the history of Gloucester in volume I. The poem breaks open, but in volume II— unlike volume III, to which I will return in a moment—this rupture is gathered and reorganized on a new level or scale of formal coherence. On one page we read the words

>   tesserae
>   commissure

which is dated "Jan 19th 1962."[19] Here the dialectic of broken boundedness is figured as a mosaic, wherein tablets or tiles are joined even as their separation is displayed. Similar figures occur throughout the last two volumes, as the poem is compared to a reticule, a mesh (II.184), a sewn textile with visible seams (II.173), to a "weave / of interlocking / pieces" (II.24). In the so-called Gravelly Hill poem toward the end of volume II, Olson meditates on the contingency of boundaries and the boundedness of contingency. "Gravelly hill was the 'source and end (or boundary' of / D'town" the poem begins, and it rejects any legally imposed framework of land surveying, or any poetic measure external to the poem itself, in favor of an immanently relational approach to recognizing boundaries:

>   It is not bad
>   to be pissed off

> where there is *any*
> condition imposed, by whomever, no matter how close
>
> any
> quid pro quo
> get out. Gravelly Hill says
> leave me be, I am contingent, the end of the world
> is the borders
> of my being
>
> I can even tell you
> where I run out; and you can find
> out. I lie here
> so many feet up
> from the end of an old creek
> which used to run off
> the Otter ponds. There is a bridge
> of old heavy slab stones
> still crossing the creek on
> the 'Back Road' about three rods
> from where I do end northerly, and from my Crown
> you may observe, in fact Jeremiah Millett's
> generous pasture
> which, in fact, is the first 'house'
> (of Dogtown) is a part of the slide of
> my back, to the East: it isn't so decisive
> how one thing does end
> and another begin to be very obviously dull about it
> I should like to take the time to be dull[20]

Here "projective verse" deploys free verse to inscribe and to voice the contingencies of being and of borders, of where one thing ends and another begins. Gravelly Hill says "the end of the world / is the borders / of my being," and what makes sense of that enunciation is a sense of the world in which there is no *decisive* border between the local and the global, between something and everything, yet wherein relations among objects and elements of experience *do* constitute discrete things amid which one moves and with which one writes: a letter, a word, a line, an old creek, the

Otter ponds, a bridge, the heavy slab stones of which it is made, Jeremiah Millett's generous pasture, or the slide of the gravelly hill itself. Projective verse, rejecting the imposition of conditions not in order to be conditionless but to arrive at its own conditions, attempts to sustain a sense of the world as a "project": not a project in the sense of "an opportunity for some 'alert' person," to make good on "the modern useableness / of any thing," but rather as the subjective embryo of a developing object, as a fragment of the future conditioned by a feeling for fragments of the past. "My memory is / the history of time,"[21] we read on another page of volume II: The subjective is immersed in a history that radically exceeds it and is included in a developing object whose objectivity is never complete insofar as it remains a fragment of the future toward which it is projected. The famous inscription with which the Gravelly Hill poem concludes—"(boundary / Disappear."[22]—incisively formulates this condition: A period marks the end of the line and of the poem, but the parenthesis which opens the enunciation does not close. The end of the poem is cast like a spell, in the imperative, disappearing the boundary as it is inscribed. It is a formal synecdoche of the condition of the long poem, mediating the insoluble codetermination of project and fragment.

Volume III, unfinished, is the point at which the poetic rendering of this insoluble codetermination evades authorial intention. Death is the terminus of intention, and this is what Olson both anticipates and recalls in the poem beginning, "the whole thing has run so fast away it breaks my heart." The poem could be described in Heideggerian terms: We are thrown into a world that precedes us, that was already there, the historicity of which we can never quite account for, though we are accountable to it; and we project ahead of our thrownness, anticipating death and are therefore bound to an economy of temporal finitude, of planning, of *projects*, while aware that our existence will remain a fragment of an unknown future. Riven between fragments of the past and fragments of the future, we never coincide with ourselves, are always exterior to ourselves, a fragment of projects constructing projects of fragments, already fallen and trying not to fall. It is worth remembering that Martin Heidegger develops the core of his existential analytic through an interpretation of Immanuel Kant's *Critique of Pure Reason*, and thus to some degree through an intellectual inheritance that also formed the context of Jena Romanticism. In his remarkable readings of Kant's transcendental deduction and transcendental schematism, Heidegger ungrounds the unity of apperception—of the "I think"—through which Kant understood the identity of the subject beneath or amid the flux of time as a form of intuition, and through which he held together the cognitive system of the categories of the understanding. Heidegger shows that the imagination's synthesis of concepts and intuitions must be understood as ungrounding the very unity of the "I" that would hold together the temporality of experience with its categorial determinations. He thus draws from the repressed substrate of Kant's thinking a constitutive temporality of the subject, a subject divided by the exteriorizing rift of recollection and anticipation, of thrown-projection, such that the I that thinks is never identical to itself but always at once ahead and behind: The supposed unity of apperception deduced by Kant must be riven by temporality.

But if such a Heideggerian framework is certainly relevant to thinking through the existential situation we encounter in volume III of *The Maximus Poems*, it is through a transformation of Heidegger's own project (in some ways akin to his modification of Kant) that I want to approach the conceptual questions at issue in thinking the codetermination of project and fragment at issue in Olson's modernist long poem. Like Kant and Heidegger, Jean-Luc Nancy is a thinker of finitude, and he describes what he calls finite thinking in terms strikingly similar to Schlegel's description of the feeling for projects inherent to romantic poetry:

> A finite thinking is one that, on each occasion, thinks the fact that it is unable to think what comes of it. Of course, it isn't a matter of refusing to see ahead or to plan. Rather, a finite thinking is one that is always surprised by its own freedom and by its own history, the finite history that produces events and sense across what is represented as the infinity of a senseless process.[23]

Like Schlegel, Nancy theorizes that which "cannot be exhausted by a theory," since finite thinking is oriented toward a future it anticipates yet cannot know, and thinks this deficit on each occasion. The surprise of its freedom and its own history are productive of sense within what seems to be a senseless process. Here, *meaning* is generated by the *contingency* of sense, because it is the finitude of knowledge and of existence that makes events significant: If they could be known in advance and as a totality their advent would be shorn of the very *feeling* of their happening, of the pleasure and the suffering bound up with unpredictability.[24] What is notable about

Nancy's work is that while Heidegger's existential analytic is concerned primarily with the relation between being and time, Nancy develops and radicalizes the role of space in Heidegger's concept of world, and it is this development that makes his thinking consonant with the formal specificity of the modernist long poem.

For Heidegger, the anticipation of death, and thus the temporalizing structure of thrown-projection, is what distinguishes *Dasein* as a modality of human being from that of animals or inorganic objects. And this is indeed the kind of distinction Olson seems to note in his winter day poem, as "all but me" is equally new and forever upon this earth, while death casts its dart of dirt and shadow across his existence and thus singles him out, like a line break. But if it is true that the anticipation of death and the finite economy of human projects it entails do indeed distinguish the temporal structure of our existence from that of other beings, for Nancy it is equally important to think the manner in which embodiment, spatial existence, and indeed the prospect of death also intimately bind us to those elements of physical being, of inorganic and animal existence, that also traverse us and constitute our being in the world. Referring to Heidegger's distinctions between modalities of being proper to man, animal, and stone, Nancy argues that

> this world beyond humanity is the effective exteriority *of humanity itself*, if the formula is understood in such a way as to avoid construing the relation between humanity and world as a relation between subject and object. For it is a question of understanding the world not as man's object or field of action, but as the spatial totality of the sense of existence, a totality that is itself *existent*, even if not in the mode of *Dasein*.[25]

Nancy's point is not to promulgate a vulgar anthropomorphism as a supposed antidote to anthropocentrism, as is the case with so many invocations of the "nonhuman" in contemporary theory. He does not mean to *collapse* distinct modalities of being, or differences between humans, other animals, and inorganic objects into irrelevance, or to consider them indifferently as "agents" in the mode of actor network theory. Rather, in his meditations on what he calls "the sense of the world" Nancy tries to think the specific dimension of exteriority passing *among* and *between* discrepant modalities of being as a surface of sense, as the contact of bodies constituting a plane of exteriority to the propriety of individual beings, as the *ex-position* of discrete things. He writes of "the general texture of being qua being-something-somewhere, being a 'fragment' of world whose matter is the very fraying or fractality of fragments, places, and takings-place . . . and this is always a *body*, a *res extensa*, in the sense of extension . . . an exposition" that is "an exposed body," and this is what he means by existence.[26]

When Olson articulates, in "Projective Verse," a stance toward reality he calls "objectism,"[27] I think this is the sense of the world he has in mind. Olson understands the human animal *not only* in terms of a capacity for thinking or for normative judgment differentiating our existence from that of other beings, but *also* in terms of the body's being an object among objects, of the poem and the world in which it participates as a field of tensions among objects, a physical field in which form is precisely the spatial *extension* of whatever content we bring to and glean from our sense of the world.[28] This is the way in which the relation between the *project* of the long poem and the finitude of existence—the possibility of its form falling into incomplete *fragments* through the interruption of intention by death—is bound up with the stance toward reality Olson articulates. We die and our bodies disintegrate into the world we are part of, or are dispersed as ashes, such that death and our anticipation of its interruption of our projects finds in the incompleteness and fragmentation of the unfinished long poem the formal correlate of our exposure to a world that we form but in which we also come undone, a formal correlate of the manner in which our existence exceeds our mortal life and includes, at once within and outside of that life, our mortal remains. Thus, Olson writes,

> I live underneath
> the light of day
>
>   I am a stone
> or the ground beneath
>
> My life is buried,
> with all sorts of passages
> both on the sides and on the face turned down
> to the earth
> or built out as long gifted generous northeastern Connecticut stone
>   walls are

through which 18th century roads still pass
as though they themselves were realms,

the stones they're made up of
are from the bottom such Ice-age megaliths

and the uplands the walls are the boundaries of
are defined with such non-niggardly definition

of the amount of distance between a road in & out
of the wood-lots or further passage-ways, further farms
are given

    that one suddenly is walking
in Tartarian-Erojan, Geaan-Ouranian
time and life love space
    time & exact
analogy time & intellect time & mind time & time
spirit

    the initiation

    of another kind of nation[29]

The closing rhyme itself dawns as if a contingent happenstance, as something that merely takes place, and it has that sense *because* there is no formal requirement of rhyme. The poem draws together a sense of physical immersion in the earth, of the inorganic elements of our existence traversing and interior to organic bodies and thinking minds—the physical being of spirit—while situating this among fragments of the past including Ice-age megaliths and fragments of the future like "another kind of nation," projected at the end of the poem as a hope that goes beyond the boundaries of the poem and of a life. Suddenly—surprised by our own freedom and our own history—one is walking in a world suffused with myth as well as divided into wood-lots and opening onto further passage-ways, since it is not so obvious how one thing begins and another ends. But literature is also the interruption of myth, such that the opening of a mythic time to which Olson alludes is also delimited by the finite extension of the poem and of moral existence. The poem does not quite end in a triumphant fusion of mythos, eros, and polis, but with a fragmentary whimper, as Silliman says, though we are now in a position to see how that could be understood as the essence of the poem's contingent project rather than a contingency by which that project is compromised.

Consider how this sense of the world, wherein finite existence is gathered and dispersed through broken-bounded articulations at the crux of fragment and project, might be regarded as implicit in free verse itself, or at least how free verse is a formal practice enabling its articulation. One page of Lorine Niedecker's *Lake Superior* harbors the following inscription:

> The smooth black stone
> I picked up in the true source park
>   the leaf beside it
> once was stone
>
> Why should we hurry
>   Home[30]

The lines range from one to eight syllables. "The smooth black stone" gets a line of its own, formally marked as a solitary particular. Then we learn its origin, or at least the place in which it came into relation with the "I" of the poem. Then that place and time (the past tense) are drawn into relation with another particular: "the leaf beside it," marked off by indentation as if to leave a place for what was once there. The poem moves from the present tense of noticing or recollection into the time recalled, and it demarcates relations of contiguity ("beside") or belonging ("in") while designating and tracing the boundaries of particulars through line breaks, such that the poem itself participates in the spatiotemporal making of what it apparently describes. We move into a deeper past, extending far beyond the space of a life: "the leaf beside it / once was stone." The organic is drawn back to inorganic origins just as the stone is drawn back to where it was picked up, in "true source park." And now we move across an empty line into a concluding couplet, "Why should we hurry / Home." We are addressed by a rhetorical question, the posing of which is divided by a line break that renders its sense ambiguous. "Why should we hurry home?" is a simple question, but the force of the break, giving

Home its own line, is to suggest that Home is the place we already are as well as where we might end up were we to hurry elsewhere: thus, that we do not need to hurry home since it is already where we are. The complex temporality of the poem is woven into the immediacy of an asynchrony, wherein now and then, already and not yet, are coimplicated. It is free verse that enables the isolation of the word "Home" on the final line, just as it allows the isolation of "The smooth black stone" on the first line, their slant rhyme emphasizing their formal bond as units, while the indentation of Home draws it likewise into formal proximity to "the leaf beside it." The word "Home" *gathers* one thing and another, "in" and "beside," "I" and "it," "once" and "why" together into what seems to be at once the word that concludes a query and the answer to that question: Question and answer are contained in a fragment of sense, unmarked by the punctuation that would seal its grammar. We are in the time and space of *existence* in the strict sense, the written articulation of our exteriority to ourselves and therefore our interiority to the world wherein we make sense precisely by dividing it from a sense that would merely be given. We find the stone, we make the poem, but it is the poem itself that makes the sense of stone, and park, and leaf, and word, since it exceeds the intentions of authorship or the totality of interpretive closure. The poem participates in the project of the world it describes with such fragile precision. And writing is the inorganic inscription of that participation by a living body, by a thinking mind: In the element of time, it marks the space of what remains of thought and feeling, of memory and desire, in the form of a thing endowed with sense.

The formal contingency of the long poem whose author dies amid its making incompletes the whole of the poem, and thereby makes that incompleteness the correlate of the minimal affordances of free verse: the capacity to fracture, to demarcate, to isolate, to ambiguate relation through the contingency of measure and the immanence of form to its unfolding. Olson's scattered fragments aspire to hold together that which drifts apart or is found together, which he knows to be undergoing a formal dispersal:

> That's
> the combination the ocean
> out one window rolling
> 100 yards from me, the City

> out the door on the next quarter up a hill was a dune
> 300 years covered very little so that, a few years back
> a street crew were and I picked up the white
> sand
>
> On my back the
> Harbor and over it the long arm'd shield of Eastern
> point.   Whenever I turn or look in whatever direction,
> and near me, on any quarter, all possible combinations of
> Creation even now early year Mars blowing
> crazy lights at night and as I write in the day light snow
> covering the water and crossing the air between me and
> the City.   Love the World—and stay inside it.
>   Concentrate
> one's own form, holding
> every automorphism
>
>   2 Feb. 1968[31]

"100 yards," "300 years," "a few years back", "the City / out the door," "the white sand," "the Ocean," "the Harbor," and "the long arm'd shield of Eastern point": The poem enumerates particulars and approximations as "the combination" by which the speaker is surrounded, and extending "wherever I turn or look in whatever direction" into "all possible combinations of / Creation." The body is a mobile point accreting *particular* relations amid extensions of sense exceeding its capacity to grasp them while nevertheless denoting consciousness of that excess. Light snow covers the water and crosses the air between poet and city *as* he writes: Emptiness is traversed by particles of exteriority that come to occupy the space between one combination and another, producing new combinations. The imperative to "Love the World—and stay inside it" implies the concentration necessary to do so, and the pathos of this imperative is that one remains inside the world once one no longer has the capacity to love, since death entails an absorption by the world of a body that is shorn of intention. The written poems are an effort at "holding every automorphism"; yet their unwritten dispersion and posthumous combinations are, in a sense, an automorphism of its own, shaped by editors and assembled by readers into unanticipated configurations of meaning and feeling. Snow becomes a major figure in volume III, its particulate fragility and amassed concentrations—heaps of singularity—offering a visual, meteorological, and affective sign of the beauty, strangeness, and exteriority of what it looks like and how it feels to fall into and within a world from which death demarcates us even as it holds us within it.

In bringing the contingent, incomplete form of the modernist long poem interrupted and constituted by death into conversation with theories of fragment and project drawn from German romanticism and relayed, in different ways, by Heidegger and Nancy, I mean to situate it in a longer and discrepant unfolding of philosophical and literary questions, concepts, and forms that is punctuated and redirected by the development of free verse. Free verse opens the formal capacity of poetry to inscribe the codetermination of project and fragment, not only at the scale of the imagist miniature but also at the scale of composition stretching across decades. Forever becoming and never perfected, the endlessness of the romantic project and the inability of finite thinking to think what comes of it finds its adequate form in poems whose contingent terminus fragments their completeness into fragments of their project whose formal significance both relays and goes beyond that of free verse: They expose the malleable openness of form to the shipwreck of intention.

NOTES

1. Charles Olson, *The Maximus Poems*, ed. George F. Butterick (Berkeley: University of California Press, 1983), 483 [III.108].
2. William Shakespeare, "Sonnet 73," in *The Sonnets*, ed. Stephen Orgel (New York: Penguin, 2001), 76.
3. Olson, *The Maximus Poems*, 604 [III.206].
4. Olson, *The Maximus Poems*, 618 [III.217].
5. Mark Scroggins, "*'A'* to *ARK*: Zukofsky, Johnson, and an Alphabet of the Long Poem," *Facture* 1 (2000), 146.
6. Ronald Johnson, *ARK* (Albuquerque, NM: Living Batch Press, 1996), n.p.
7. Ron Silliman, "Un-scene, Ur-new: The History of the Longpoem and 'The Collage Poems of *Drafts*,'" in *Drafting Beyond the Ending: On Rachel Blau DuPlessis*, ed. Patrick Pritchett, *Jacket2* (2011), n. p. http://jacket2.org/article/un-scene-ur-new.
8. Silliman, "Un-scene, Ur-new," n.p.

9. George Oppen, *New Collected Poems*, ed. Michael Davidson (New York: New Directions, 2008), 167.
10. Rachel Blau DuPlessis, "After the Long Poem," *DIBUR Literary Journal* 4 (2019): n.p. https://arcade.stanford.edu/dibur/after-long-poem.
11. Rachel Blau DuPlessis, *Surge: Drafts 96–114* (Cromer, UK: Salt Publishing, 2013), 159.
12. DuPlessis, *Surge*, 159.
13. Nathaniel Mackey, "Preface," in *Splay Anthem* (New York: New Directions, 2006), xi.
14. Friedrich Schlegel, "Athenaeum Fragment 22," in *Friedrich Schlegel's Lucinde and the Fragments*, trans. Peter Firchow (Minneapolis: University of Minnesota Press, 1971), 164.
15. Schlegel, "Athenaeum Fragment 116," 175.
16. Jed Rasula, *History of a Shiver: The Sublime Impudence of Modernism* (Oxford: Oxford University Press, 2016), 54.
17. Rasula, *History of a Shiver*, 54.
18. Rasula, *History of a Shiver*, 74, 73.
19. Olson, *The Maximus Poems*, 269 [II.99].
20. Olson, *The Maximus Poems*, 331 [II.161].
21. Olson, *The Maximus Poems*, 256 [II.86].
22. Olson, *The Maximus Poems*, 320 [II.150].
23. Jean-Luc Nancy, "A Finite Thinking," trans. Edward Bullard, Jonathan Derbyshire, and Simon Sparks, in *A Finite Thinking*, ed. Simon Sparks (Stanford, CA: Stanford University Press, 2003), 15. Nancy's work is deeply influenced by and attentive to early German romanticism. See, in particular, Philippe Lacoue-Labarthe and Jean-Luc Nancy, *The Literary Absolute: The Theory of Literature in German Romanticism*, trans. Philip Barnard and Cheryl Lester (New York: State University of New York Press, 1988).
24. See Martin Hägglund, *Dying for Time: Proust, Woolf, Nabokov* (Cambridge, MA: Harvard University Press, 2012).
25. Jean-Luc Nancy, *The Sense of the World*, trans. Jeffrey S. Librett (Minneapolis: University of Minnesota Press, 1997), 56.
26. Nancy, *The Sense of the World*, 58.
27. Charles Olson, "Projective Verse," in *The Collected Prose of Charles Olson*, ed. Donald Allen and Benjamin Friedlander (Berkeley: University of California Press, 1997), 247.

28. Olson, "Projective Verse," 243–44.
29. Olson, *The Maximus Poems*, 633 [III.228].
30. Lorine Niedecker, *Collected Poems*, ed. Jenny Penberthy (Berkeley: University of California Press, 2002), 236.
31. Olson, *The Maximus Poems*, 582 [III.188].

BIBLIOGRAPHY

DuPlessis, Rachel Blau. "After the Long Poem." *DIBUR Literary Journal* 4 (2019). N.p. https://arcade.stanford.edu/dibur/after-long-poem.
DuPlessis, Rachel Blau. *Surge: Drafts 96–114*. Cromer, UK: Salt Publishing, 2013.
Hägglund, Martin. *Dying for Time: Proust, Woolf, Nabokov*. Cambridge, MA: Harvard University Press, 2012.
Johnson, Ronald. *ARK*. Albuquerque, NM: Living Batch Press, 1996.
Lacoue-Labarthe, Philippe, and Jean-Luc Nancy. *The Literary Absolute: The Theory of Literature in German Romanticism*. Translated by Philip Barnard and Cheryl Lester. New York: State University of New York Press, 1988.
Mackey, Nathaniel. "Preface." In *Splay Anthem*, ix–xvi. New York: New Directions, 2006.
Nancy, Jean-Luc. "A Finite Thinking." In *A Finite Thinking*, edited by Simon Sparks, translated by Edward Bullard, Jonathan Derbyshire, and Simon Sparks, 3–30. Stanford, CA: Stanford University Press, 2003.
Nancy, Jean-Luc. *The Sense of the World*. Translated Jeffry S. Librett. Minneapolis: University of Minnesota Press, 1997.
Niedecker, Lorine. *Collected Poems*. Edited by Jenny Penberthy. Berkeley: University of California Press, 2002.
Olson, Charles. *The Maximus Poems*. Edited by George F. Butterick. Berkeley: University of California Press, 1983.
Olson, Charles. "Projective Verse." In *Collected Prose*, edited by Donald Allen and Benjamin Friedlander, 239–49. Berkeley: University of California Press, 1997.
Oppen, George. *New Collected Poems*. Edited by Michael Davidson. New York: New Directions, 2008.
Rasula, Jed. *History of a Shiver: The Sublime Impudence of Modernism*. Oxford: Oxford University Press, 2016.

Schlegel, Friedrich. *Friedrich Schlegel's Lucinde and the Fragments*. Edited by Peter Firchow. Minneapolis: University of Minnesota Press, 1971.

Scroggins, Mark. "*'A'* to *ARK*: Zukofsky, Johnson, and an Alphabet of the Long Poem." *Facture* 1 (2000): 143–52.

Shakespeare, William. *The Sonnets*. Edited by Stephen Orgel. New York: Penguin, 2001.

Silliman, Ron. "Un-scene, Ur-new: The History of the Longpoem and 'The Collage Poems of *Drafts*.'" In *Drafting Beyond the Ending: On Rachel Blau DuPlessis*, edited by Patrick Pritchett. *Jacket2* (2011): n.p. https://jacket2.org/article/un-scene-ur-new.

Chapter Three

"A Restless Surface"

Everyday Phenomenology in James Schuyler's Long Poems

Matthew Carbery

> I can't get over
> how it all works in together
> —James Schuyler, "February"

INTRODUCTION

James Schuyler's poetry explores the intersubjective world from the perspective of a finite subject position. He displays at all times, as Andrew Epstein writes, "attentiveness to the here and now."[1] His long poems constitute acts of framing a self-critical and self-reflexive I. In addressing the "restless surface" of both life and text, he "accommodate[s] the random trivialities of experience without either loading them with significance, or making them seem mere illustrations of chaos and contingency."[2] His work dramatizes the act of perception itself and how perception is articulated in language. His attention is attuned to, for example, the way colors shift in our sensory apprehension, denying nominal signification, like "the blue looking pink" of February in the poem that bears "February" as its title.[3] But it is not enough to understand Schuyler as *merely* a poet of the everyday. Epstein suggests that in thinking "of Schuyler as primarily a poet of realism and mimesis, the quotidian snapshot and the limpid lyric, we overlook some of what makes his poetry so powerful, lasting and timely."[4] Schuyler's writing foregrounds its own process of composition by reflecting throughout on the specificity of certain words and phrasings in their contingently determined contexts. His poetry reflects on, as Daniel Katz writes, "the alterity of what is beyond him and beyond subjectivity."[5] Indeed, this is crucial to an understanding of Schuyler's long poems as long poems. It could reasonably be suggested that his long poems are short in comparison to the mighty book-length works of Charles Olson, Rachel Blau DuPlessis, or Ron Silliman. We should by now, however, be beyond superficial readings of quantity in works of poetic extension. As my book *Phenomenology and the Late Twentieth Century American Long Poem* sought to show, the "long" of long poems can be achieved in a variety of ways.[6] A long poem is not simply a double-digit page count, or above a certain number of lines. One of the most famous examples of a long poem ever, T. S. Eliot's *The Waste Land*, is plumped up with a series of explanatory notes at the end; many other poets create long poems by stitching many short poems together. This, however, is not the place for a detailed discussion of all the various ways in which poets create long poems. What matters is that a poet carries out an act of extension in their writing, which is to say that the long poem necessarily has to be a relative measure. One poet's long poem is not the equivalent of another's. It is precisely through Schuyler's decision to extend his usually short lyrical observations into margin-to-margin, expansive, meandering, multipage poems that he qualifies as a writer of long poems.

As this essay will explore, the openness to alterity in Schuyler's work can be better understood with reference to the phenomenology of Emmanuel Levinas. Writing out of the Husserl-Heidegger tradition, Levinas developed a version of phenomenology focused closely on ethics. In *Poetic Obligation: Ethics in Experimental American Poetry After 1945*, Matthew Jenkins writes:

> Unique in the philosophy of ethics is Levinas's definition of the Other, which he develops after the end of World War I through the 1970s and that can help us understand the ethics behind experimental poetics. Neither oppositional nor dialectical, Levinas's "Other" explicitly avoids a negative definition because he sees this "allergy" as the source of a deeply unethical strain in Western philosophy that seeks totality. Instead, he defines subjectivity as "welcoming the Other, as hospitality". His notion of the Other is marked by an alterity that cannot be captured by thought or category because it is a relation with infinity.[7]

The meeting between subjectivities in Levinas's conception is not a confrontation, but rather a welcoming, a site of hospitality and ultimately of ethics. In *Ethics and Infinity*, he argues, "In the communication of knowledge one is found beside the Other, not confronted with him."[8] This "besideness" is a reciprocal position. In what Levinas terms the "face" of the other, their "living presence," we are compelled by the fact that we also present as the Other to all other Others. This sense of nonconfrontation also establishes a situation in which "being in direct relation with the Other is not to thematize the Other and consider him in the same manner one considers a known object."[9] We cannot objectify the Other without objectifying ourselves. The Other necessarily transcends the knowledge we can obtain of them in their presence. In *Totality and Infinity*, Levinas argues that "We can proceed from the experience of totality back to a situation where totality breaks up, a situation that conditions the totality itself. Such a situation is the gleam of exteriority or of transcendence in the face of the Other. The rigorously developed concept of this transcendence is expressed by the term infinity."[10] Our encounters with Others are transcendent in that they take us outside ourselves, and, as Levinas claims, this going beyond has an infinite potential. It cannot, he argues, be totalized.

Important work has already been carried out by Peter Baker on the integration of Levinas's ethical phenomenology in American poetics. His 2004 book *Obdurate Brilliance: Exteriority in the Modern Long Poem* explicitly portrays long poems as being intersubjectively motivated, concerned foremost with responding to that which is exterior to subjectivity. Baker therefore offers the first example of a critical model in which the American long poem is read in phenomenological terms. Baker's rubric of "exteriority" is developed from Levinas's *Totality and Infinity*. Baker writes, "The philosophy of Levinas claims that an ethical stance, open to the address of the truly other, will keep faith with the need to resist violence. [...] This openness to the other he terms exteriority."[11] This openness to the alterity of the Other, the exploration of exteriority, is a hallmark of Schuyler's poetics. Furthermore, as will be the focus of this chapter, Schuyler's acts of poetic extension, his construction of long poem forms, arise from this desire toward exteriority. In light of this, this chapter will explore Schuyler's long poems "The Morning of The Poem," "Hymn to Life," and "A Few Days" in parallel with Levinas's phenomenology.

What links Schuyler and Levinas is precisely this radical conception of the encounter with the Other. This "Other" for Schuyler is often a person, close to him but frequently unknown to the reader. The site in which these encounters take place within his poems is a notion of "life" conceptualized as "the what of which you are a part."[12] In order to fully explicate this site of the encounter with the Other, I will first explore Schuyler's conception of life. Second, I will describe the ways in which Schuyler's long poems utilize time and temporality to prolong the encounter with the Other, with reference to the diaristic structures of his longer works. Third, and by way of conclusion, I will link these ideas about the experience of the ethical encounter to Levinas's phenomenology of radical empathy.

LIFE AND PHENOMENOLOGY

How do we approach a poet philosophically if the poet himself does not "read" philosophy in his work? It is clear that Schuyler's work has philosophical dimensions, and while it might mimic a kind of purely mimetic poetry, it is dealing with much broader questions of representation and reality. As Epstein reflects, "Schuyler's poems relentlessly explore the set of contradictions proposed by Lefebvre, Blanchot, and other philosophers: that the everyday is always both impoverished and bountiful, boring and fascinating, forgettable and memorable, repetitive and different, familiar and surprising at the exact same time."[13]

Schuyler did not engage explicitly with poetic theory or philosophy in his work, though this should not disqualify him from being read in relation to philosophy or theory. Schuyler is not a poet who alludes to Heidegger like Oppen, or weaves Whitehead into his verse like Olson; the sources he cites, as in "The Faure Ballade," consist of a coterie of friends (Frank O'Hara, John Ashbery, and Ron Padgett) as well as diarists (Sir Thomas Browne, Rev. Francis Kilvert, and Madame de la Tour du Pin), French poets (most notably Rimbaud), and art criticism. Schuyler's body of work is, as Epstein argues, "aesthetically and philosophically complex,"[14] but it hides its depth behind the more immediate impression of being a poetics of the everyday, of the surface of our lives. It is important, therefore, to avoid any conception of Schuyler as a poet who is deliberately carrying out a philosophical project; rather, we can adopt the terms of Schuyler's poetry itself in order to more accurately arrive at an authentic picture of his work. One such term is the deceptively simple "life," which appears frequently in his long poems, most prominently in "Hymn to Life." Schuyler's "life" is not meant as a mere metaphysical category, a synonym for "humanity" or "the world," but rather the experience of his living. As Epstein writes, "Although Schuyler clearly takes the everyday to be a central facet of human existence, he never views it as one-dimensional or as an easily understood aspect of experience."[15] Schuyler gleans his observations about life from life itself, rather than from a body of thought that might estrange the poet from this lived experience and the things and people that are proximate to him.

This notion of proximity, and the role it plays in the creation of art, is discussed in Schuyler's own art criticism. In "An Aspect of Fairfield Porter's Paintings," Schuyler sees in Porter's work "an unquestioning instinctive feeling for what are his natural subjects: the people and places he knows best."[16] He continues: "It is doubtful that he would paint well a subject with which he was not well acquainted, if only by way of a prototype. He once said to a painter who was thinking about moving away from a familiar landscape to an unknown one: 'Any place becomes interesting when you get to know it.'"[17]

So too in Schuyler's work we can see a desire to remain proximate with the people and things that populate his life in order to get to know them. One of the most prominent features of Schuyler's art criticism is that he knew most of the painters he was writing about and that he was close enough with them that the reviews themselves are populated with anecdotes and personal details that evoke the world in which the painting was composed. In "Appearance and Reality," for example, Schuyler writes of Porter and his group: "Bowden, Dash, Koehler, Burckhardt, Button, Katz, Porter know the fogs and water of Maine and/or Sausalito: the new reality that abstract painters create they find already there, in changing light and weather: in seeing."[18] In a likewise manner, Schuyler's own new reality is found already there, in the "restless surface" of life, and the desire to "see" is what drives the act of poetic composition, in both his shorter and longer works.

If the principles from which Schuyler's longer and shorter poems are composed are similar, how then might we explain the act of poetic extension itself? What makes his long poems "long" and why? Almost all of Schuyler's poems could be termed descriptions of a given poetic voice reflecting on its immediate phenomenal circumstances and the thoughts they provoke. In his long poems, self-evidently, this process is extended; we see Schuyler's poetic voice framing and reframing the day as the subject position it gives voice to necessarily modulates over the course of time. There is a sense, real or not, that many of Schuyler's poems could be "extended" into longer poems. The purpose of dwelling on the close relationship between Schuyler's shorter works and his long poems is to establish the sense in which Schuyler's poetics are largely consistent regardless of length, and that therefore what we find in Schuyler's *Collected Poems* is a variety of differently sustained framings of Schuyler's conception of life. This is to say, the contents of, for example, a short poem like "February" and a long poem like "Hymn to Life" have the same source in life, but the difference in length indicates the extent to which Schuyler wished to bear witness not only to this life but to the process of living. In this sense, one can describe Schuyler's poetry as framing life, and the poems themselves as constituting this frame.

This sense of the frame can be extracted from Schuyler's commentary on the process of writing an early poem, "February":

> The poem turned out to be laborious and flat, and looking out the window I saw that something marvelous was happening to the light, transforming everything. It then occurred to me that this happened more often than not (a beautiful sunset I mean) and that it was "a day like any other," which I put down as a title. The rest of the poem popped out of its own accord. Or so it seems now.[19]

The fact that for Schuyler, the process of composition was compelled by the realization that the poem framed "a day like any other" establishes the relationship between the act of writing poetry and the day. The window, which frames a perspective on the day, "transform[s] everything" by virtue of the way it holds the "restless surface" of the daily within a consistent measure.

SCHUYLER'S FRAMES

Raphael Allison comments that "it has become axiomatic in commentary on James Schuyler to call him a poet who celebrates everyday experiences and ordinary things."[20] Many of the aspects of Schuyler's poetry that are critical commonplaces—that, for example, Schuyler is a poet who accurately and joyously observes particulars in quotidian contexts—arise from Schuyler's attention to framing life. While these are certainly not entirely incorrect observations (he is a poet of the everyday, after all) they fail to consider the importance of Schuyler's poetics as a self-reflexive framing of a perceiving subject. As indicated, the term framing will become pivotal as my argument develops: It is appropriate in the context of Schuyler's occupation as an art critic and it furthermore underscores the sense in which Schuyler's long poems enact a framing of both quotidian incidents and of the poet-subject himself. The term captures the idiosyncrasy of Schuyler's poetics. It is pitched toward the visual, in the sense that much of Schuyler's life was spent looking at framed things: the world through the window and the painting in the frame. One such example can be seen in Schuyler's "February":

> I can't get over
> how it all works in together
> like a woman who just came to her window
> and stands there filling it
> jogging her baby in her arms.
> She's so far off.[21]

Here Schuyler's lyric reads as a joyous appraisal of life. But, as Allison argues, Schuyler's poetry is also "deeply skeptical of the everyday and ordinary, and 'celebration' is only half the story."[22] This skepticism is evident here in the ambiguity of Schuyler's phrase "I can't get over." It draws our attention to a number of things, not only amazement but also the nature of voice perception; that is, how one really cannot get over, in the sense of explaining, "how it all works in together." Paul Bauschatz claims that Schuyler's method consists of "creating order and structure for a sequence of seemingly unregulated events."[23] Daniel Katz offers a means of coming to terms with this: "The prevailing tendency of Schuyler's work is to deny that a 'literal description' can ever exist outside a network of comparisons, differentiations and discriminations."[24] This is evident in Schuyler's reflection that "Not knowing / a name for something proves nothing."[25] Together, this sense of a restless structure holding together restless language can be seen to exemplify the way in which Schuyler's poems *become long*.

In this regard, the phrase "I can't get over" from "February" seems to refer to the aporetic situation of attempting to give voice to subjective perception. The woman and her baby are "so far off," distanced from the poetic voice by the very act of articulation. The seemingly innocuous closing phrase ("It's a day like any other") ends the poem with a further ambiguous use of an idiomatic locution that simultaneously celebrates the quotidian while acknowledging that the inability to "get over / how it all works in together" is the condition of "the everyday" and every day. Epstein comments on the ambiguity of this seemingly conclusive line: "Schuyler deliberately leaves open what 'it' is meant to refer to—is 'it' the meaning of this specific everyday moment? February? Life? Poetry?"[26] Another term we might justifiably add to this list is "day," a term of great importance in Schuyler's work. Both a constant temporal reference and an essential measure throughout his work, the day is framed. For him, a day is distinct as a specific type of human endeavor rather than merely an ongoing present. David Herd highlights this perceptual openness in Schuyler's procedure, drawing attention to the term "life" as key to Schuyler's poetics: "In the process and experience of composing, Schuyler opened his writing up; to other voices, but also, as he was able to confidently put it in 'Slowly' to 'the what of which you are a part'; where 'the what' was, as Schuyler called it, 'life'—as distinct from a Romantic 'nature,' or, say, from a Heideggerian sense of 'being'—and with which he understood himself to be continuous."[27]

Herd suggests here an idea of process that is both continuous and yet to be systematically determined. His selection of the phrase "the what of which you are a part" is apt; here, Schuyler's diction steers from formally appropriating "the what" as anything other than something that can be vaguely gestured at. Herd's reading highlights Schuyler's own equivocation of "the what of which you are a part" as "life." In attempting to illuminate Schuyler's poetics, it is crucial to come to an understanding of Schuyler's "life," which to him is the phenomenal site where meaning plays out. In this regard, Maurice Merleau-Ponty writes: "I am not a 'living being,' a 'man,' nor even a 'consciousness,' possessing all of the characteristics that zoology, social anatomy and inductive psychology acknowledge in these products of nature or history. Rather, I am the absolute source. My existence does not come from my antecedents, nor from my physical or social surroundings; it moves out towards them and sustains them."[28]

As "the absolute source," the subject can be said to be self-consciously aware of their investment of meaning in any given perceptible phenomena, be that an object, a person, a judgment, an opinion, or a word. The immanent experience of life, however, commonly transcends this phenomenological perspective—we exist, and we call this living—and while it cannot strictly be denied that our window onto life is our own subjectivity, it can be counterargued that life is not necessarily always experienced as an emanation from the self as the "absolute source." This is to say that "life" seems to have a life itself, separate to ours. Rather than seeking to decide the distinct parameters of what constitutes self and life, Schuyler proposes a chiasmic situation in which life and self constitute each other. As Schuyler writes in "Hymn to Life":

> [...] each day is subjective and there is a totality of days
> As there are as many to live it. The day lives us and in exchange
> We it.[29]

The "totality of days" that constitute "life" lives us, which is to say, we are an object of life as much as it is our object of intention. What this means for Schuyler's practice is that just as writing about the self portrays life at large, so writing about life and its "totality of days" reveals the self. The poet-speaker of Schuyler's long poems is therefore always caught in this double-play of describing the external and revealing the internal. Later in "Hymn to Life," he writes:

> Time brings us into bloom and we wait, busy, but wait
> For the unforced flow of words and intercourse and sleep and dreams
> In which the past seems to portend the future which is just more
> Daily life.[30]

Schuyler's seemingly anticlimactic conclusion—"just more / Daily life"—should be read as a gesture toward the importance of the diurnal as a measure for Schuyler. In the act of writing about his days and portraying "dailiness," Schuyler can be said to present propositions about life while acknowledging the finite subjectivities responsible for such propositions. Though he only rarely reflected publicly on his own work, he comments in his "Letter to Miss Batie": "In the past I have declined to comment on my own work: because, it seems to me, a poem is what it is; because a poem is itself a definition, and to try to redefine it is to be apt to falsify it; and because the author is the person least able to consider his work objectively."[31]

Here Schuyler argues that poems speak for themselves; they do not need, in his mind, exegesis from their writers. There is potentially something disingenuous about this expression of values given that much of Schuyler's life was spent writing art criticism. If read generously, however, the comment can be seen to form a fundamentally phenomenological understanding of the poetic. A poem being simply what it is, without need for further explanation, conceptualizes it as being continuous with life, simply another object of our perception. In this sense, Schuyler's long poems frame subjectivity, for both us and the poetic voice. In "The Morning of the Poem," Schuyler writes:

> What's the problem?
> No innate love of
> Words, no sense of
> How the thing said
> Is in the words, how
> The words are themselves
> The thing said [...]³²

The lines here recall his "Letter to Miss Batie," where the poem "is what it is." Schuyler states that the problem of life lies in there being no "innate love of words," or a conception that would hold that "The words are themselves / The thing said." Schuyler seems to be gesturing toward a conception of language wherein language itself inaugurates "the thing"; it does not, strictly speaking, exist without it. This sense of language playing a role in granting things their existence is evoked in Schuyler's notion of "a restless surface," where the restlessness in question refers not only to the contingency of perception but also to the role language plays in giving reality to the objects of our perception.

THE RESTLESS SURFACE OF THE DAY

This play of language and perception is dramatized in one of Schuyler's most important works: "Hymn to Life," a long lyrical poem that reflects on the passage of months and their effect on Schuyler's environment and moods, the external and the internal, the objective and the subjective. Toward the end of "Hymn to Life," Schuyler writes:

> In
> A dishpan the soap powder dissolves under a turned on faucet and
> Makes foam, just like the waves that crash ashore at the foot
> Of the street. A restless surface. Chewing, and spitting sand and
> Small white pebbles, clam shells with a sheen or chalky white.
> A horseshoe crab: primeval.[33]

The phrase "a restless surface" stands out among a dense series of clauses on either side. This restlessness is one of disjunction in many senses. Structurally, Schuyler's long poems oscillate in a seemingly aleatoric fashion between the observed and the reflective. William Watkin describes this process as "an ongoing parenthetical series of interruptions of interruptions, negotiating between the two forces of the poem, the general and the specific."[34] Watkin's phrasing is apt: Schuyler's deviations are parenthetical and interruptions of interruptions, suggesting that the ontology of his poetry is shifting, as Schuyler writes: "A story / Not told: so much not understood, a sight, an insight, and you pass on."[35] While it is true that Schuyler's tone moves between addressing things generally and specifically, to make this distinction risks misunderstanding the modulation at work in his texts as strictly dialectical rather than more indeterminate and contingent. There is always the "not told" and "not understood."

It is in this context that turning to the key concepts of Merleau-Ponty's phenomenology is useful. His writings evoke a sympathetic sense of our perceptual experience as being a contingent interaction between self and world. For him, phenomenology "is an ever-renewed experiment of its own beginning, that [...] consists entirely in describing this beginning."[36] For Schuyler, this "ever-renewed experiment" takes place within the site of the everyday, and he gives voice to this contingency with the kind of disjunctive self-reflection we have witnessed in his long poems. His longer works, by virtue of the fact that they frame multiple and contradictory perspectives over the course of an extended period of time, present an "ever-renewed" contact with the daily that necessarily modulates as the day progresses. Schuyler's first-person poetic voice is at once deeply subjective in the sense that it acknowledges its temporal and perspectival finitude, while being an object in the sense that it is a deliberate construction by the poet, manifested by the text itself. This hints at the profoundly intersubjective nature of his long poems: they extend not just in terms of textual quantity but in an empathetic reach out into the perceptual world. This view of Schuyler is developed by Watkin: "The poet must attend at each turn, not merely as to how his observing and inscribing point of view relates to the things he is observing and writing about, but also how this process itself is not only changing the nature of the things being written about, but how the very act of writing is a thing in itself."[37]

Superficially, Schuyler inscribes subjectivity in his texts by writing almost exclusively from the first-person perspective of the poet-subject, but additionally, he frames the subject by opening his poems to authorial digression, self-critique, or editing that remains in the text. He rarely, if ever, deviates from this mode. Most significantly, Schuyler's long poems maintain this revelation of subjectivity over a space and duration that allows for multiple shifts and modulations in tone.

Schuyler's framing of subjectivity in turn frames the everyday, in the sense that there is only ever "a restless surface" to "the what of which [we] are a part," which can be constituted, rather than reflected upon, in language. Schuyler's attention is directed toward, to use Merleau-Ponty's phrase, "the vibration of appearances which is the cradle of things,"[38] and the forms Schuyler creates to embody this attention undergo a likewise vibration or restlessness. The consistent measure in Schuyler's long poems is the "day," which, "a restless surface" itself, is both an event in the poet-subject's life and a manifestation of that life.

Schuyler's "Each day is subjective" in "Hymn to Life" invokes a sense of revelation.[39] This revelation is achieved in a sensitivity to the minutiae of the diurnal. This is evinced in the passage quoted earlier from "Hymn to Life," which develops a motif of dish washing that stands in tension between its place as a quotidian observation and a meditation on the substance of the daily. While in places the poetic voice adopts a stance (for example, "the truth is / that all these household tasks and daily work [. . .] are beautiful"),[40] these moments of reflection and self-interrogation are themselves, for Schuyler, the truth of his everyday. Kaufmann describes this temporal aspect of Schuyler's poems as an "attempt to seek the world in a day or series of days that can never quite encompass it"[41]:

> Attune yourself to what is happening
> Now, the little wet things, like washing up the lunch dishes. Bubbles
> Rise, rinse and it is done. Let the dishes air dry, the way
> You let your hair after a shampoo. All evaporates, water, time, the
> Happy moment and—harder to believe—the unhappy.[42]

Schuyler asks us and himself to attune to "what is happening / Now," a phrase the deixis of which echoes "the what of which you are a part" of "Slowly."[43] The gesture itself is polysemic; it suggests not only that Schuyler's poetic voice is attuned to the act of composing its immediate perceptions, but also that there is something to be discovered or learned from a daily routine. The simple process of dishwashing is described briefly, but provokes and extends into a meditation on the transience of the "all" that constitutes life. This bathetic shift in tone, where a desire to "attune" to "the little wet things" of life leads to a conclusion that "all evaporates," evokes an analogous sense of the flow of life evaporating in its moments. In this instance, the framing of a daily task becomes a site of revelation in which life itself is also framed. Kaufmann describes Schuyler's "day" as "serv[ing] as the background of Schuyler's experience while it is also the experience itself."[44] This sense of the inner and outer of Schuyler's writing underscores the fact that his poems are both expressions and manifestations of life.

This revelation of life in the daily occurs not only in the carrying out of routine tasks but also in all the various contingencies of the lived day: chance meetings, tiredness, hunger, memory, accident. Later in "Hymn to Life," Schuyler writes, "A bird shits on my window ledge. Rain will wash it off / Or a storm will chip it loose. Life, I do not understand."[45] The tone ambiguously hangs between marvel and grim resignation at having his window ledge shat on, either reading of which makes Schuyler's conclusive remark comedic in its exasperation, and "daily" in that the event of watching the bird is as much the "what of which you are a part" as the act of composition the poem frames. Furthermore, the fact that this seemingly conclusive passage is embedded in a ten-page poem that elsewhere contains contrary estimations of life emphasizes the sense in which the poetic voice is "attuned to what is happening / Now" and responds repeatedly to life as it continues to live him, and he it.

The ongoing revelation of subjectivity in Schuyler's long poems takes place through his framing of daily perceptions. The measure of the day in Schuyler's work is often contained within larger orders, most commonly in seasons and months, for example in the evocation of "March," "April," and "May" in "Hymn to Life." "May" acts as a clear example of how Schuyler illuminates the experience of a temporal event that occurs over a significant span. In this manner, temporality acts as a further frame in which Schuyler's poet-speakers are constituted.

TEMPORALITY AND SCHUYLER'S "MONTHS"

As we have seen in his meditations on the everyday, Schuyler's poems frame temporality as an ontological restlessness. His evocations of the commingling particulars of dailiness echoes Merleau-Ponty's figuration that "Time is neither a real process nor an actual succession that I could limit myself simply to recording. It is born of my relation with things."[46] Temporality is, as Kaufmann writes, "Schuyler's great subject."[47] His longer poems are all voicings of a phenomenal world taking place from the finite perspective of the poet reflecting on the process at hand. This has the effect of framing them each as events with a temporality both personal and objective. It is as if the processes of thought in his long poems *occur* as we read. Schuyler's works are often directly concerned with the specific evidence of objective time (growth, the seasons, the weather, natural cycles, the day, the month) but these are only ever given in the texts through subjective espousals of the personal relevance of that specific unit of time. Merleau-Ponty describes the phenomenal event as being subject to a contingency and a coalescence: "Chance happenings offset each other, and then this dust of facts coalesces, outlines a certain way of taking a position in relation to the human situation, an *event* whose contours are defined and about which we can speak."[48]

This seems true of Schuyler's framing of subjectivity in his long poems, in the sense that the proximity his texts develop across their span with the poet-subject itself constitutes an event. The contours of Schuyler's language include not only the lived events he describes but also the very event of describing these events. By framing the events of friendship, love, longing, desire, and care, Schuyler exposes empathy as a temporal process, an active event that must take place in the poem, rather than merely be projected as a sentiment. What Levinas describes as the "disturbance of [. . .] rememberable time" of the proximate relation is akin to the restless temporal surface in Schuyler's compositions.[49] This epitomizes Schuyler's poetics in that while he writes within the units of days and months, the range of temporalities invoked with reference to events that have occurred in the past or that are soon to occur creates a sense in which temporal duration is itself subject to the same digressions that populate Schuyler's texts. This suggests a sense of temporality as textual, which is to say that it functions through a series of signifiers, including objective indications like the setting of the sun or human need for sleep, and so its expression in a text constitutes a framing of time.

Schuyler's last long poem "A Few Days" can be seen to present this sense of temporality as itself being textual. The poem ostensibly concerns the death of Schuyler's mother, but the revelation of this fact ("the weary journey done")[50] only occurs in the tightened closing lines of the poem. Prior to this, the reader is confronted with a variety of meditations on the phrase "A few days":

> [A few days] are all we have. So count them as they pass. They pass
>   too quickly
> Out of breath: don't dwell on the grave, which yawns for
>   one and all.
> [...]
>   A few days: how to celebrate them?
>   It's today I want
> to memorialize but how can I? What is there to it?
>   Cold coffee and
> a ham-salad sandwich?
> [...]
>   There is
> No place to put
> anything. These squandered minutes, hours, days. A few days, spend
>   them riotously.[51]

The first of these passages, which opens the poem, might suggest at first a fairly sentimental reflection on time and life. This sense of sentiment, however, gives way to Schuyler addressing the contents of the day: travel, reported conversations, observations of landscapes, flowers, and animals. The second passage quoted above then cuts short these meditations, making explicitly synonymous the regularity of the day with the problem of how to celebrate life in the poem. The third reflection, which advises to spend life riotously, exhibits a variation in thought from the opening passage. The structural effect is one of a restless process of thought as the poet-subject portrays its phenomenal world and simultaneously reflects on this portrayal. That the poem ends with the speaker's bereavement shows that the temporal process of the poem is one of having sat down to write a poem the overarching subject of which—bereavement—exerts a cumulative pressure on the sentiments expressed. Schuyler's equivocation of life with a few days gives way by the poem's end to an embedded phone call in which the news is broken. The poem in this regard is a contingent elegy, a self-reflexive expression of grief. Again, emphasized throughout by Schuyler is the overwhelming significance of paying attention to the minute details of the daily. He writes:

> Tomorrow is another day, but no better than today if
>   you only realize it.
> Let's love today, the what we have now, this day, not
>   today or tomorrow or
> yesterday, but this passing moment, that will
>   not come again.
> Now tomorrow is today, the day before Labor Day,
>   1979.[52]

"The what we have now" is both a temporal and an existential statement. In fact, the two qualifications are almost indistinct from each other in this context.

As suggested earlier, Schuyler's measure of the day is often framed within the context of its respective month. This is frequently the case in his long poems, where the passage of time between seasons is marked for Schuyler by the weather and the effect this has on his mood and tone. In "Hymn to Life," Schuyler addresses March:

> After snowball time, a month, March, of fits and starts, winds,
> Rain, spring hints and wintry arrears. The weather pays its check,
> like quarrelling in a D.C. hotel, "I won't quarrel about it, but I made
> No local calls."[53]

The "fits and starts" of short paratactic clauses evoke not only Schuyler's experience of the month but the days that constitute it, distinguished by the weather they bear witness to. There are no quarrels, as Schuyler voices it, because the season is ambiguous, a commingling in which "spring hints and wintry arrears" blur the clarity of the relation between March as a fixed notion and as a transitional "restless surface." Earlier in the poem, Schuyler writes:

>   The turning of the globe is not so real to us
> As the seasons turning and the days that rise out of early gray
> —The world is all cut outs then—and slip or step steadily down
> The slopes of our lives where the emotions and needs sprout.[54]

The realness of the seasons here lies in that they and the days are the sites where "emotions and needs sprout." Emotions and needs—the content of the daily—are more real than the "turning of the globe," because the day is lived and the turning of the globe is not. This is profoundly phenomenological. Schuyler bears witness to life—and the act of writing a long poem—as an ongoing project that is perpetually beginning. In the same manner, the days in his poems are lived in succession and constitute a recurring determination of Schuyler's "day." He further distinguishes March with reference to April:

> And if you thought March was bad
> Consider April, early April, wet snow falling into blue squills
> That underneath a beach make an illusory lake, a haze of blue
> With depth to it. That is like pain, ordinary household pain,
> Like piles, or bumping against a hernia.[55]

What might be an allusion to T. S. Eliot's "The Waste Land" undermines the tone of the latter by reimagining the cruelty of April as being akin to the pain of piles. This does not dominate the passage, however; it stands in contrast to Schuyler's earlier evocation of March in that the subjective "ordinary household pain" evoked (Schuyler's speaker tells us he has suffered a hernia earlier in the poem) marks the month as a sensation rather than through its formal denotations. This sense of the month as a manifestation of the poet-speaker's mood is continued in Schuyler's conversation with May:

> Thank you, May, for these warm stirrings. Life
> Goes on, it seems, though in all sorts of places—nursing
> Homes—it is drawing to a close. Abstractions and generalities:
> Grass and blue depths into which the evening star seems set.[56]

"Warm stirrings" suggests an exchange between Schuyler and life, and furthermore draws attention to the poetic voice's self-consciousness by allowing "stirring" to mean both the desire to articulate and those articulations themselves. The exchange that takes place between the speaker and "May" and other temporal figurations (March and April; life; the day; the seasons) is the driving impetus of the poem. "Hymn to Life" concludes with a dialogue with May itself: "May mutters, 'Why ask questions?' or,

'What are the questions you wish to / ask?'"[57] The questions May asks are themselves concerned with the poet-subject's relation to his world, and effect a kind of paradox, first questioning the need to ask questions before inviting further questions. This is typical of Schuyler; as Epstein writes, he "constantly casts the quotidian in terms and images charged with contradiction and paradox."[58] This oscillation captures the stance we frequently find Schuyler adopting: He has a desire not to question, to commit to "the pure pleasure of simply looking,"[59] but he finds life prompting him to question. Merleau-Ponty voices a similar view of the artistic process in reference to Paul Cézanne, who, he writes, desired not to have to "choose between feeling and thought, as if he were deciding between chaos and order. He did not want to separate the stable things that appear before our gaze and their fleeting way of appearing. He wanted to paint matter as it takes on form, the birth of order through spontaneous organization."[60] In a similar manner, Schuyler seeks to give voice to this restless surface, and to bear witness to, for example, the day or the month as "spontaneous organization" rather than as an objective totality. This is not to say, however, that the revelation of subjectivity in Schuyler's work is consistently maintained; rather, the acts of composition the poems frame adhere to an internal logic of contingency, in which digression is difficult to define because of the digressive character of the poem itself.

Levinas expresses this necessity for digression as a form of transcendence. He writes: "To contain more than one's capacity does not mean to embrace or to encompass the totality of being in thought, or, at least, to be able to account for it after the fact by the inward play of constitutive thought. To contain more than one's capacity is to shatter at every moment the framework of a content that is thought, to cross the barriers of immanence."[61]

Schuyler "contains more than [his] capacity" in his long poems by creating a poetic voice that can articulate proximity not only with the phenomena of the month or of the day, but also with the lives of others. This is not to say that Schuyler's poetry succeeds at the task of "cross[ing] the barriers of immanence," but that his long poems portray, as Katz writes, "what is beyond him and beyond subjectivity."[62] One aspect of that which is "beyond subjectivity" is, of course, the Other, and the intersubjective realm. In order to more fully explicate and understand this, it is necessary to turn to Levinas to better enumerate the ways in which Schuyler's poetry explores what is "beyond subjectivity."

EMPATHY AND PROXIMITY

"Empathy and New Year" describes empathy through a series of observations and encounters around the heavy snowfall of the season. It opens with an epigraph from Claude Lévi-Strauss: "A notion like that of empathy inspires greater distrust in us, because it connotes a further dose of irrationalism and mysticism."[63] After describing the indeterminate weather (which "isn't raining, snowing, sleeting, slushing, / yet it is doing something") Schuyler states that "To look out a window is to sense / wet feet."[64] Schuyler comes to terms with the world outside the window, populated by other subjectivities like his own, through an empathetic attempt to understand what it is like to be outside. This extends Schuyler's description of the weather to include a proximate example of the effect it has on an imagined other. The following line self-consciously shifts the poem's focus ("now to infuse / the garage with a subjective state") and gestures toward Lévi-Strauss's sense of "irrationalism and mysticism" in its desire to "infuse" a sight with subjectivity. This empathetic stance is developed later in the poem when Schuyler writes, "New year is nearly here / and who, knowing himself, would / endanger his desires / resolving them / in a formula?"[65]

This state can be likened to Levinas's figuration of "the one-for-the-other" that indicates the extent to which our perception automatically signifies for others in our intersubjective world.[66] The site for all meaning and thought is itself constituted of the relation between "Same" and "The Other." As Levinas writes, this relation involves both the risk of endangering the self and of totalizing the other:

> The absolutely other is the Other. He and I do not form a number. The collectivity in which I say "you" or "we" is not a plural of the "I." I, you—these are not individuals of a common concept. Neither possession nor the unity of number nor the unity of concept link me to the Stranger, the Stranger who disturbs the being at home with oneself. But Stranger also means the free one. Over him I have no *power*. He escapes my grasp by an essential dimension even if I have him at my disposal. He is not wholly in my site.[67]

The phenomenological "site" marks the ambiguous point at which Same and Other meet in "uncommon" terms. The double bind this creates (wherein our subjectivity is absolutely subject to the plural world, while the

Stranger is subject to our meeting with him) is developed further by Levinas with reference to the "site" as conversation. He writes: "Conversation, from the very fact that it maintains the distance between me and the Other [...] cannot renounce the egoism of its existence; but the very fact of being in a conversation consists in recognizing in the Other a *right* over this egoism."[68] In this figure, engaging with the words and intentions of others constitutes a recognition of the "right" this Other has to express its own subjectivity.

Merleau-Ponty's notion of subjectivity as always being entangled in "certain relationships with others" and Levinas's conception of intersubjectivity as "one-for-the-other" are useful means of coming to terms with Schuyler's poetics. This is particularly true of his longest poem, "The Morning of The Poem,"[69] which at various times directly addresses a number of "yous": family members, poets, artists, friends. In these examples, it is the particularity of the relation that characterizes Schuyler's empathetic exchange. In the Anne Dunn section of "The Morning of The Poem," for example, Schuyler quotes a letter from his recently bereaved friend Anne, followed by his reflections:

> [...] I know how harrowing it must
>   have been for you, but, though I'm not much of
> A mystic, I'm sure in that last long handclasp he gave you
>   something: not just love, the electric flow of his failing
> Power: a gentle charge: and in exchange took with him from your
>   physical grip all that you felt for him all those
> Years, condensed in a red pulsation.[70]

Schuyler considers life, in a series of paratactic clauses coalesced into a process by the connective colons, as "the electric flow of [...] power." The passage is caught in a tension between the empathy being articulated and the inadequacy of the medium, leaving Schuyler to conclude "yes, / I wish I had been with you,"[71] a phrase that addresses the significance of the encounter over its inscription in the text. This, however, reveals a logic wherein, for Schuyler's poet-subject, the encounter occurs in the text itself, in his expression of it as an event. In a certain sense, this bereavement is textual. The phrases "touch," "handclasp," "a red pulsation," "your physical grip," "condensed," and, in particular, "exchange" emphasize the extent to which Schuyler wishes his textual encounters to be "proximate" to the encounters they detail.

In *Otherwise than Being*, Levinas writes that "Proximity is to be described as extending the subject in its very subjectivity."[72] Proximity, the being-with-an-other, is a situation that forces a kind of extension, a transcendence beyond the self. We see this proximate situation at work everywhere in Schuyler's poetry, but further, this "extension" of the subject bears relation to the form Schuyler's long poems take. Schuyler, as we have seen, extends his poems in order to make further empathetic reaches toward the various Others in the worlds of his poetic-speakers. Schuyler's long poems are therefore acts of proximity in the sense that, as he indicates in "Letter to Miss Batie," "a poem is what it is"; and a long poem is what it is, at length: an effort to give voice to the self, the other, and the "restless surface" of the relationship between Self and Other.

A further example of this conundrum can be seen in "The Morning of the Poem," where the second person "You" shifts throughout, implying the address of various people, including the poet himself. Schuyler reflects on this:

> When you read this poem you will have to decide
>   Which of the "yous" are "you." I think you will have no trouble,
> as you rise from your chair and take up your
>   Brush again and scrub in some green, that particular green,
> whose name I can't remember.[73]

This gesture toward particularity is ironic in its situation, in that the deictic "you," itself without a specific referent, evokes through its address a sense of the particular. The closing line echoes this ambiguity in its inability to name "that particular green." This ambiguity, however, evokes proximity in the sense that the particularity in question has been witnessed by both the "I" and the "You." And by forgetting its name but leaving this omission in the poem, Schuyler refuses to appropriate the Other's perception, instead evoking the green through "that-ness." This kind of deixis is used throughout Schuyler's interactions with Others in his work.

As mentioned previously, Baker's *Obdurate Brilliance* uses Levinas's work to establish a sense of the long poem as an inherently intersubjective and ethical practice. He frames this in terms of the relationship between the writer of the long poem and its readers: "The modern long poem, often through experimental strategies, works to break down the identification of the poetic speaker and the poet/author. [. . .] As readers, our ethical response is thus engaged, as we are confronted with works in which the very structure of intersubjectivity is worked out."[74]

The "ethical response" here requires an understanding of the minute ways in which intersubjectivity is "worked out." In stressing this intertwining of terms, it is essential to address the extent to which intersubjectivity, concerned as it is with the Other, cannot become generalized. It is irreducibly proximate. "Otherness" is not a vague exoticism encountered in the not-I; it is the very recognition of I-ness in the lives of Others. In *Totality and Infinity*, Levinas writes, "A calling into question of the same [. . .] is brought about by the other. We name this calling into question of my spontaneity by the presence of the Other ethics. The strangeness of the Other, his irreducibility to the I, to my thoughts and my possessions, is precisely accomplished as a calling into question of my spontaneity, as ethics."[75]

Here, Levinas's work allows the other to remain absolutely other. This task requires the polarities of "same" and "other" in that the latter cannot ethically be comprehended in the terms of the former. In a similar manner, Schuyler's long poems, especially when they address the lives of others, never attempt to fully apprehend these alien subjectivities into neat or easily comprehensible figurations. They are ambiguous, unclear, hard to identify, and regularly go unnamed, a mystery for the reader. This is not because of any lack of familiarity on the poetic voice's part, but rather as a precise result of familiarity or of proximity. Just as we rarely use the formal full names of the people we spend the majority of our time with, Schuyler's long poems create and nurture intimacy in their overfamiliar rendering of Others.

Schuyler is, therefore, a profoundly phenomenological poet in a variety of ways. It is obvious that his poems explore subjectivity and intersubjectivity, but crucially these themes are the basis of how his poems, as it were, become long. Epstein suggests that Schuyler even "reinvents" the long-poem form as a response to the paradoxes of the everyday.[76] In comparison to his shorter works, his long poems dwell at length on these complicated relationships between self and other. Furthermore, Schuyler delves into the processes by which subjectivity and intersubjectivity are produced by language. By turning to phenomenology, and specifically the work of Levinas, we have been able to gain an insight into the role long poems can play in allowing the creation of a space for working out the dynamics of self and other. In Schuyler's work, the self is a naturalistic construction via the poetic voice, and his others are the perceptual phenomena not only of daily life, but of the relationships with friends, family, and strangers that inhabit it. The long poem, then, becomes a frame for the everyday; not merely a stream of consciousness narrating the poet's thoughts, but a purposeful framing of the poetic act as a phenomenological experience.

NOTES

1. Andrew Epstein, *Attention Equals Life: The Pursuit of the Everyday in Contemporary Poetry and Culture* (New York: Oxford University Press, 2018), 70.
2. James Schuyler, *Collected Poems* (New York: Farrar, Strauss & Giroux, 1995), 215; Mark Ford, "James Schuyler and Englishness," *Poetry Review* 92, no. 3 (2002): 61.
3. Schuyler, *Collected Poems*, 4.
4. Epstein, *Attention Equals Life*, 70.
5. Daniel Katz, "James Schuyler's Epistolary Poetry: Things, Postcards, Ekphrasis," *Journal of Modern Literature* 34, no. 1 (2010): 143.
6. Matthew Carbery, *Phenomenology and the Late Twentieth Century American Long Poem* (Cham: Palgrave Macmillan, 2019).
7. Matthew Jenkins, *Poetic Obligation: Ethics in Experimental American Poetry after 1945* (Iowa City: University of Iowa Press, 2008), 11.
8. Emmanuel Levinas, *Ethics and Infinity*, trans. Richard A. Cohen (Pittsburgh: Duquesne University Press, 1985), 57.
9. Levinas, *Ethics and Infinity*, 56.
10. Emmanuel Levinas, *Totality and Infinity: An Essay on Exteriority*, trans. Alphonso Lingis (Pittsburgh: Duquesne University Press, 1999), 24–25.
11. Peter Baker, *Obdurate Brilliance: Exteriority and the Modern Long Poem* (Gainesville: University of Florida Press, 1991), 6.
12. Schuyler, *Collected Poems*, 4.
13. Epstein, *Attention Equals Life*, 71.
14. Epstein, *Attention Equals Life*, 71.
15. Epstein, *Attention Equals Life*, 97.
16. James Schuyler, *Selected Art Writings of James Schuyler* (Santa Rosa, CA: Black Sparrow Press, 1998), 35.
17. Schuyler, *Selected Art Writings*, 36.
18. Schuyler, *Selected Art Writings*, 36.
19. James Schuyler, "A Letter to Miss Batie," *Lingo* 8, no. 1 (1999): 3.
20. Raphael Allison, "James Schuyler's Beef with Ordinary Language," *Journal of Modern Literature* 34, no. 3 (2011): 106.
21. Schuyler, *Collected Poems*, 4.
22. Allison, "James Schuyler's Beef with Ordinary Language," 107.
23. Paul Bauschatz, "James Schuyler's 'A Picnic Cantata': The Art of the Ordinary," in *The Scene of My Selves: New Work on New York School Poets*, ed. Terence Diggory and Stephen Paul Miller (Orono, ME: National Poetry Foundation, 2001), 146.
24. Katz, "James Schuyler's Epistolary Poetry," 147.

25. Schuyler, *Collected Poems*, 77.
26. Epstein, *Attention Equals Life*, 78.
27. David Herd, *Enthusiast! Essays on Modern American Literature* (New York: Palgrave MacMillan, 2007), 168.
28. Maurice Merleau-Ponty, *The Phenomenology of Perception*, trans. Donald A. Landes (London: Routledge, 2012), lxxii.
29. Schuyler, *Collected Poems*, 215.
30. Schuyler, *Collected Poems*, 215.
31. Schuyler, "A Letter to Miss Batie," 3.
32. Schuyler, *Collected Poems*, 268.
33. Schuyler, *Collected Poems*, 223.
34. William Watkin, "Let's Make a List: James Schuyler's Taxonomic Autobiography," *Journal of American Studies* 36, no. 1 (2002): 31.
35. Schuyler, *Collected Poems*, 215.
36. Merleau-Ponty, *The Phenomenology of Perception*, lxxviii.
37. Watkin, "Let's Make a List," 88.
38. Maurice Merleau-Ponty, "Cézanne's Doubt," in *The Merleau-Ponty Reader*, ed. Ted Toadvine and Leonard Lawlor (Evanston, IL: Northwestern University Press, 2007), 77.
39. Schuyler, *Collected Poems*, 215.
40. Schuyler, *Collected Poems*, 218.
41. David Kaufmann, "James Schuyler's Specimen Days," in *A Schuyler of Urgent Concern*, ed. David Kaufmann, *Jacket 2* (2012): n.p. https://jacket2.org/article/james-schuylers-specimen-days.
42. Schuyler, *Collected Poems*, 219.
43. Schuyler, *Collected Poems*, 105.
44. Kaufmann, "James Schuyler's Specimen Days," n.p.
45. Schuyler, *Collected Poems*, 223.
46. Merleau-Ponty, *The Phenomenology of Perception*, 434.
47. Kaufmann, "James Schuyler's Specimen Days," n.p.
48. Merleau-Ponty, *The Phenomenology of Perception*, 66.
49. Levinas, *Totality and Infinity*, 43.
50. Schuyler, *Collected Poems*, 349.
51. Schuyler, *Collected Poems*, 354, 356, 357.
52. Schuyler, *Collected Poems*, 362.
53. Schuyler, *Collected Poems*, 215–16.
54. Schuyler, *Collected Poems*, 215.

55. Schuyler, *Collected Poems*, 217.
56. Schuyler, *Collected Poems*, 223.
57. Schuyler, *Collected Poems*, 217.
58. Epstein, *Attention Equals Life*, 98.
59. Schuyler, *Collected Poems*, 220.
60. Merleau-Ponty, "Cézanne's Doubt," 73.
61. Levinas, *Totality and Infinity*, 27.
62. Katz, "James Schuyler's Epistolary Poetry," 145.
63. Schuyler, *Collected Poems*, 77.
64. Schuyler, *Collected Poems*, 77.
65. Schuyler, *Collected Poems*, 78.
66. Emmanuel Levinas, *Otherwise than Being or Beyond Essence* (Pittsburgh: Duquesne University Press, 1999), 80.
67. Levinas, *Totality and Infinity*, 39.
68. Levinas, *Totality and Infinity*, 40.
69. Schuyler, *Collected Poems*, 259–303.
70. Schuyler, *Collected Poems*, 299.
71. Schuyler, *Collected Poems*, 299.
72. Levinas, *Otherwise than Being*, 86.
73. Schuyler, *Collected Poems*, 294.
74. Baker, *Obdurate Brilliance*, 35.
75. Levinas, *Totality and Infinity*, 63.
76. Epstein, Attention Equals Life, 74.

BIBLIOGRAPHY

Allison, Raphael. "James Schuyler's Beef with Ordinary Language." *Journal of Modern Literature* 34, no. 3 (2011): 106–27.

Baker, Peter. *Obdurate Brilliance: Exteriority and the Modern Long Poem*. Gainesville: University of Florida Press, 1991.

Bauschatz, Paul. "James Schuyler's 'A Picnic Cantata': The Art of the Ordinary." In *The Scene of My Selves: New Work on New York School Poets*, edited by Terence Diggory and Stephen Paul Miller, 267–86. Orono, ME: National Poetry Foundation, 2001.

Carbery, Matthew. *Phenomenology and the Late Twentieth Century American Long Poem*. Cham: Palgrave Macmillan, 2019.

Epstein, Andrew. *Attention Equals Life: The Pursuit of the Everyday in Contemporary Poetry and Culture*. New York: Oxford University Press, 2018.

Ford, Mark. "James Schuyler and Englishness." *Poetry Review* 92, no. 3 (2002): 60–71.

Herd, David. *Enthusiast! Essays on Modern American Literature*. New York: Palgrave MacMillan, 2007.

Jenkins, Matthew. *Poetic Obligation: Ethics in Experimental American Poetry after 1945*. Iowa City: University of Iowa Press, 2008.

Katz, Daniel. "James Schuyler's Epistolary Poetry: Things, Postcards, Ekphrasis." *Journal of Modern Literature* 34, no. 1 (2010): 143–61.

Kaufmann, David. "James Schuyler's Specimen Days." In *A Schuyler of Urgent Concern*, edited by David Kaufmann. *Jacket 2* (2012): n.p. https://jacket2.org/article/james-schuylers-specimen-days.

Levinas, Emmanuel. *Ethics and Infinity*. Translated by Richard A. Cohen. Pittsburgh: Duquesne University Press, 1985.

Levinas, Emmanuel. *Otherwise than Being or Beyond Essence*. Pittsburgh: Duquesne University Press, 1999.

Levinas, Emmanuel. *Totality and Infinity: An Essay on Exteriority*. Translated by Alphonso Lingis. Pittsburgh: Duquesne University Press, 1999.

Merleau-Ponty, Maurice. "Cézanne's Doubt." In *The Merleau-Ponty Reader*, edited by Ted Toadvine and Leonard Lawlor, 69–84. Evanston, IL: Northwestern University Press, 2007.

Merleau-Ponty, Maurice. *The Phenomenology of Perception*. Translated by Donald A. Landes. London: Routledge, 2012.

Schuyler, James. *Collected Poems*. New York: Farrar, Strauss & Giroux, 1995.

Schuyler, James. "A Letter to Miss Batie." *Lingo* 8, no. 1 (1999): 3–4.

Schuyler, James. *Selected Art Writings of James Schuyler*. Santa Rosa, CA: Black Sparrow Press, 1998.

Watkin, William. "Let's Make a List: James Schuyler's Taxonomic Autobiography." *Journal of American Studies* 36, no. 1 (2002): 43–68.

PART II

Matter

Chapter Four

Matter, Rhetoric, and Ambient Form in Susan Howe's Poetic Space

Brian J. McAllister

> The future seemed to lie in this forest of letters, theories, and forgotten actualities. I had a sense of the parallel between our fragmentary knowledge and the continual progress toward perfect understanding that never withers away.
> —Susan Howe, *Souls of the Labadie Tract*

Susan Howe's "Personal Narrative" introduces her long poem "Souls of the Labadie Tract," both included in the book also titled *Souls of the Labadie Tract*. In that personal narrative, Howe recalls her production of the earlier poem *Articulation of Sound Forms in Time*. Wandering the book stacks at Yale's Sterling Library, Howe followed the "inexorable order only chance creates,"[1] stumbling upon the lost and fragmented voices of the past within hidden and dissolving books. Through these fragmentations ("ghosts wrapped in appreciative obituaries by committee members, or dedications presented at vanished community field meetings")[2] she recognizes disjointed possibility. Through the jerks and starts of historical fragments, the lost "letters, theories, and forgotten actualities" on the library shelves,[3] Howe's poetry reconstitutes the past. The forgotten remains of the past, if not fully recoverable, can be recognized as forgotten and placed before us in their collective fragmentation. In our engagement with those fragments, we attune ourselves and our world to their absent presence. The metaphorical "forest" created through the ambient conditions of these collective materials implies an ecological concern central to Howe's practice. But this poetic attention is not with ecology, per se—as it is in landscape poetry, pastoral poetry, or other poetic reflections on environment—but, instead, with poetic practice *as* ecology; that is, poetry as a site of engagement with and attunement to the materiality of the world.

To understand and articulate this poetic attunement, I consider the roles of ambience, atmosphere, and assemblage in poetic form. First, I turn to Timothy Morton's ambient poetics, which critiques aesthetic representations that seek to holistically render an environment. Jane Bennett connects Morton's ambience to the conditions of agency, rejecting individualized, subjective agency to consider ways that environment produces ecologically contingent forms of emergent agency. As Seth Kim-Cohen and others have noted, however, this new materialist approach to agency often elides political conditions in these emergent processes. For Kim-Cohen, ambience is "hopelessly interstitial," dangerously apolitical, and leads ultimately to "the exhaustion of its own ontological status."[4] To avoid this exhaustion and maintain the political possibilities of ambient form, I turn to N. Katherine Hayles, who approaches the ontological concerns of new materialism with more nuanced attention to the conditions of emergent agency. In tandem with Hayles's more careful approach to agency, Thomas Rickert's concept of ambient rhetoric acknowledges the presence of other beings within situations of engagement and considers influences that those beings have on rhetorical encounters. Through this ambient and rhetorical lens, I highlight poetry's emergent characteristics, which attunes readers to an author's sense of world through the materially contingent assemblages of poetic form. My attention to rhetorical attunement emphasizes poetry's shifting sense of the world and draws critical attention to the strategies by which that attunement happens.[5]

This ambient trail leads to a renewed consideration of the rhetorical conditions of poetic form that complicates relationships between author, text, and reader. To model this approach and explore its possibilities in the contemporary long poem, I turn to Howe's later poetry and its performance adaptations with sound artist David Grubbs, comparing the performed versions to their print counterparts. First, I show how relationships between poetic voice and collective vision in the printed version of "Souls of the Labadie Tract" reveal implicit political possibilities of this ambient form, negotiating archival fragmentation and utopian totality in its rendering of the world. Then, in Howe's 2008 performance adaptation of this poem, I describe ways that Howe and Grubbs exploit ambient possibilities in relationships between textual materiality, spoken language, and music. Ultimately, I claim that the thematic and political possibilities of Howe's poetry build on rhetorical interactions implicit in emergent, material conditions of creation and engagement, mediated through the idiosyncratic affordances of print and recorded form.

FROM AMBIENT MUSIC TO AMBIENT RHETORIC

Situating these ambient sensibilities within broader narratives of contemporary aesthetics requires a brief look at an anecdote from the history of ambient music: Brian Eno lies in bed in January 1975, injured after an automobile accident. He struggles to the record player to listen to a performance of eighteenth-century harp music. When he returns to bed, he realizes that the amplifier volume is too low. In too much pain to rise again, Eno just listens to the nearly inaudible music. As he does so, he notices "a new way of hearing music—as part of the ambience of the environment just as the colour of the light and the sound of the rain were parts of that ambience."[6] This new way of hearing leads Eno to create a series of ambient albums, beginning in 1975 with *Discreet Music* but perhaps most famously in 1978 with *Ambient 1: Music for Airports*.[7] In the liner notes to that album, he explains how his ambient music seeks to enhance "acoustic and atmospheric idiosyncrasies," retain a "sense of doubt and uncertainty," and "induce calm and a space to think." Eno's ambience complicates relationships between performer, audience, and environment. Ambient music must "accommodate many levels of listening attention without enforcing one in particular; it must be as ignorable as it is interesting."[8]

Eno's approach to ambience emphasizes relationships between art objects and their conditions of engagement. In order to extend this relational emphasis to poetry as a site of ambient emergence, recent work seeking to complicate agency and engagement offers a shaky, problematic, but potentially useful foundation. For instance, Morton's concept of ambient poetics understands ambience as an aesthetic practice that seeks to "denote a sense of a surrounding world."[9] These works blur boundaries between subject and object to render the immediacy of nature. This practice, which Morton terms "ecomimesis," struggles to construct "a fantasy of nature as a surrounding atmosphere, palpable but shapeless" and appears most tellingly in the genre of nature writing.[10] Conjuring the natural world is always already unsuccessful, sinking back into self-constructed artificialities rather than escaping into a supposedly "real" natural situation. But Morton sees "liberating potential" in this failure, turning ecological aesthetics inward to imagine new relationships between inside and outside, art and nature, subject and object. For Morton, ambience is an aesthetic impossibility. Nevertheless, its structures, which are produced within and highlight the material conditions of textual engagement, are "the extended phenotype of the poem, the way in which text and the environment develop together."[11] These structures reveal sites for imagining new ecological relationships between reader, text, and environment.

Morton's turn to materiality links his concerns with Jane Bennett's attention to material relationships of the assemblage, what she calls "ad hoc groupings of diverse elements."[12] Bennett situates objects within ecological networks, diffusing agency among a variety of beings. For her, the agency of the assemblage is greater than—or at least different from—the sum of its parts. It is an emergent property in which "each member and protomember of the assemblage has a certain vital force, but there is also an effectivity proper to the grouping as such."[13] These assemblages are entangled relationships that produce an agency different from any agency present within the individual objects of the assemblage. This approach, which flattens ontological difference to explore agencies developed within interrelationships of being, is not without its critics. Nathan Brown, for instance, though not specifically addressing Morton's notion of ambience, dismisses his larger philosophical framework and methodological approach. In his review of *Realist Magic*, one of Morton's earlier, ontologically driven projects, Brown notes Morton's inconsistent engagement with scientific discourse, charging him with "picking and choosing the interpretive framing of his remarks without much attention to their consistency with his own ideas or their position within debates that already exist."[14] Morton's disconnect with scientific discourse leads to a methodology rife with "obscurantism" that "reinforce[s] incomprehension, rather than alleviating it."[15]

Where Brown attacks the conceptual and methodological heart of Morton's ontological approach, Kim-Cohen directs his critical attention beyond Morton to the concept of "ambience" itself, both in its aesthetic and philosophical usage. Lamenting the recent popularity of ambience— seen in the rising popularity of artists like James Turrell, Olafur Eliasson, and LaMonte Young, among others—Kim-Cohen describes it as "an artistic mode of passivity" that offers "no resistance" to political pressure.[16] He describes this ambient passivity in the following manner: "The artistic material surfs the threshold of perception, mingling with other environmental stimuli. The listener, rather than fighting to discern the former from the latter, accepts their symbiosis. Of course, this is always more or less true. Art never takes place in a vacuum. Listeners and spectators always have to negotiate the work and its environment. All art is inevitably, often unintentionally, site specific. The ambient, however, foregrounds a devaluation of foregrounding."[17]

For artists like Turrell—whose light-based works Kim-Cohen sees as engaged in this devaluing process—and in Morton's own use of the term, the ambient produces a kind of ontological purity that is ultimately "an abnegation of participation in the social, communicative, and critical realms."[18] The discursive and political possibilities of art are washed away in a purified and mystified aesthetic process.

Hayles offers a critical path away from this abnegation, which recognizes the value of these new materialist approaches while avoiding their more problematic relationship with scientific and political contexts. For her, the key problem in new materialists like Morton, Bennett, Karen Barad, Luciana Parisi, and others is their untethering of agency from cognition. This separation weakens their attempt to foreground materiality, erasing "the critical role played by materiality in creating the structures and organizations from which consciousness and cognition emerge."[19] Rather than continuing to employ these overgeneralizing moves of erasure, Hayles refines agency by recentering cognition. She distinguishes what she calls "actors," those that can make choices and decisions, from what she calls "agents," those things that cannot make choices or interpretations. Where actors are capable of cognition and include living beings and some technical systems, agents include noncognizing entities and forces (like rocks, weather patterns, glaciers, etc.). A boulder is not an actor. It cannot decide to roll down the hill to crush a house, though the material forces of erosion and gravity may still produce that result. But when incorporated into materially contingent assemblages, that same boulder becomes an agent within emergent agencies: camouflaging a lizard from a stalking predator, baking in the sun to warm the belly of a resting goat, or, with the aid of tools and physics, rolling down the hill to crush the house of one's enemy. Its role as agent in these assemblages shapes each emergent form of agency.

Moreover, rather than establishing a stable binary between agents and actors, Hayles calls for "interpenetration, continual and pervasive interactions that flow through, within, and beyond the humans, nonhumans, cognizers, noncognizers, and material processes that make up our world."[20]

In other words, Hayles draws attention to the nuances implicit within ontological conditions of agency and ways that agency involves complicated webs of engagement and interaction. That attention, moreover, builds from empirical research in cognitive science. Rather than embracing the dehierarchized ontology of new materialism, she calls for a more careful and contingent consideration of interacting relationships that produce these different forms of agency.

Like Hayles, recent work in rhetorical studies has also complicated and refined agency and intention. Rickert, for instance, has sought to ground rhetoric within material relations as "an embodied and embedded practice" that results from "environmentally situated and interactive engagements."[21] This interactive situatedness produces the "always ongoing disclosure of the world" that shifts "our manner of being."[22] For Rickert, rhetoric is "a responsive way of revealing the world for others, responding to and put forth through affective, symbolic, and material means, so as to (at least potentially) reattune or otherwise transform how others inhabit the world to an extent that calls for some action."[23] This ontological approach to rhetoric still recognizes intentionality but also considers "the dispersal and diffusion of agency," which complicate "more traditional notions of human agency."[24] For Rickert, "intent is only one element in a large array of things, feelings, peoples, and forces all complexly interacting" in this disclosure of world.[25] Where traditional rhetoric elides those other elements in the service of "humanist notions of willing," Rickert's approach considers ways that attunement between speaker and audience emerges from and is embedded within ontological conditions of the occasion.

While never mentioning Rickert, Lucy Alford also notes ways that poetic form extends beyond traditional rhetoric's attention to persuasion. For Alford, poems are "attentional acts and modalities that are fundamentally noninstrumental, not subjugated to the conveyance or extraction of information, and not in the service of rhetorical persuasion."[26] Instead, Alford notes relationships between reader, writer, and text that are constituted by both "attentional dynamics" of the poetic encounter and the "environmental factors […] surrounding both the act of writing and the act of reading."[27] In other words, to return to Hayles's notion of emergent agency, choices made by actors in the poetic encounter—that is, encounters between poets and audiences—exist within and are shaped by conditions involving various cognizing actors and noncognizing agents. Moreover, if we accept Rickert's expansion of rhetoric from intentional, purposive persuasion to emergent attunement with the conditions of the world, then poetic form has agency within this attunement processes. Much as physical forces like gravity and weather contribute to emergent forms of agency within the ontological conditions of the world, so too might poetic phenomena serve as rhetorical forces of attunement, shaped by and shaping various agencies involved in rhetorical encounters. This rhetorical and ambient approach to poetic form attends to processes by which readers integrate texts into their own senses of being in the world and highlights ways that form contributes to attunements between author, reader, text, and world.

AMBIENCE IN *SOULS OF THE LABADIE TRACT*

Howe's poetic practice offers a powerful example of this ambient rhetoric. For Howe, agency emerges within processes of poetic creation, in her engagement with and manipulation of material text. In that engagement and manipulation, Howe is just one actor within the larger agency of the creative process. In her book *Spontaneous Particulars: The Telepathy of Archives*, she describes the emergent properties of her archival work:

> Poetry has no proof nor plan nor evidence by decree or in any other way. From somewhere in the twilight realm of sound a spirit of belief flares up at the point where meaning stops and the unreality of what seems most real floods over us. The inward ardor I feel while working in research libraries is intuitive. It's a sense of self-identification and trust, or the granting of grace in an ordinary room, in secular time.[28]

For Howe, the archive's material conditions are central: "We need to see and touch objects and documents."[29] With this materiality in mind, her language of "grace" and "a spirit of belief" exemplifies the emergent assemblage of actors and agents. In the archive's material conditions, the individual enters into entangled relationships with other objects and voices. For Howe, uncomplicated, individualized agency gives way to the "granting of grace in an ordinary room, in secular time," religious language describing conditions of emergence within the archival assemblage.

This graceful, archival engagement produces interactive forms of attunement and reaches utopian fervor in "Souls of the Labadie Tract."

The poem, which incorporates writing from members of the Labadist community, an early American utopian project, models rhetorically ambient relationships between poet, poem, and reader while resisting the apolitical pitfalls of ambience and diffused agency. Moreover, the poem's utopian concerns situate Howe's poetics within longer critical narratives of the American long poem. For Paul Naylor, Howe's work lies at the end of a line that stretches back to Wallace Stevens, or from a "pure" to an "impure" poetry. For Naylor, pure poetry attempts two kinds of purification: (1) a separation from the "real world landscape" and (2) a separation from prose.[30] Howe's poetry, on the other hand, is deeply embedded in the real-world landscape, as poems like "Thorow" and its attention to the landscape of Lake George, New York, might indicate. As "a poetry of phrases and fragments," her poetry depends on an ambivalent position between poetry and prose.[31]

Craig Dworkin describes reading practices that engage these prosaic and paratactic strategies as "paragrammatic." Quoting Leon Roudiez, Dworkin defines paragrammatics as "any reading strategy that challenges the normative referential grammar of a text by forming 'networks of signification not accessible through conventional reading habits.'"[32] This demand for unconventional reading is most clear in the poems that disrupt page space, where lines cross over one another, are positioned upside down, or shaped in ways that make traditional reading difficult, if not impossible. We see this strategy in "Fragment of a Wedding Dress of Sarah Pierpont Edwards," published with "Souls of the Labadie Tract." The poem disrupts reading to such an extent that it is effectively "unreadable." At one point, the text appears to blow off the page;[33] another page includes only a small slit of indecipherable print.[34] Inability to access semantic meaning becomes central to the reading experience. Through that experience, Howe renders both the materiality of dress fabric and the invisibility of the dress's historical wearer. The dress, constructed, worn, removed, and preserved as archival cloth cutting, makes visible the invisibility of its subject. "Reading" becomes paragrammatical, establishing sensibility through metaphorical relationships between the materiality of text and dress.

Though "Souls of the Labadie Tract" is less disruptive, it still employs a paragrammatic form. Each page contains little text relative to white space, situated centrally on the page. With few variations, verso and recto pairings mirror one another, including the same number of lines and the same stanzaic structure. Dworkin recognizes paragrammatic possibilities in these mirrored pages, which "echo both her own ironic citational techniques as well as what her *détournements* teach her readers about the historical abuses and dangers of language: that the same words can always be turned around, or made to say the opposite, that the voices of others—like the type on the page—can be all too easily manipulated and twisted."[35] Text shape calls attention to both its materiality and Howe's appropriative act. These poems appear pasted onto a page from somewhere else, highlighting appropriative power in lost or suppressed voices.

For Michael Davidson, Howe's appropriation of lost voices "reveal[s] a hermeneutic of power in the nation's early exploration and colonization that [. . .] attempts to inscribe a divine intent (and, later, a market imperative) upon a 'virgin' wilderness, figured as female."[36] While "Souls of the Labadie Tract" explores this hermeneutic of power within the utopian history of its subject, it does not immediately dismiss that utopian potential. In fact, its unstable, shifting voices exemplify Howe's complicated relationship with utopian thinking. Throughout the poem, a collective, archival "we" often seems to speak to the poet ("You may amend as you find," "What do you wake us for," "You can't / hear us without having to be / us knowing everything we // know," among others).[37] Is this the "we" of the collective, utopian Labadist community? If it is, there are other passages where the "we" is far more ambiguous ("We needn't dot any i's / We know what we know / We needn't dot any i's").[38] And is the "you" Howe? At times, "you" also appears to be "poetry," addressed through a fragmented apostrophe ("Poetry you may do the / map of Hell softly," "You look ramshackle / extract poem").[39] There are also moments where the "you" is spoken by an "I," potentially the poet, though this identity is also ambiguous ("I am too much your mother," "Will you forget when I forget / that we are come to that").[40] And, of course, any use of "you" always implicates the reader, highlighting their textual engagement and position within the rhetorical encounter. These ambiguities of voice and audience reinforce slippery relationships between pronoun and antecedent. Some passages create systems for understanding these slippages, such as references to aspects of the historical Labadists or phrases that hint at their utopian ideology. The opening page concludes, "That we are come to that / Between us here to know / Things in the perfect way."[41] The lines "Millennial hopes / are certainly a part of it" offer no clue as to what "it" is (The Labadist project? The poem? The "white wall" that precedes the passage? All three? None?).[42] There are direct mentions of Labadist thinking and history. But with each connection to the Labadists or each recognition of a citational passage, the order of the text spins itself out from underneath this controlling framework.

McHale recognizes this problematic relationship between fragment and whole when he states that, in Howe's corpus, "it is seldom clear whether, in her own view, these parts add up to a 'whole,' and if they do, what exactly the scope and character of that 'whole' might be."[43] Readers are torn between understanding the poem as a cohesive whole and understanding it as a fragmented collection. But rather than coming down on either side of this binary, understanding the text's politics requires sustained ambivalence between these two positions. Dworkin clarifies this political vision:

> Even critical and scholarly work that pays close attention to the disruptive possibilities of visual prosody runs the risk of neutralizing the very disruptive potential it identifies. Such work must try to avoid co-opting those disruptions for its own rhetorical ends, and might instead attempt to communicate noise in the way one might communicate a disease. There is a strong temptation to recuperate the resisting and unsettling potential of "noise" as a "message" which can be absorbed into the very code it challenges, so that it can then be safely consumed by traditional hermeneutic strategies as simply another part of the message's "meaning."[44]

Howe's poem sits between the potential for a totalizing meaning and a fragmentation that denies meaning. It demands interpretive caution in order to avoid co-opting the text for one's own rhetorical ends.

Linking the poem's formal instability to its political vision, this ambivalence between unified potential and resistant fragmentation exhibits formal features implicit in what David Harvey calls "dialectical utopianism."[45] He distinguishes dialectical utopianism from two historically prevalent utopian forms. The first, utopias of spatial form, are concerned exclusively with the manipulation of space (e.g., More's Utopia or Disney's Epcot).[46] The other, utopias of social process, involve temporal processes of change, embodied for Harvey in Hegel and Marx.[47] These utopianisms fail in their ignorance of historical process (for spatial utopias) and spatial restriction (for social utopias). To avoid abandoning utopian thinking, Harvey proposes a utopianism that addresses "the multiple intersecting material processes that so tightly imprison us in the fine-spun web of contemporary socio-ecological life."[48] This dialectic recognizes the need for closure at the same time that it sees problems in such closure. Similarly, Howe's poetry recognizes and resists the impulse toward closure. Its formal processes implicate readers, evoking the potential for a systematized understanding of the text but simultaneously undermining such holistic systematization through fragmentation and instability.

Ultimately, though, Harvey calls for any utopian project to make a decision that produces meaning, an actionable political vision. While his dialectical utopianism "confronts the problematics of closure," the project seeks to "pull together a spatiotemporal utopianism [. . .] that is rooted in our present possibilities at the same time as it points towards different trajectories for human uneven geographical developments."[49] Does Howe's poetic utopianism do this political work? While not identical to Harvey's project, Howe's poetic voice does something very similar. As Gerald Bruns explains, Howe's composition process constructs a "dimension of intersubjectivity" in which "she is always herself and others [. . .] formed out of her library encounters with other subjects, each of which is, moreover, historically, geographically, and (there being no better term) ideologically situated."[50] No single voice, quotation, or system of meaning making produces poetic identity, yet the collective work, culled from spatially and temporally disparate locations, circles around the possibility of a unified identity. Poetic voice becomes ambient, emerging from interrelationships between author, archive, text, and reader. At the same time, that ambient condition collapses on itself through fragmentation and illegibility. In other words, the poetic identity implicit in this fragmented and resistant form gestures toward a unified identity while simultaneously undermining such unity. The millennial hopes of the poem are, in this sense, the deferred construction of a unified poetic subject. Howe's ambient rhetoric and poetic politics are formed in the countermeasurement of these two forces: between the fragmented, unstable collectivity culled from archival quotations at the heart of her identity formation and her desire for a "perfect understanding that never withers away."[51]

All this talk of utopianism might stay at the level of form if "Souls of the Labadie Tract" did not incorporate voices from the seventeenth-century utopian Labadist community. While Howe's poem focuses on the American iteration of the Labadists, which began in 1684 and ended in 1722, the movement's history stretches back to early seventeenth-century France. The group practiced a strict version of Protestant Christianity that called for the separation of community and world. As Howe states in her preface, "They held all property in common (including children) and supported themselves by manual labor and commerce."[52] Like many separatist religious communities of the time, Labadists were transient, forced to move often due to religious persecution.[53] The leader of the American colony, Peter Sluyter, ruled with an iron fist, going so far as to ban the use of firewood.[54] Nevertheless, by the end of its existence in Maryland, the community had abandoned its more radical practices, dividing and privatizing its land, growing tobacco (a crop they originally found sinful), and purchasing slaves to work the fields. Despite their attempt to escape European repression on American soil, the Labadists, like so many other utopian communities before and after, ended up engaging in those same repressive practices.

Howe's poem appropriates voices from this problematic community, recognizing the dangers of utopia without abandoning its political possibilities. The poem's emergent, ambient intersubjectivity attunes readers to conditions of utopian thinking. They become aware of moments when those conditions failed while also remaining sensitive to possibilities that those conditions carry. Rather than a utopian manifesto that etches political vision onto a space or historical narrative, "Souls of the Labadie Tract" offers an emergent model of utopian poetic form, attuning readers to modes of utopian thinking through their engagement with form. In this sense, Howe's poetic project is not necessarily historical reconstitution but, instead, poetic seance. Her archive of lost voices can no longer be wholly resurrected and incorporated into our world. But Howe's medium, in both aesthetic and paranormal senses, reconnects and attunes our world to these other, fragmented senses of being: tenuously, problematically, and always through engagement with and negotiation of form.

This archival reconstitution of lost voices offers a way to reconsider Howe's position in the long-poem tradition. In his own attempt to reconcile the relationship between textual fragment and poetic whole in Howe's practice, McHale notes her poetry can be read both within and outside the definition of the long poem, and that poetic double vision produces "a series of countermeasures against the received version of literary historiography" that exclude the marginalized and fragmented voices she resurrects in her poems.[55] In the long poem, Howe's emergent subjectivities assemble and gesture toward a possible coherence, without ever fulfilling that possibility. Approached only as fragments, these voices lose that condition of potentiality and unrealized congruity. In this sense, the utopian possibilities of Howe's poetic practice are only realized in the context of the long-poem form.

POETIC SOUND AND AMBIENCE

The emergent conditions of Howe's work take on new possibilities when adapted from print to spoken-word performance. In the past twenty years or so, Howe and Grubbs have worked together on a number of projects that merge Grubbs's sound art with Howe's readings of her strongly visual poems. The resulting performances take on the characteristics of ambient music: long drones, limited dramatic development, occasional, incomprehensible sonic interruptions, and so on. Their adaptation of "Souls of the Labadie Tract," recorded in 2008, offers a convenient site for considering ways that these adaptations integrate audiences into their idiosyncratic rhetorical relationships, attuning performer, text, and listener through the ambient conditions of form. The album consists of four tracks that are each around nine to ten minutes long. The first track begins with three minutes of droning, harmonious chords, played by Grubbs on the VCS3 synthesizer. Grubbs's playing drops out and Howe then reads, unaccompanied, the opening preface to the poem, in which she describes her archival encounter with the Labadists and offers a brief history of the community. As she concludes, Grubbs's synthesizer returns, this time more dissonant and metallic. This opening track grounds the listening experience, preparing audiences for the historical content, thematic concerns, and formal structure of the remaining pieces.

In the three remaining tracks, Howe reads the poem, with Grubbs's drones rising and falling throughout the recording. In one sense, Howe's reading is fairly traditional: moving more or less methodically through the print version from left to right and from top to bottom. Long pauses separate each printed page, "translating" page materiality to the recorded voice and emphasizing the poem's citational and appropriated conditions. These remain manipulated voices, brought together through the agency of the poet but still maintaining a fragmented and tenuous agency of their own. The recording differs from the printed poem, however, in its foregrounding of Howe's voice. Rather than engaging with silent, printed text on the page, listeners access the poem's ambient, emergent conditions through Howe's actual voice, with its distinctly American accent. Howe's recorded voice more thoroughly melds the fragmented voices appropriated from archival material. There is a struggle, then, between two conditions here: the fragmentary nature of her citation material, which creates the disjointed effects present in the print version, and the unifying effects of Howe's recorded voice, which undermine that disjointedness. Through its foregrounding of language's physicality, the spoken-word recording shifts the conditions of emergence for voice within the poem.

Grubbs complements this material emphasis. His layering drones, produced through the synthesizer and a Khaen Baet, a Southeast Asian mouth organ, create a space of attention for the listener, in Eno's sense "induc[ing] calm and a space to think."[56] Shifting between harmony, dissonance, and silence, Grubbs's performance frames audience engagement with Howe's reading, creating a complementary atmosphere: we know when Howe is speaking and when Grubbs is playing. This stable relationship draws readers to Howe's voice, to the sounds of his performance, or to interactions between her voice and his performance. In its shifts from dissonance to harmony and in its altering relationships with Howe's spoken performance, Grubbs's accompaniment moves back and forth between what David Toop sees as the two poles of ambient music: "calm, therapeutic sounds for chilling out or music which taps into the disturbing, chaotic undertow of the environment."[57] Each sonic possibility shapes listener attention, attuning them differently to the sound of Howe's voice.

In other collaborations between the two—for instance, in their 2010 recording of the poem "Frolic Architecture"—the relationship between Howe's reading and Grubbs's performance creates very different rhetorical conditions for audience engagement.[58] In this later recording, Grubbs employs similarly layered droning chords. In addition, however, he includes overprocessed sounds—e.g., cicadas, crunching gravel—that resemble the landscape sounds of field recordings, but only slightly. The metallic and mechanical screeches of the cicada and gravel sounds feel anything but "natural." Grubbs also splices incomprehensible, recorded snippets of Howe's voice into the recording. These small clips of consonant and vowel sounds intrude upon Howe's reading, breaking through the droning chords (which resemble those in "Souls of the Labadie Tract") and disrupting Howe's spoken-word performance. Without the text in front of us, it becomes impossible to distinguish her "reading" of the poem from the sampled segments of her voice. The added sounds are so brief and so similar to Howe's fragmented reading practice that distinguishing spoken and sampled voice is nearly impossible.

In both "Souls of the Labadie Tract" and "Frolic Architecture," the shift from print to recording highlights formal conditions and rhetorical processes by which listeners attune these pieces to their own senses of being in the world. Whereas Grubbs's accompaniment frames and guides audiences through Howe's reading of "Souls of the Labadie Tract," reinforcing the unified poetic voice, his inclusion of dissonant and disorienting soundscapes challenges stable listening practices in "Frolic Architecture," reinforcing fragmentation and instability in poetic voice. Attention to those medium-specific structures of attunement highlight emergent conditions of poetic production and rhetorical engagement. The affordances of form attune author/musician, text/recording, and reader/listener differently, highlighting form's role in these processes of attunement. While the material conditions of print are elided in these performances, materiality returns with a difference. For instance, the disruptive sounds in "Frolic Architecture" gesture toward a world outside the recording. Howe's voice becomes ecologically embedded, though in a way that disorients and confuses any "authentic" environmental condition. In "Souls of the Labadie Tract," Grubbs's more complementary ambience focuses our attention on the materiality of Howe's spoken voice. Listeners are drawn to the embodied conditions that produce her mid-Atlantic, American accent and her articulations of words and sound fragments within the long poem.

Moreover, in the context of Howe's position within the long-poem tradition, these sound recordings and their idiosyncratic materiality reinforce emergent relationships between fragment and whole that situate Howe's practice within that tradition. The unifying effects of her voice may even strengthen the case for considering these works as long poems. If, as McHale argues, her poetry "can be read as a single book-length poem, though it *need not* be read that way,"[59] the unifying effects of her voice and Grubbs's sonic effects reinforce the wholeness and singularity of these texts. The ghostly voices and textual fragments from the Labadist community that make up Howe's poetic practice are cohered through her spoken-word performance, emphasizing more traditional characteristics of poetic voice that may be elided or obscured in the print form. Here, her role as medium—as reconstituting voice for these scraps of historical documentation—is far more pronounced and thematically relevant to our engagement with the text. The struggle between fragment and whole is less fraught. And while we *could* listen to these pieces in fragments, the conditions of listening make that fragmentation more difficult than in the print versions, reinforcing the uniformity of these recordings. These performances and their emergent, material conditions bring these texts clearly into the domain of the long poem.

CONCLUSION

Ambient poetics are particularly fruitful when looking at works by poets like Howe, who foreground material conditions of poetry and embrace intermedial collaboration. But the implications of these questions within larger critical narratives of North American long poetry seem equally productive. Howe's own engagement with these other poems offers an initial, speculative step in that direction. In *Spontaneous Particulars*, Howe describes similarities she senses between her local, New England shoreline and William Carlos Williams's *Paterson*:

> Reading *Paterson* reminds me of walking barefoot across a small strip of common land near my house that's littered with beach glass, broken oyster shells, razor clams and kelp. It's called a beach, but no one swims there because even at high tide what is euphemistically referred to as "sand" quickly becomes marl, mud, and marsh grass. I feel the past vividly here—my own memories and the deeper past I like to explore in poems.[60]

Howe's comparison of *Paterson* and her local shoreline links poetic form to ecology and points to emergent, ambient features in Williams's text. In Howe's New England, the material amalgamation that constitutes geographical space both becomes a beach and resists that label through its idiosyncratic, emergent characteristics. Similarly, Williams's long poem offers a site of entanglement, in which its various components both cohere and resist coherence.[61] Moreover, that affinity between poetry and ecology reinforces Howe's own poetic practice, uniting the present space of the shoreline with the historical concerns of her poetry.

Here, Howe's comparison of poetic and ecological conditions invites an ambient reading of form in Williams's modernist poem. I want also to suggest that this approach is particularly valuable for reading contemporary long poetry. For instance, this lens might enrich our engagement with Tan Lin's own idiosyncratic "ambient stylistics." Lin rejects the expectation that poetic language be innovative, instead calling for poetry that is "repetitive," "boring," and "merely involv[ing] the passing of its own temporal restraints."[62] For example, in "Ambient Fiction Reading System 01: A List of Things I Read Didn't Read and Hardly Read for Exactly One Year," Lin notes the text, time, and location of everything he reads, from January 10 to June 28, 2006. This project rejects poetic transcendence, reminiscence, or ambition. Lin even admits that "most of the stuff I read I don't read at all and never remember reading afterwards."[63] In this recording practice, poetry is not "morally uplifting." Instead, it "inspire[s] a deep sense of relax" and "merely evoke[s] a mood."[64] For Lin, rather than being like music, with "recognizable harmonies and melodic threads," poetry should resemble code, or "meaning embedded in language field as undistinguishable sounds."[65] His conscription of passivity, uncreativity, and the formal structures of code might be understood as foregrounding the diffused agency and attunements central to ambient rhetoric.

While I have focused primarily on rhetorical engagements between authors, texts, and readers, these emergent conditions are implicit in the adaptive systems produced in the process of "writing in real time,"[66] as Paul Jaussen has noted, or in the development of these long poems over extended periods of time, responding to the changing conditions of the world within those periods. In that sense, Ronald Johnson's *Ark*, for example, written and published over twenty years, might model the processes of emergence and diffused agency both in terms of its extended production and in terms of its formal structure. The emergent materiality of poetic production may also complicate our sense of the long poem, opening that tradition to new possibilities. If Johnson's *Ark* responds to changing conditions of the world over its twenty years of production and if Howe's fragmented practice flickers between part and whole, how might we consider the poetic practice of someone like Scottish poet Ian Hamilton Finlay in this tradition? By incorporating a vast array of poetic objects into the space of his garden, Little Sparta, Finlay's decades-long project (ending only with his death in 2006) offers clear similarities to both Howe's and Johnson's poetic practice and may serve as one possible site for rethinking the material conditions of the long poem. Is Little Sparta a long poem in line with Howe's fragmentations and Johnson's adaptive writing, with the important difference that Finlay's work emerges within the material conditions of landscape?

Lastly, attending to poetry's ambient conditions might also open new paths of engagement between poetry studies and developments in ecocriticism and environmental humanities in work like Morton's and Rickert's, but also in others, like Cary Wolfe's interest in nonrepresentational "ecological poetics," or Margaret Ronda's historicizing concept of "great acceleration poetics."[67] The diffused agencies of poetic production and readerly engagement, which meet via the material and rhetorical forces of poetic form, offer any number of paths for enriching our critical understanding of poetry in general and the long poem in particular.

NOTES

1. Susan Howe, *Souls of the Labadie Tract* (New York: New Directions, 2007), 14.
2. Howe, *Souls of the Labadie Tract*, 15.
3. Howe, *Souls of the Labadie Tract*, 14.
4. Seth Kim-Cohen, *Against Ambience and Other Essays* (London: Bloomsbury, 2016), 32.
5. Rickert and Morton are by no means the only theorists taking up ambience and atmosphere. Though their approaches to emergence and rhetoricity are particularly salient to the specific interests of this article, a variety of ambient approaches can be found in Malcom McCullough, *Ambient Commons: Attention in the Age of Embodied Information* (Cambridge, MA: MIT Press, 2015); Gernot Böhme, *The Aesthetics of Atmospheres*, ed. Jean-Paul Thibaud (New York: Routledge, 2017); Paul Roquet, *Ambient Media: Japanese Atmospheres of Self* (Minneapolis: University of Minnesota Press, 2016); Karen Pinkus, "Ambiguity, Ambience, Ambivalence, and the Environment," *Common Knowledge* 19, no. 1 (2013): 88–95; and Anna McCarthy, *Ambient Television: Visual Culture and Public Space* (Durham, NC: Duke University Press, 2001).
6. Brian Eno, Liner Notes, in *Ambient 1: Music for Airports* (Polydor Records, 1978), n.p.
7. This story has become a kind of creation myth in musical circles, but to call Eno the "founder" of ambient music is a gross exaggeration. For longer and more detailed histories of ambient music that stretch its origins to late romantic composers like Mahler and Debussy, see Mark Prendergast, *The Ambient Century: From Mahler to Trance* (London: Bloomsbury, 2001);

and David Toop, *Ocean of Sound: Ambient Sound and Radical Listening in the Age of Communication* (London: Serpent's Tail, 2018).
8. Eno, Liner Notes, n.p.
9. Timothy Morton, *Ecology without Nature: Rethinking Environmental Aesthetics* (Cambridge, MA: Harvard University Press, 2007), 33.
10. Morton, *Ecology without Nature*, 77.
11. Timothy Morton, *The Ecological Thought* (Cambridge, MA: Harvard University Press, 2010), 104.
12. Jane Bennett, *Vibrant Matter: A Political Ecology of Things* (Durham, NC: Duke University Press, 2010), 23.
13. Bennett, *Vibrant Matter*, 24.
14. Nathan Brown, "The Nadir of OOO: From Graham Harman's *Tool-Being* to Timothy Morton's *Realist Magic: Objects, Ontology, Causality*," *Parrhesia* 17 (2013): 66.
15. Brown, "The Nadir of OOO," 68.
16. Kim-Cohen, *Against Ambience*, 32.
17. Kim-Cohen, *Against Ambience*, 33.
18. Kim-Cohen, *Against Ambience*, 29.
19. N. Katherine Hayles, *Unthought: The Power of the Cognitive Nonconscious* (Chicago: University of Chicago Press, 2017), 66.
20. Hayles, *Unthought*, 32–33.
21. Thomas Rickert, *Ambient Rhetoric: The Attunements of Rhetorical Being* (Pittsburgh: University of Pittsburgh Press, 2013), 18.
22. Rickert, *Ambient Rhetoric*, xii.
23. Rickert, *Ambient Rhetoric*, 162.
24. Rickert, *Ambient Rhetoric*, 16.
25. Rickert, *Ambient Rhetoric*, 36.
26. Lucy Alford, *Forms of Poetic Attention* (New York: Columbia University Press, 2020), 8.
27. Alford, *Forms of Poetic Attention*, 7.
28. Susan Howe, *Spontaneous Particulars: The Telepathy of the Archive* (New York: New Directions, 2014), 63.
29. Howe, *Spontaneous Particulars*, 9.
30. Paul Naylor, *Poetic Investigations: Singing the Holes in History* (Evanston, IL: Northwestern University Press, 1999), 44.
31. Naylor, *Poetic Investigations*, 55. Similarly, Brian McHale claims that Howe's antinomianism distinguishes her work from typical avant-garde poetry; rather than implying "a break with the poetry of the past," Howe's work

"implies a revisionist dialogue with the past." Brian McHale, *The Obligation toward the Difficult Whole: Postmodernist Long Poems* (Tuscaloosa: University of Alabama Press, 2004), 206.

32. Craig Dworkin, *Reading the Illegible* (Evanston, IL: Northwestern University Press, 2003), 12.
33. Howe, *Souls of the Labadie Tract*, 123.
34. Howe, *Souls of the Labadie Tract*, 125.
35. Dworkin, *Reading the Illegible*, 38.
36. Michael Davidson, *Ghostlier Demarcations: Modern Poetry and the Material Word* (Berkeley: University of California Press, 1997), 81.
37. Howe, *Souls of the Labadie Tract*, 41, 50, 58.
38. Howe, *Souls of the Labadie Tract*, 52.
39. Howe, *Souls of the Labadie Tract*, 30, 53.
40. Howe, *Souls of the Labadie Tract*, 65, 69.
41. Howe, *Souls of the Labadie Tract*, 27.
42. Howe, *Souls of the Labadie Tract*, 43.
43. McHale, *The Obligation toward the Difficult Whole*, 209.
44. Dworkin, *Reading the Illegible*, 49.
45. David Harvey, *Spaces of Hope* (Berkeley: University of California Press, 2000), 182.
46. Harvey, *Spaces of Hope*, 164.
47. Harvey, *Spaces of Hope*, 173.
48. Harvey, *Spaces of Hope*, 199.
49. Harvey, *Spaces of Hope*, 196.
50. Gerald L. Bruns, "Voices of Construction: On Susan Howe's Poetry and Poetics (A Citational Ghost Story)," *Contemporary Literature* 50, no. 1 (2009): 43.
51. Howe, *Souls of the Labadie Tract*, 14.
52. Howe, *Souls of the Labadie Tract*, 24. See T. J. Saxby, *The Quest for the New Jerusalem, Jean de Labadie and the Labadists, 1610–1744* (London: Springer, 1987), 103–34, for more on Labadist communitarianism. I recommend this tentatively, however. While this work is the only lengthy discussion of Labadists that I could find, Saxby engages in some questionable historiography. The clearest example: When explaining why the group was unsuccessful in converting the local Native population to Christianity, Saxby states, "The chief reason for this [failure to convert the Indians] was the readiness of supposedly Christian planters to flout state law in order to ply a lucrative liquor trade with the indians [*sic*], who were then reduced

by alcohol to the level of bestiality." Saxby, *The Quest for the New Jerusalem*, 297.
53. Places where the Labadists lived include Bordeaux, Amiens, Bazas, Montauban, Geneva, Middleburg, Veere, Amsterdam, Herford, Altona, Wieuwerd, Surinam, and, finally, Bohemia Manor, Maryland.
54. Saxby, *The Quest for the New Jerusalem*, 303.
55. McHale, *The Obligation toward the Difficult Whole*, 205.
56. Eno, Liner Notes, n.p.
57. Toop, *Ocean of Sound*, 40.
58. Susan Howe and David Grubbs, *Frolic Architecture* (Blue Chopsticks, 2018).
59. McHale, *The Obligation toward the Difficult Whole*, 210. Here McHale is discussing Howe's earlier work, *The Europe of Trusts*, but his claims about the open possibilities of reading seem equally valid for these more recent publications.
60. Howe, *Spontaneous Particulars*, 37.
61. For a reading of *Paterson* in terms of emergence in a systems theoretical sense, see Paul Jaussen's contribution to this volume.
62. Tan Lin, "Ambient Stylistics," *Conjunctions* 35 (2000): 127.
63. Tan Lin, "Ambient Fiction Reading System 01: A List of Things I Read Didn't Read and Hardly Read for Exactly One Year," *Ambientreading*, n.p., 2011, http://ambientreading.blogspot.com/.
64. Lin, "Ambient Stylistics," 140.
65. Lin, "Ambient Stylistics," 138.
66. Paul Jaussen, *Writing in Real Time: Emergent Poetics from Whitman to the Digital* (Cambridge: Cambridge University Press, 2017).
67. See Cary Wolfe, *Ecological Poetics; or, Wallace Stevens's Birds* (Chicago: University of Chicago Press, 2020) and Margaret Ronda, *Remainders: American Poetry at Nature's End* (Stanford, CA: Stanford University Press, 2018), 5.

BIBLIOGRAPHY

Alford, Lucy. *Forms of Poetic Attention*. New York: Columbia University Press, 2020.
Bennett, Jane. *Vibrant Matter: A Political Ecology of Things*. Durham, NC: Duke University Press, 2010.

Böhme, Gernot. *The Aesthetics of Atmospheres*. Edited by Jean-Paul Thibaud. New York: Routledge, 2017.

Brown, Nathan. "The Nadir of OOO: From Graham Harman's *Tool-Being* to Timothy Morton's *Realist Magic: Objects, Ontology, Causality*." *Parrhesia* 17 (2013): 62–71.

Bruns, Gerald L. "Voices of Construction: On Susan Howe's Poetry and Poetics (A Citational Ghost Story)." *Contemporary Literature* 50, no. 1 (2009): 28–53.

Davidson, Michael. *Ghostlier Demarcations: Modern Poetry and the Material Word*. Berkeley: University of California Press, 1997.

Dworkin, Craig. *Reading the Illegible*. Evanston, IL: Northwestern University Press, 2003.

Eno, Brian. Liner Notes. In *Ambient 1: Music for Airports*. Polydor Records, 1978.

Harvey, David. *Spaces of Hope*. Berkeley: University of California Press, 2000.

Hayles, N. Katherine. *Unthought: The Power of the Cognitive Nonconscious*. Chicago: University of Chicago Press, 2017.

Howe, Susan. *Souls of the Labadie Tract*. New York: New Directions, 2007.

Howe, Susan. *Spontaneous Particulars: The Telepathy of the Archive*. New York: New Directions, 2014.

Howe, Susan, and David Grubbs. *Frolic Architecture*. Blue Chopsticks, 2018.

Howe, Susan, and David Grubbs. *Souls of the Labadie Tract*. Drag City, 2008.

Jaussen, Paul. *Writing in Real Time: Emergent Poetics from Whitman to the Digital*. Cambridge: Cambridge University Press, 2017.

Kim-Cohen, Seth. *Against Ambience and Other Essays*. London: Bloomsbury, 2016.

Lin, Tan. "Ambient Fiction Reading System 01: A List of Things I Read Didn't Read and Hardly Read for Exactly One Year." N.p. *Ambientreading*, 2011. http://ambientreading.blogspot.com/.

Lin, Tan. "Ambient Stylistics." *Conjunctions* 35 (2000): 127–45.

McCarthy, Anna. *Ambient Television: Visual Culture and Public Space*. Durham, NC: Duke University Press, 2001.

McCullough, Malcom. *Ambient Commons: Attention in the Age of Embodied Information*. Cambridge, MA: MIT Press, 2015.

McHale, Brian. *The Obligation toward the Difficult Whole: Postmodernist Long Poems*. Tuscaloosa: University of Alabama Press, 2004.

Morton, Timothy. *The Ecological Thought*. Cambridge, MA: Harvard University Press, 2010.

Morton, Timothy. *Ecology without Nature: Rethinking Environmental Aesthetics.* Cambridge, MA: Harvard University Press, 2007.
Naylor, Paul. *Poetic Investigations: Singing the Holes in History.* Evanston, IL: Northwestern University Press, 1999.
Pinkus, Karen. "Ambiguity, Ambience, Ambivalence, and the Environment." *Common Knowledge* 19, no. 1 (2013): 88–95.
Prendergast, Mark. *The Ambient Century: From Mahler to Trance.* London: Bloomsbury, 2001.
Rickert, Thomas. *Ambient Rhetoric: The Attunements of Rhetorical Being.* Pittsburgh: University of Pittsburgh Press, 2013.
Ronda, Margaret. *Remainders: American Poetry at Nature's End.* Stanford, CA: Stanford University Press, 2018.
Roquet, Paul. *Ambient Media: Japanese Atmospheres of Self.* Minneapolis: University of Minnesota Press, 2016.
Saxby, T. J. *The Quest for the New Jerusalem, Jean de Labadie and the Labadists, 1610–1744.* London: Springer, 1987.
Toop, David. *Ocean of Sound: Ambient Sound and Radical Listening in the Age of Communication.* London: Serpent's Tail, 2018.
Wolfe, Cary. *Ecological Poetics; or, Wallace Stevens's Birds.* Chicago: University of Chicago Press, 2020.

Chapter Five

Paterson's Analogies

Iteration, Recursion, and Contingency

Paul Jaussen

The North American long poem is regularly out of time. By that I mean it is a tradition of works preoccupied with the crossing of historical and phenomenological temporalities, where the past is a persistent force and the present is that which is perceived, felt, or experienced in the moment (which can, but does not always, include the scene of writing itself). That neither of these categories is stable or entirely isolated from each other is obvious, as experiential time is historical, a mode of attention emerging from the material and contingent realities that make it possible: the built environment within which we live, the languages we speak, the people we encounter. So many iconic North American long poems write out of these dynamics,[1] despite the divergent literary, imaginative, political, and aesthetic commitments of the individual poets, commitments that, in turn, shape the very meaning of the "historical," the "experiential," or the "material." These poems often then become self-conscious manifestations of the very historical-phenomenological crossings they track, reinserting themselves into the conditions that have brought them into being.

As I have argued elsewhere, this continual reinvention can be understood through concepts like recursion and iteration, which are formal devices of the long poem that enable adaptive engagements with real-time events. Iteration is the repetition of a single unit (such as anaphora) while recursion is an embedded series of similar functions (think of a refrain with slight variations). They become complementary operations in many long poems, where "iterative elements [create] the formal condition for continuity, while recursive elements provide the formal condition for change, adaptation, modification, and evolution."[2] Through these twinned processes, the long poem is able both to orient itself in a material, changing world and adaptively to respond to that environment, fluctuating between the historical and the phenomenological as interrelated fields unfolding in unexpected ways.

In what follows, I extend this approach to the long poem through a reading of William Carlos Williams's *Paterson*, informed by Yuk Hui's recent philosophical work on recursion and contingency. For Hui, recursion "is the movement that tirelessly integrates contingency into its own functioning to realize its *telos*."[3] By contingency, Hui indicates the confrontation with exteriority that forces recursive operations, whether organic or technological, to reconsider their own terms. Thus, the "telos" he has in mind is best understood not as "the finality [. . .] assumed by mechanisms like interferences of linear causal propositions," a kind of logical necessity or inevitability, "but rather [as] attempts to arrive at such an end by recursively turning back to itself to determine itself. The form it determines is accomplished by combating contingency, not to eliminate it but rather to integrate it as necessity."[4] Hui's paradigm, while primarily developed as a philosophy of technology, is also fruitful for thinking of the relationship between recursion and contingency as the struggle to produce *poetic* form, by integrating the outside through a self-referential movement. In Williams's case, the contingencies of historical pressures, material encounters, and contemporary experiences are made visible and meaningful through the poem's similarly recursive logic, which brings together the past and the present while continually reinventing the very composition that makes such crossings possible. Poetic writing and imagination are best understood as a function whose activity is constantly cashing itself out in new writing perpetually in search of its own form. A primary operation within that function is *analogy*. *Paterson* is a recursive and iterative analogy machine, tapping local archives and experiences in order to construct dynamic poetic forms adequate for contingent encounters with a changing, material present.

Williams anticipates the recursive logic of *Paterson* in the prose reflections he called *In the American Grain*, first published in 1925. The latter text, his most direct and explicit historical writing, offers an account of the past that exceeds the national narratives one might expect from the work's title. Historiography, for Williams, was not merely an explanation of received and recognized facts but a task of imaginative proportions, an act of creation as well as accounting. That Williams called such a writing "history" challenges several cultural assumptions about the discipline (often not shared by actual historians), including beliefs about accuracy, objectivity, and representation. For Williams the past is not something merely to be studied, the purview of academics, but a physical encounter, something to be swallowed, chewed, spat out, gripped with the "bare hands," and even repeated in a violent and monstrous recreation.[5] This recreation follows a recursive logic: "However hopeless it may seem," Williams writes, "we have no other choice: we must go back to the beginning; it all must be done over; everything that is must be destroyed."[6] This destruction and recreation is precisely the kind of writing that *In the American Grain* displays. Williams tells a story of Western expansion and bloody extermination in a narrative style that moves fluently between the figurative and the literal, attempting both to attend to the details and actively to project what that history has to offer life in the present moment and in a specific place. Such a version of history, to adapt Williams's own terms, reflects the stringency of an imaginative structure: "I have told you, this / is a fiction, pay attention."[7] In bringing these two forms of knowledge together, Williams implies that "fictional" writing becomes a crucial means by which we comprehend history, while historical materials, in turn, provide a necessary ground for the fictional to emerge. Perhaps the best formulation of this interplay can be found toward the end of *Spring & All*: "As birds' wings beat the solid air without which none could fly so words freed by the imagination affirm reality by their flight."[8] The written, imaginative word is not a mere (or poor) representation of material reality but a necessary complement to it. For the Williams of *Spring & All*, the interdependence of history and imagination is essential; without the imagination, the world remains mere potential, at best, or at worst, horrifically oppressive.

These often paradoxical and shifting combinations between the historical and the fictional, the imaginative and the material, are also at the heart of *Paterson*. In Book III, for instance, events from the history of Paterson, New Jersey, are imaginatively converted into structural devices and central metaphors. In 1902, the city was savaged by a flood, a fire, and an unusual cyclone, each disaster leveling large parts of the city the previous tragedies had left intact.[9] Williams converts these destructive events into doubles for the imagination, particularly as the latter destroys the "structures" of books stacked in library shelves, those inert records of prior mental acts. Books, in this section of the poem, are a liability, bearers of a deadening poetic tradition and a barrier to new metaphorical work (and, in this instance, represent a clear departure from, say, Pound's use of the tradition).

Thus, just as the fire, flood, and cyclone tore through and opened up the buildings of Paterson, so too the poem must break open the library, the metonymic representative of its bound volumes, giving air to the "library stench."[10] This complicated series of figurations is made visible as a chain of interrelated and shifting analogies: the library is to the tornado as books are to the imagination; books are to the library as the library is to the other buildings in Paterson; the buildings of Paterson are to the city's language as the bound volumes are to the poem *Paterson*. Similarly, as Book III unfolds we see each natural event linked to the next in an extending aggregation of figures: a flood is a tornado is a fire is, ultimately, the Passaic Falls, one of the many-faced symbolic terms recurring throughout the poem. In Book III, the fire mirrors and inverts the falls: "the waterfall of the / flames, a cataract reversed, shooting / upward (what difference does it make?)."[11]

The parenthetical question is not merely rhetorical, for while the poem's analogies bring these different historical events together by converting them into imaginative figures, the work is keenly attentive to the complications arising from analogic composition. The figures make a great deal of difference, in fact, and the precise distinctions whereby water is *not* fire, nor a cyclone the imagination, disrupts the metaphors, opening up their terms to new possible significations, other contingent encounters. For instance, while the rushing water of the falls is, for Williams, the mind imaginatively at work, which allows him to link the falls as mind to the flood, a flood also has negative and detrimental effects, precisely opposite to those of the vital imagination. The waters, in their receding, leave behind not a "fertile (?) mud" but "Rather a sort of muck, a detritus, / in this case—a pustular scum, a decay, a choking / lifelessness."[12] The ooze recalls the stench of the library's shelves and an earlier description of textuality:

> And there rises
> a counterpart, of reading, slowly, overwhelming
> the mind; anchors him in his chair. So be
> it. He turns   .   O Paradiso! The stream
> grows leaden within him, his lilies drag. So
> be it. Texts mount and complicate them-
> selves, lead to further texts and those
> to synopses, digests and emendations. So be it.
> Until the words break loose or—sadly
> hold, unshaken. [...][13]

The endless accumulation of texts threatens to drag down the internal stream of the imagination, suppressing the mind. The promise that eventually the words may "break loose" offers some hope, but the overall tone of the passage is a lamentation, bemoaning the fact that writing is mere detritus, that the water of the imagination can produce infertile flood-scum.

It is precisely at this point that the work of Book III explodes through an act of self-reference, the multiplied and shifting analogies turning back on the act of writing. For *Paterson* III, as an imaginative recollection and transformation of local history, is also a textual remainder in its own right, a new digest and emendation. It may want to offer a difference, an imaginative "breaking loose" of the words, or it may be yet one more layer of the packed and poisoned dirt. The analogic chain has generated an ironic self-awareness, subjecting the poem to its own critique. But instead of invalidating the work, this moment of self-reference prompts *Paterson*'s recursive gesture of sundering the analogic chain to reforge it again, to contingently reconstitute history and fiction, imagination and word into another form yet to come.

This brief sketch of Book III, in which one analogy collapses only to be transformed into another, clearly demonstrates the way in which Williams's long poem recursively propels itself to imagine the lived experience and historical archives of the local. *Paterson*'s movements, which led Williams to eventually recognize its own structured endlessness, can be understood as the manufacture of an analogic chain by which the local language, culture, events, and history are turned into an imaginative historico-fictional poetic space. Williams claimed, famously, that a poem was a "machine made out of words,"[14] and while the shorter lyrics leave readers with the sense that they are engaging a well-tuned engine, *Paterson* confronts us like a complex, adaptive system, a self-modifying assemblage, through which the force of the local is channeled and reformed into alternative configurations. Recursivity and contingency: This work in language brings the force of the imagination theorized in *Spring & All* into the material history of a local place. In doing so, *Paterson* takes up in a more thoroughgoing manner the task of historiography of *In the American Grain*, an intervention into a history understood, in Brian A. Bremen's terms, as "the continuing story of discovery, violence, and enslavement—a story whose analogue in literary history includes the 'violent torsions' of Gertrude Stein and James Joyce 'to divorce words from the enslavement of the prevalent clichés.'"[15] As will be shown, Williams's analogies are powerful things, and so the violent literary "torsions" of a Stein or a Joyce or a *Paterson* not only mark the violence of history but actually provide a counterpressure to it, a shaping liberation of past and language.

Analogy as a central technique is visible from the opening epigraph of the work, one that begins with a colon and becomes a paratactic aggregation that ceases but does not end. The colon can be read as an open form of predication, or, more properly, predication without a single or named subject. Thus, by implication, *Paterson* / Paterson / Paterson (is) "*: a local pride; spring, summer, fall and the sea* [. . .]."[16] Each term creates a new possible configuration of the city, Paterson the main character, and the poem, and, by extension, each term in the list is distantly but potentially linked. Furthermore, linguistic substitutions, such as replacing the expected "winter" with "the sea," allow both senses to exist simultaneously, one term layered over, analogically read within, the other. As the list continues, we see that "confession" is also, or can be, "a column," "a reply to Greek and Latin with the bare hands," and "a celebration."[17] The many reorganizations suggested in this chain made out of words thus offer not merely a summary prospective outline of the poem's dramatic action but convey its central poetic and imaginative activity as an analogy machine. The final term in the list appropriately marks this multiplicity as "a dispersal and a metamorphosis"; where Pound's metamorphosis hinted at the mystical and Dionysian, Williams's shape shifting will occur through the endless writing that disperses and recreates from the local environment, an entirely immanent, materialist activity. The "distinctive terms" of "local pride," though "hard put to it," will inevitably force one to come up with "a plan for action to supplant a plan for action,"[18] recursively embracing and integrating its contingent encounters with the material world. At the beginning, it would appear, *Paterson* is already beginning again.

These affirmations of metamorphosis and repetition, grounded in the immediate configurations of the local, are made explicit as the poem's generative principle:

>   Yet there is
> no return: rolling up out of chaos,
> a nine months' wonder, the city
> the man, an identity—it can't be
> otherwise—an
> interpenetration, both ways. [. . .][19]

The poem rejects a classicist or Eurocentric nostalgia in its declaration that there will be no return to a mythic past. Instead, there is an accumulation presented as reproduction, the new text born out of the numerous manifold. The allusion to human birth, that "nine months' wonder," will become one of the recurring themes throughout the poem, imaginative fertility contrasted with rationalized and impersonal divorce.[20] Nevertheless, each instance of fertility conveys different and specific valences; in this case, the sexual dynamic exists between "the city" and "the man" in which "interpenetration" occurs "both ways." In Book I, "a man" is like a "city," and, on that register, the fertility alluded to in this passage is born from a homoerotic figuration, subtly destabilizing at the outset the traditionally gendered fertility images Williams regularly employed. Further expanding the figure, the passage can also be read as a multiplication of desires, since the city and man both produce and are interpenetrated by the third, an "identity"; one, as Olson will insist in *The Maximus Poems*, makes many.[21]

This early manifestation of some of the poem's recurring motifs reveals a fundamentally productive instability, a kind of contingency, which Williams exploits at every step, namely the "interpenetration" between the figure and its referent, the fact that we are faced, in this passage, not with a metaphor but a series of shifting and multivalued terms. The man is not merely like the city, or the identity like a "nine months' wonder," or a return like a rolling up. Instead, this passage is merely one of the possible constructions these words provide. As the poem moves forward, it offers alternative configurations, new orders among the terms, accumulating meanings and adding to the previous articulations even as it continues to navigate the language of the city by aggregating it into the poem. As new analogies emerge from sources as diverse as the local paper to private letters, imaginatively comprehending and articulating these shifting linguistic possibilities becomes the task of the poem. As Piotr Parlej argues, Williams "breaks down the distinction between ground and figure, between vehicle and tenor, because for him metaphoricity is transitive: all categories are real, all categories are imaginary."[22] In the case of *Paterson*, the imagination in place *is* this transitive movement, measurable and generated in the process of writing.

Like all figurative constructions, however, *Paterson* may tempt readers with the desire for a stabilizing symbol, an organizing motif or master term that will afford the poem an underlying coherence amid its multiplications. Williams at times seemed to search for such a figure; the note published at the beginning of the text includes his statement that after writing Book IV he realized that "there can be no end to such a story [. . .] with the terms which [he] had laid down for [himself]."[23] One of the major "terms" that could have afforded a stabilizing center was the figure of the Passaic River, and a consideration of its multiple signifying possibilities, its evolving metaphoricity, affords a clear understanding of the work's analogic recursivity. Early in Book I, the "common language to unravel"[24] becomes the Passaic Falls, "combed into straight lines / from that rafter of a rock's / lip."[25] The rock as lip turns the stone into a human mouth, from which the words pour like the water falling into the air with their engulfing roar. The common language sounds through the city as do the falls, inarticulate yet inescapable, and, important for the poem's own efforts, at least potentially capable of being "combed into straight lines" and thus made newly legible. From the falls-as-language it is merely a half-step to the falls-as-thought, namely the thought of the individual Paterson:

> Jostled as are the waters approaching
> the brink, his thoughts
> interlace, repel and cut under,
> rise rock-thwarted and turn aside
> by forever strain forward [. . .][26]

As these thoughts "fall, fall in air!," they become both weightless and undefined, only to regain "their course" by striking, once again, the riverbed.[27] Here, the river becomes a notable figure for *Paterson*'s famous "no ideas but in things." Thought has no weight, floats ambivalently, and thus lacks *force*, until it is coupled to the material and concrete reality of things, the rocks and pathways of the riverbed. The earlier association of the falls with language impinges upon the second formulation of the falls as thinking, bringing together words and thoughts at least associatively, if not explicitly. No ideas but *among* things, in this case, a dynamic interplay figured by the shaping work of the water on the land and the land on the water. Finally, for the Williams of *Spring & All*, the river's inseparability from either the land or the water, moving endlessly, recalls the necessary relationship between the imagination and material reality.

The Passaic River has thus moved from the roar of common language to the thought of an individual to the dynamism and materiality of the imagination. But these analogies are intertwined with others, and thus the proliferation of poetic structures is amplified. The "man is a city" link claimed at the poem's beginning breaks through, adding itself to the analogic chain:

> Say it! No ideas but in things. Mr.
> Paterson has gone away
> to rest and write. Inside the bus one sees
> his thoughts sitting and standing. His
> thoughts alight and scatter—
>
> Who are these people (how complex
> the mathematic) among whom I see myself
> in the regularly ordered plateglass of
> his thoughts, glimmering before shoes and bicycles?[28]

Paterson the character, off for a bourgeois and literary vacation, attributes the bus riders of the city to "his thoughts," depersonalizing these others in a metamorphic gaze while linking the "thought : (common) language" chain to the people themselves. These "thought : people" "alight and scatter," recalling the water hitting the bottom of the falls. By extension, the falls have now become a bus, carrying their load of individuals through the town along a regular pathway (a mapped and coursed schedule) but producing through that regularity manifold dispersals, movements of selves and bodies that the poet's mind cannot entirely contain. The "thought : person" in the bus, under the figurative eye of the poet, can thus only be encountered imaginatively through the already developed poetic terms established through the falls and, as the time/space coordinates change (one bus stop leading to another), the meeting cannot last. This "complex mathematic" is driven home by the emergence of Paterson's "I," now, in a partial gesture away from his individual imagination, identifying himself "among" the anonymous crowd ("Who are these people [. . .]?), a collective identification solidified by the shifting pronoun from "I" to "his," which, turning on the link between the two "Patersons," suggests that the "thoughts" can be understood as those of the city itself. The interplay between movement and stasis that marks the passage is reinforced through a new figure, the pouring water giving way to the "regularly ordered plateglass / of his thoughts."[29] The "regularly ordered" glass here could be derived from the windows of the bus through which the "thought : people" can be seen, along with their quotidian "shoes and bicycles." As a clear medium, the glass makes the city's movement visible, which in turn illuminates the imagination, causing it to "glimmer." In the movement from the Passaic to the plateglass, sound has become sight in this passage: "I" has become "them" has become "him" has become "thoughts."

These complications point not only to the poem's movement or its productive instability but, as well, to the cognitive potential of analogy. Paterson is Paterson's thought in this passage, that interpenetration described in the preface. Thought, thus, is a *function*, not simply a moment of subjectivity or limited to the human. The poem's analogic structures have made the notion of the city as a thinking entity visible, successfully yet tenuously mediating a new vision of the local and allowing, in turn, the reader and the poet to conceptualize the city anew. One could also claim that the poem itself is thinking by generating these analogic multiplicities, cognitively mapping the interactions of the many things bearing the name "Paterson." The figure of the falls allows these complex contingencies to be worked out even as that figure refuses to be reduced to any single formulation.

Because of those many possible readings, the poem's inherently instable analogic chains "interlace, repel and cut under" to create an expansive and aggregating semiotic space, one capable of integrating a seemingly endless amount of material. The generation of that material through the historical existence of Paterson the place is never far from the poem, revealing itself in the form of textual excerpts, newspaper accounts, and even economic reflections. "The province of the poem," Williams asserts in Book III, "is the world."[30] Clearly, in its analogies *Paterson* does not merely replicate the local, but, instead, assembles it, endlessly reshaping it to offer a new language of the place. This constructivist aesthetic challenges the notion that the poem is seeking an originary or pure "authentic language" that the poet and reader must "separate [. . .] from the dross."[31] There is no more or less authentic word or utterance in *Paterson*; there are, instead, iterative and recursive patterns and rhythms made and remade out of the multiple streams of everyday interactions and the contingencies of historical materials. It is this self-conscious act of continuous formation that gives the poem its energy and identity, not its recovery of a lost Presence or forgotten Word.

The analogic imagination is particularly visible in the famous passage describing the "Two halfgrown girls":

> two, bound by an instinct to be the same:
> ribbons, cut from a piece,
> cerise pink, binding their hair: one—
> a willow twig pulled from a low
> leafless bush in full bud in her hand,
> (or eels or a moon!)
> holds it, the gathered spray,
> upright in the air, the pouring air,
> strokes the soft fur—
>
> Ain't they beautiful![32]

The resonances of this passage in the context of the rest of Book I are multiple, as Mark Gorey has pointed out,[33] but there are also major analogic movements at work that demonstrate precisely how poetic recursion can generate its own dispersal and transformation. The girls as women, albeit "half-grown" ones, recall Williams's predictable and all-too-traditional figure of "woman as flower."[34] This analogy is doubled by the fact that one of the girls is holding a "willow bud," a vegetative growth on the verge of reproduction. This reproduction can be read as cut off ("divorced," perhaps, in the language of *Paterson*) by the girl when she plucks it from its bush. Aesthetic appreciation may destroy biological intent, but the same reproductive impulse is mirrored in the girls themselves, who are "bound by instinct to be the same."[35] As the bud grows instinctively, so too do the girls unconsciously imitate each other, another possible "flower: women" resonance in that there are "innumerable women, each like a flower," a field of individuals.[36] The parenthetical aside "(or eels or a moon!)," seemingly out of place, opens the preceding line into many different directions. The "eels" will appear later in the book as a historical anecdote that demonstrates the fertility of water,[37] thus providing one more addition to the "girls: bud: reproduction" chain, as could the "moon," which can be described as "full," like the bud, another established metaphor for female sexuality. The "gathered spray" evokes the many associations with the river and the falls previously sketched, multiplying the possibilities even further.

Clearly, these few lines contain within them not one but many analogic mechanisms, uniting numerous patterns that have been generated by the poem and that the passage both sustains and expands. But this formation contains within it, as well, the conditions for its own dispersal, activated by the final "Ain't they beautiful!"[38] As Gorey points out, this "performative line" can be read as either coming from the girls, which means it "could be read as an example of false language," or it can "also be read as the persona's observation about the girls," producing a moment in which identity is uncertain not only in terms of the speaker but also the referent of "they."[39] In doing so, the line collapses and scatters the potential symbolic structures the poem has thus far attempted to create. "They" can be flowers, girls, the girls with the flowers, the buds, women in general, even, in a metapoetic reaffirmation of *Paterson*'s quest, the lines themselves, and in each possible subject, the predication of beauty changes as well. "Ain't they beautiful!" thus recursively disassembles the iterative analogies that the song has just produced, demonstrating that the poem can compose many more relations,[40] and, furthermore, proving that new links can be (and will be) added to this particular analogic chain.

As if reflecting on this explosive potential at work, the poem later notes that the "theme / is as it may prove," acknowledging that *Paterson* cannot predict its own future identity since it is attempting "a mass of detail / to interrelate on a new ground, difficultly; / an assonance, a homologue."[41] The interrelation of these masses of detail, the expansive production of assonances and homologues, figurative constructions that are inevitably transformed into other improvisations, signals a poetic process that is both projective and unpredictable. Composition as analogy assembling is further complicated by the notion of the local as shifting and temporal, wherein "it is the new, uninterrupted, that / remoulds the old, pouring down."[42] As Williams demonstrates time and again, Paterson as a space includes not only the present activities witnessed by the poet but also the past uses of the place, the stories of those who previously claimed it with their cruel violence. No single narrative will account for those conflicted analogies, and neither will any ultimate or closed poetic structure. As an alternative, *Paterson* offers thus not a symbolic *order*, an anthem codifying the law of an inevitable history, but an imaginative *mechanism*, a means for self-modifying cultural and poetic production. The machine made out of words becomes a self-modifying feedback loop (that is, a mechanics of recursion) for creating and destroying the world (that is, the contingencies of fact).

After roaming through the library of Book III, Paterson recognizes that he "cannot stay here / [. . .] looking into the past" and, at the same time, "the future's no answer."[43] Instead, the present calls, the "sliding water" that marks the moving articulations of the moment, and so the speaker cries "Let / me out! (Well, go!) this rhetoric / is real."[44] The apparent contradiction of the phrase "real rhetoric" does not indicate language trapped in the illusion of unmediated "authentic" speech, but instead can be read as a description of language actively transforming its own material and representational conditions. As Joseph Riddel has famously pointed out, Williams's "language is 'immediate' precisely because he does not nostalgically lament a violated purity, or lost origin; for this poet, language is originally diacritical"; the work of language in *Paterson* and in Paterson, then, is to "[expose] the illusion of totalization in [...] recorded history," which opens it "in the same way the fire opened the closed language of the library."[45] Williams's cry to escape the closure of the library onto the streets of real rhetoric is thus not an effort to sidestep the past but to enter into historicity as such, to engage the present as a meaning-making activity. Writing wants to imitate speech not as that which is unmediated but as that which does not cease in mediation, which continues to create.

For this reason, the library reflects not only the paradoxes of *Paterson*, but also that of the long poem as a practice. For as the poem moves forward in its creative analogic iterations and recursions, it generates bound volumes to be placed on shelves, adding to the historical record (and rhetoric) from which it is made. In a now-familiar modernist gesture that goes back at least to Charles Baudelaire, the moment of affirmation and recreation gives birth to the old.[46] For Williams's concern with the present language, this is a very real problem: The conditions of poetic existence, of active writing, are rapidly converted into mere bookish being. "Let / me out!" in this sense can be read as a cry to escape the bound volume as well as the space in which the volumes are contained.

In formal terms, the anxiety over the book is displaced into the question of an ending, a dilemma presaged by *Paterson*'s introductory evocation of metamorphosis and anticipated throughout the multiple volumes of the work. The arc of the first four books, concluding with the central figure of Paterson emerging from the water and "headed inland," has been attractive to readers as the formal conclusion of the original plan. This inland journey does not necessarily guarantee symbolic closure, however. Peter Schmidt, in his essay on "*Paterson* and Epic Tradition," reads Book IV as primarily satirical and ironic, which implies that "We leave Dr. Paterson as he stands on the dunes contemplating an endless series of other Odyssean descents into history—and, consequently, an endless series of further losses and self-defeats."[47] Trapped in a circle of repetition, Book IV's "final somersault / the end" cannot afford consolation, much less the rigor of beauty. Schmidt goes on to argue that it was for this reason that Book V was required by Williams and that the new movement from I through V means that "the poem ends classically, with the hero symbolically returning to the Falls, to a world where the eternal and the time-bound, the creative and the decadent, may be held in balance."[48]

This reading equates analogy making with a resigned consciousness of defeat; the poem can never catch up with the world it seeks to engage. In contrast, throughout this chapter I have sought to demonstrate the affirmative, if no less humbling, metamorphic and shifting symbol-making *ana*logic of the poem, which figures the falls not as a "world where the eternal and the time-bound" may be "held in balance" but one in which there are *no* guarantees of symbolic, psychic, or social closure. If anything, whatever balance the poem achieves is a temporary one at best, a momentary pause generated by an analogy that contains within it the conditions of its own recursive transformation, what Hui might call the necessary integration of contingency.[49] For this reason, the falls, like Paterson the city, can be nothing more than a site for *writing*, and so if Dr. Paterson returns home, he also recursively takes up the endless task of poetry, the effort in language that attempts to fill, or at least bridge, the space between history and the imagination.

Schmidt's reading of Book V is useful, however, for calling our attention to an image of endless creation, for such figures can tentatively conclude an iterative and recursive text. As Williams firmly establishes throughout the poem, a place, no matter how modest, is too vast and complicated to be adequately contained in any narrative, no matter how epic. The early admission that "we know nothing, pure / and simple, beyond / our own complexities" does not, itself, adequately represent the extent of those multiplicities. Furthermore, as the poem continues it contains more and more incidents of displaced desire, violence, and disaster, making Williams's ultimate goal of a community-building common language seem remote. A striking example of this darkness can be found in the tale of Fred Goddell Jr., related toward the end of Book IV, who killed his infant child "by twice snapping the wooden tray of a high chair into the baby's face [...] when her crying annoyed him."[50] These stories are far from "pure / and simple," and mock any claim for a balancing myth or ultimate code; the "complexities" may be more than a single structure can handle. This may be the reason that the end of Book V converts the epistemological ground:

> We know nothing and can know nothing .
>   but
> the dance, to dance to a measure
> contrapuntally,
>   Satyrically, the tragic foot.[51]

Paterson's complexities resist capture, at the end, and so they must be (re)formed, (re)iterated, played out and sung with, "contrapuntally" measured. The figure of the dance becomes another articulation of the analogic movement, and so the "end" that Book V offers is not a unified closure but a call to performance. The logic of the poem, in its analogy assembling, leads to this open conclusion. The poetic work of *Paterson* has allowed the poet to think numerous connections, to make new analogies, across many material landscapes, and in doing so to affirm a new conceptual reality that intersects with the multiplicity and contingency of a time and place. But that reality, in turn, can only be imaginatively sustained through additional analogic acts, new performances of unification marrying the chain to new links. Such a poetic cannot cease; *Paterson* is, as it were, condemned to iterative and recursive dancing.

Thus, the poem continues into the unfinished Book VI, its fragment shuffle-steps, new symbolic makings born out of elder experiences and recovered histories. *Paterson* demanded its own continuation, calling attention to the inescapable fact that "Words are the burden of poems, poems are made of / words," a negotiation that forces one to "Dance, dance!"[52] In these gestures toward yet another movement, one finds evidence for Clark Lunberry's suggestion that the poem became "the poignant record of an impossible knowledge, an unsustainable image, always requiring additional appendices for its story to even be partially, provisionally told."[53] Dancing as writing as speech as river may be one way to enact such an impossible knowledge, a recursive movement through a contingent world, a song to take one forward into the night.

NOTES

1. I am thinking of the poems all scholars of the North American long poem regularly have in mind: Ezra Pound's *Cantos*, Muriel Rukeyser's *The Book of the Dead*, Melvin Tolson's *Harlem Gallery*, H.D.'s *Helen in Egypt*, Charles

Olson's *The Maximus Poems*, Rachel Blau DuPlessis's *Drafts*, Nathaniel Mackey's *Song of the Andoumboulou*, Juliana Spahr's *This Connection of Everything with Lungs*, as just a cross-sampling.
2. Paul Jaussen, *Writing in Real Time: Emergent Poetics from Whitman to the Digital* (Cambridge: Cambridge University Press, 2017), 24.
3. Yuk Hui, *Recursivity and Contingency* (London: Rowman & Littlefield, 2019), 15.
4. Hui, *Recursivity and Contingency*, 15.
5. William Carlos Williams, *Paterson* (New York: New Directions, 1963), 10.
6. William Carlos Williams, *In the American Grain* (New York: New Directions, 1956), 205.
7. Williams, *Paterson*, 275.
8. William Carlos Williams, *Imaginations* (New York: New Directions, 1970), 150.
9. Benjamin Sankey, *A Companion to William Carlos Williams's* Paterson (Berkeley: University of California Press, 1971), 117.
10. Williams, *Paterson*, 126.
11. Williams, *Paterson*, 146.
12. Williams, *Paterson*, 167.
13. Williams, *Paterson*, 156.
14. William Carlos Williams, *Selected Essays* (New York: New Directions, 1969), 256.
15. Brian A. Bremen, *William Carlos Williams and the Diagnostics of Culture* (Oxford: Oxford University Press 1996), 6.
16. Williams, *Paterson*, 10.
17. Williams, *Paterson*, 10.
18. Williams, *Paterson*, 10.
19. Williams, *Paterson*, 12.
20. See Walter Scott Peterson's *An Approach to Paterson* (New Haven, CT: Yale University Press, 1967) for an early reading of the poem based upon this binary.
21. Charles Olson, *The Maximus Poems*, ed. George F. Butterick (Berkeley: University of California Press, 1983), 3.
22. Piotr Parlej, "Imagine the Outside: Metaphor in William Carlos Williams," in *William Carlos Williams and the Language of Poetry*, ed. Burton Hatlen and Demetres Tryphonopoulos (Orono, ME: National Poetry Foundation, 2002), 164.
23. Williams, *Paterson*, 7.

24. The phrase "common language" functions in at least two ways: first as a language common to all, a community-creating discursive formation, and, second as the vulgarity of a tangled and insincere everyday speech. In the first sense, the "common language" would be the product of the "combing out" of the poem, while the second sense would present the language as the raw material being transformed. Williams's variant of the modernist anxiety over communication both discredits common language and aspires to precisely such a democratic articulation, a gesture elitist but with egalitarian aspirations.
25. Williams, *Paterson*, 15.
26. Williams, *Paterson*, 16.
27. Williams, *Paterson*, 16–17.
28. Williams, *Paterson*, 18.
29. Williams, *Paterson*, 18.
30. Williams, *Paterson*, 122.
31. Joel Conarroe, *William Carlos Williams' Paterson: Language and Landscape* (Philadelphia: University of Pennsylvania Press, 1970), 137.
32. Williams, *Paterson*, 29.
33. Mark Gorey, "Reading *Paterson* Book One: The Interpenetration of Metaphor and the 'Gathered Spray' of Language," in *William Carlos Williams and the Language of Poetry*, ed. Burton Hatlen and Demetres Tryphonopoulos (Orono, ME: National Poetry Foundation, 2002), 206–7.
34. Williams, *Paterson*, 15.
35. Williams, *Paterson*, 29.
36. Williams, *Paterson*, 15.
37. Williams, *Paterson*, 47.
38. Williams, *Paterson*, 29.
39. Gorey, "Reading *Paterson* Book One," 207.
40. That these relations are profoundly, unequally, and problematically gendered adds to the complexity of this passage. For an essential reading of *Paterson*'s gender analogies, see Rachel Blau DuPlessis, "*Pater*-Daughter: Male Modernists and Female Readers," in *The Pink Guitar: Writing as Feminist Practice* (New York: Routledge, 1990), 41–67.
41. Williams, *Paterson*, 30.
42. Williams, *Paterson*, 101.
43. Williams, *Paterson*, 173.
44. Williams, *Paterson*, 173.
45. Joseph Riddel, *The Inverted Bell: Modernism and the Counterpoetics of*

William Carlos Williams (Baton Rouge: Louisiana State University Press, 1974), 5, 19.
46. For a classic statement on this, see Paul de Man's "Literary History and Literary Modernity," in *Blindness and Insight: Essays in the Rhetoric of Contemporary Criticism*, 2nd ed. (London: Routledge, 1983), 142–65. As de Man points out (150), that gesture cannot separate itself from the very past it disavows: "As soon as modernism becomes conscious of its own strategies [. . .] it discovers itself to be a generative power that not only engenders history, but is part of a generative scheme that extends far back into the past."
47. Peter Schmidt, "*Paterson* and Epic Tradition," in *Critical Essays on William Carlos Williams*, ed. Steven Gould Axelrod and Helen Deese (New York: G. K. Hall, 1995), 173.
48. Schmidt, "*Paterson* and Epic Tradition," 175.
49. Hui, *Recursivity and Contingency*, 15.
50. Williams, *Paterson*, 229.
51. Williams, *Paterson*, 278.
52. Williams, *Paterson*, 282.
53. Clark Lunberry, "So Much Depends: Printed Matter, Dying Words, and the Entropic Poem," *Critical Inquiry* 30 (2004): 650.

BIBLIOGRAPHY

Bremen, Brian A. *William Carlos Williams and the Diagnostics of Culture*. Oxford: Oxford University Press, 1996.
Conarroe, Joel. *William Carlos Williams' Paterson: Language and Landscape*. Philadelphia: University of Pennsylvania Press, 1970.
de Man, Paul. "Literary History and Literary Modernity." In *Blindness and Insight: Essays in the Rhetoric of Contemporary Criticism*, 2nd ed., 142–65. London: Routledge, 1983.
DuPlessis, Rachel Blau. "*Pater*-Daughter: Male Modernists and Female Readers." In *The Pink Guitar: Writing as Feminist Practice*, 41–67. New York: Routledge, 1990.
Gorey, Mark. "Reading *Paterson* Book One: The Interpenetration of Metaphor and the 'Gathered Spray' of Language." In *William Carlos Williams and the Language of Poetry*, edited by Burton Hatlen and Demetres Tryphonopoulos, 201–18. Orono, ME: National Poetry Foundation, 2002.

Hui, Yuk. *Recursivity and Contingency*. London: Rowman & Littlefield, 2019.
Jaussen, Paul. *Writing in Real Time: Emergent Poetics from Whitman to the Digital*. Cambridge: Cambridge University Press, 2017.
Lunberry, Clark. "So Much Depends: Printed Matter, Dying Words, and the Entropic Poem." *Critical Inquiry* 30 (2004): 627–53.
Olson, Charles. *The Maximus Poems*. Edited by George F. Butterick. Berkeley: University of California Press, 1983.
Parlej, Piotr. "Imagine the Outside: Metaphor in William Carlos Williams." In *William Carlos Williams and the Language of Poetry*, edited by Burton Hatlen and Demetres Tryphonopoulos, 157–68. Orono, ME: National Poetry Foundation, 2002.
Peterson, Walter Scott. *An Approach to* Paterson. New Haven, CT: Yale University Press, 1967.
Riddel, Joseph. *The Inverted Bell: Modernism and the Counterpoetics of William Carlos Williams*. Baton Rouge: Louisiana State University Press, 1974.
Sankey, Benjamin. *A Companion to William Carlos Williams's* Paterson. Berkeley: University of California Press, 1971.
Schmidt, Peter. "*Paterson* and Epic Tradition." In *Critical Essays on William Carlos Williams*, edited by Steven Gould Axelrod and Helen Deese, 167–76. New York: G. K. Hall, 1995.
Williams, William Carlos. *Imaginations*. New York: New Directions, 1970.
Williams, William Carlos. *In the American Grain*. New York: New Directions, 1956.
Williams, William Carlos. *Paterson*. New York: New Directions, 1963.
Williams, William Carlos. *Selected Essays*. New York: New Directions, 1969.

Chapter Six

Against Spectatorship

"Being with" in Claudia Rankine's Long Poems

Kathy Lou Schultz

Claudia Rankine's *American Lyric* long-poem project spans two books with the same subtitle: *Don't Let Me Be Lonely: An American Lyric* (2004) and *Citizen: An American Lyric* (2014).[1] *Lonely* is Rankine's first book to feature collaged visual components that appear in combination with the text. Some of these images are: a small, cube-like television; an X-ray; photographs; maps; prescription labels; a diagram of an artificial heart; and a billboard. Of these, the television is most ubiquitous, a realistic image of an old-fashioned, boxy television set with black-and-white static on its screen that contains a barely discernible image of President George W. Bush that blends in with the white noise. Used to denote the book's section breaks, the television also displays scenes from movies and television news, as well as slogans from commercials. *Lonely* examines physical illness and painful emotional states (loneliness, sadness, hopelessness) as both individual and social states of being and takes up, as an ethical question, the relationship of the self to the other: "Why are we here if not for each other?"[2]

Lonely engages large-scale existential concerns about life and death, including both individual trauma that can go unrecognized, relegated to the silence of a "personal problem," and collective trauma, such as that experienced in conjunction with the AIDS crisis in South Africa and other nations, the Gulf War, and the 9/11 attacks on the Twin Towers and other US landmarks. In addition to nearly universal existential conflicts, the poem also explores the specific precarity of Black lives brought about by interpersonal and structural racism, including hate crimes and police violence. Rankine links these themes with the experience of everyday life in the twentieth century, which is deluged by the twenty-four-hour news cycle and highly mediated by the consumerist images inundating viewers from the television and other forms of media. In its multimedia, multi-genre format, *Lonely* extends the social documentary tradition of the 1930s.

Moreover, *Lonely*'s focus on affect, on "feeling the facts" of social injustice,[3] links the poem to this tradition. One of historical social documentaries' aims was to convey meaning that causes the reader to both think about and feel the facts of social inequality. As William Stott outlines in his foundational study of the emergence of social documentary writing that addressed the effects of the Great Depression on ordinary Americans, this form urges readers or viewers to "feel" in order to move them to action. Rankine's extension of this tradition, utilizing the modes of contemporary media, especially television and movies, emphasizes the ethical importance of being with, rather than simply looking at, others who are suffering. Through capturing the reader's affective responses in the mode of social documentary, responses that readers also witness in the speakers of the poem, the process of reading *Lonely* leads to intellectual, in addition to emotional, considerations of the ethical questions surrounding the relationship between self and other.

Citizen furthers this social documentary project using a diverse array of paratactically arranged visual images, including photographs, screengrabs from internet and television sources, and full-color reproductions of selected pieces of contemporary art along with text that is mostly written in prose blocks, to investigate what Rankine calls "the field of the encounter; what happens when one body comes up against another and race enters into the moment of intimacy between two people."[4] Focusing on often unremarked moments of interaction in everyday contemporary life presumed to be neutral (standing in line in a store) or even intimate (a long-term friendship), *Citizen* also investigates social relations through documentation of individual affect and feeling. As *Citizen* stresses, "What feels more than feeling?"[5] In *The Life of Poetry* (1949) Muriel Rukeyser also argues that poetry can engage the intellect but must do so by first engaging the emotions: "This response is total, but it is reached through the emotions. A fine poem will seize your imagination intellectually—that is, when you reach it, you will reach it intellectually too—but the way is through emotion, through what we call feeling,"[6] which is evident in her poem "The Book of the Dead," a Depression-era documentary poem first published in her book *U.S. 1.* (1938).

Furthermore, Rukeyser stresses that in the combination of images and words "there are separables: the meaning of the image, the meaning of the words, and a third, the meaning of the two in combination. The words are not used to describe the picture, but to extend its meaning."[7] This "third meaning," greater than word or image, created when words extend rather than describe or explain, is already laid out in "The Book of the Dead," which chronicles a car trip from New York to West Virginia to document the plight of miners in Gauley Bridge, in its explicit aim "to photograph and to extend the voice, / to speak this meaning."[8] The photograph extends the voice and vice versa as the reader constructs multiple meanings through the numerous connections available among paratactically arranged elements. Analyzing *Lonely* and *Citizen* within the lineage of social documentary poetry and film makes it clear that Rankine is expanding on a long tradition that allows many genres—lyric, archive, essay, interview, image—to coexist. Other common features of the documentary poem include narrative, description, testimony, collage, fragment, and reportage.

Reading the conversation among such disparate elements puts them into motion on the page, leading Rukeyser to seek out a new kind of expression, noting in a negative assessment of Archibald MacLeish's attempt at photo captioning in *Land of the Free* (1938) the need for something else: "Here we need something like a poem, something like movie titles, something like news in lights around the Times building."[9] Upending a hierarchical relationship between text and image, such as that employed when captions "explain" photographs, also suspends their fixed arrangements. Moving the elements on the page into cinematic motion, through a paratactic arrangement, engages the reader to make meaning in the visual gaps among the elements on the page. Rankine's emphasis on affect requires readers to rethink their relationship to the people represented in both words and pictures as they focus on the variety of meanings of the words and images in various combinations.

Moreover, in historical social documentaries, quotations attributed to human subjects—through an imagined "we" commenting on the subjects' experiences, an address to a second-person "you," or an individual lyric "I" reporting her own experience—raise questions about the ethical relationship between author and subject (and thus reader and subject); or simply, who speaks for whom? What is the connection between the representation of the person suffering and the reader/viewer of that experience?

This American documentary poem tradition is nearly a hundred years old, making Rankine's rotation of pronouns through her *American Lyric* project (including *Citizen*'s often-discussed "you") a continued investigation of individual and collective subjectivities and the ethics of representation, rather than a new invention, or a "postlyric" phenomenon. Emphasizing dominant forms of media consumption in twentieth-century America, Rankine investigates what it means to look at, or consume, images of suffering, challenging the reader to move beyond the posture of the spectator and be with others.

POEM SCRIPTS

Citizen also contains eight "poem scripts" in section VI for the "Situation" video poems on which Rankine and filmmaker and photographer John Lucas collaborate. Exploring what Rankine names "indwelling" with the collective "you," or "switching your body out with the body in the frame," the video poems create the opportunity to be inside each moment rather than a removed spectator.[10] Feeling can be a conduit for the reader to be with others as they are, rather than consuming their anguish as spectacle. This form of "switching" and experiencing, however, does not mean owning another's experience. Historian Dominick LaCapra emphasizes that through both empathy and imagination, a witness of history can place herself "in the other's position while recognizing the difference of that position and hence not taking the other's place,"[11] not assuming that person's identity, but standing with them. In addition, as Cynthia Hogue stresses, "the ability to both imagine the experience of another and also refrain from claiming that position as that of the self is crucial to any attempt to understand those affected by traumatic events in the past."[12] Thus, indwelling presents a way to be with another in their suffering, to not let them be lonely, creating new forms of citizenship in Rankine's *American Lyric*.

Both "being with" and "indwelling" are ethical modes of connecting self and other, indicated in both works through Rankine's invocations of poet Paul Celan. What Celan calls the "connective" (*das Verbindende*) is enacted through the metaphor of a handshake: "Or Paul Celan said that the poem was no different from a handshake. *I cannot see any basic difference between a handshake and a poem*—is how Rosemary Waldrop translated his German."[13] The poem, then, reaches across time to connect disparate individuals. Rankine writes, "The handshake is our decided ritual of both asserting (I am here) and handing over (here) a self to another. Hence the poem is that—Here. I am here."[14] Being "here" is to be present for the other: "We must both be here in this world in this life in this place indicating the presence of," Rankine writes, "or in other words, I am here."[15] The poem is the connection between self and other, through word and image, that brings the reader together with the other, here.

This ability to free the "I" from imprisoning isolation is dependent upon turning outward to create an encounter or connection through the poem. William Franke argues that Celan's poetry "suspends" language while also enabling what he describes as a step "to enter the outside world": "When representation and even language are suspended for the moment of a turning of the breath, an 'Atemwende,' the poem can set the I—estranged from itself—free in its encounter with the wholly Other, who is likewise set free. Poetry summons us to take a 'step,' rather than remaining purely within language, and to enter the outside world, the world outside language and representation, where otherness is encountered."[16]

Being separated from language also separates the self from static representation, taking the reader to "the world outside language," which, rather than ending in stasis, opens the possibility of encountering otherness. Thus, for Celan, and likewise for Rankine, the project becomes one of freeing the "I" from the stasis of unspeakable trauma, which also enables the freeing of the "Other."

This shared freedom is created through the encounter, a connection of selves that might engender an experience of shared humanity. In his speech "The Meridian," which he delivered upon receiving the Büchner award in 1960, Celan calls this "the mystery of the encounter," that the poem creates. "The poem is the 'connective' (*das Verbindende*), the 'meridian,' the means of an encounter with what is wholly other, and therefore of encounter with oneself, too, as genuinely human."[17] The poem can allow "I" and the "Other" to touch, to form human connection that transforms spectatorship (looking at) to being with one another.

Rankine first poses the problems of spectatorship in the epigraph to *Lonely*, quoting Aimé Césaire: "And most of all beware, even in thought, of assuming the sterile attitude of a spectator, for life is not a spectacle, a sea of grief is not a proscenium, a man who wails is not a dancing bear."[18] The quote emphasizes that the spectator's attitude is "sterile," or unmarked by the suffering of others. Spectacle, grief, and wailing in misery are viewed from the outside, an unaffecting theater. Frantz Fanon's *The Wretched of the Earth* (1961) also remains a strong influence for those seeking to recast traditional forms of spectatorship. Fanon writes, "Yes, everyone must be involved in the struggle for the sake of the common salvation. There are no clean hands, no innocent bystanders. We are all in the process of dirtying our hands in the quagmire of our soil and the terrifying void of our minds. Any bystander is a coward or a traitor."[19] In the work of filmmakers and theorists, Fanon's cowardly, traitorous "bystander" is often translated as "spectator."

The difference between a bystander and a spectator is significant for understanding not only these film projects, but also for theorizing Rankine's term "indwelling." A bystander denotes a person who is separate from an event and chooses not to participate in it. There is even the so-called bystander effect in social psychology that suggests that people are less likely to intervene to help someone being victimized when others are also present. A spectator, however, may experience heightened feelings such as revulsion or desire, gazing at the other as a separate being. Rankine and Lucas question the affective activity of spectatorship while at the same time asking us to look.

ARCHIVE OF FEELING

While Susan Sontag contends that photographing people is a violation in and of itself,[20] Rankine's work elevates the human subjects of social documentary to make them equal to the reader, not people to be looked at from a cool distance, or looked down upon. In a meta-commentary on the processes of social documentary, Rankine creates an archive of feeling that extends the document even further, advancing Rukeyser's theories about reaching the reader through the emotions. For Rukeyser, this ability to reach readers both affectively (through what "Public Feelings" scholar Ann Cvetkovich labels "sensation and feeling") and intellectually is also a marker of a good poem.[21] Like the historical social documentary tradition (but differing in the kind of media images it collects), *Lonely* uses word and image to produce both affective and intellectual responses. Rankine not only retells histories of collective and individual trauma, but also explores the ethical relationship of self and other while expanding the archive to include unique forms of personal documentation and ephemera.

One such example is a photograph of an ailing friend and his message scratched into a slate message board—"THIS IS THE MOST / MISERABLE IN MY LIFE"[22]—as he attempts to cope with the effects of Alzheimer's. The photograph of the message on the board appears twice on page 17, and twice again on page 18, this time connected to two photographs partially revealing an aging man's face and hand. The first-person speaker describes her friend: "For a while he understands he is getting ill and will die within this illness."[23] This is the period in which he permanently scratches the message "with some sort of sharp edge" into the chalkboard's surface, though it "has a built-in ledge, on the ledge is an eraser."[24] Although his illness is causing his memory, and his life, to be impermanent, the man's feelings of misery thus form a kind of permanent record that cannot be erased, and the speaker collects it after her friend's death. "I bring the chalkboard home with me and hang it on the wall in my study. Whenever I look up from my desk it is there—."[25] This is an example of what the speakers in the book do in order not to abandon one another, not to let each other be lonely, highlighting what it means to be with others.

The speaker stays with her ailing friend and preserves the chalkboard, a human document, which shows he was not left alone in his suffering, nor is he "erased" after his death. The friend's message—both "sharp" in its making and sharp in the fear that it produces of being "on the ledge" as if ready to jump or fall—preserves history outside of official documents and statistics. His archive of feeling is enabled because a friend is present to be with him in his anguish and also to preserve the record of it. Rankine's approach thus adjusts the scale of what is considered worth recording. As Rebecca Macmillan points out, showcasing such "personal effects" in *Lonely* affirms "the need to uncover and examine the connections between what appears at first to be solely individual and those broader, structural contemporary conditions."[26] This is a hallmark of Rankine's *American Lyric* project, which places individual experiences within larger social frameworks. As Cvetkovich argues, "the focus on sensation and feeling as the register of historical experience gives rise to new forms of documentation and writing."[27] Though Cvetkovich is not writing about Rankine specifically, her argument provides a heuristic for understanding how and why the *American Lyric* sequence creates new forms of documentation.

LONG-POEM LINEAGES

American women writers' long poems emerge from a variety of lineages. Yet their inclusion in historical canons of literature ebb and flow, as works also go in and out of print. For example, Rukeyser's poem "The Book of the Dead" has gone through long periods of critical disuse but has received more attention recently, including the release of a stand-alone edition by West Virginia University Press in 2018. Yet in genealogies of feminist writing, Rukeyser's name and the long poem genre are not always included. For example, in her promotion of a formalist feminist poetic practice, poet Annie Finch writes, "The historical problem is that contemporary women poets do not have a long and powerful female formal tradition to rebel against,"[28] arguing that "the only women's poetic tradition that has been influential during out [sic] century is the free-verse tradition that followed on Modernism."[29] Curiously, Finch's assertion erases now well-known women modernists, including such poets (and poems) as H.D. (*Helen of Egypt*), Gertrude Stein (*Tender Buttons*), and Mina Loy (*Anglo-Mongrels and the Rose*), all writers of the long poem.

Female modernists became (and continue to be) strongly influential for American women writers. For example, in May 1983, poet Kathleen Fraser, with associate editors Beverly Dahlen and Frances Jaffer and contributing editors Rachel Blau DuPlessis and Carolyn Burke, launched the literary newsletter *HOW(ever)*, a feminist vehicle for women's "experimentalist poetry" that also went on to focus on neglected texts by American modernist women writers, drawing an aesthetic and historical connection from early modernist to late-twentieth-century women's experimental writing. Often, the writers published in *HOW(ever)* also focused on the long poem. In *Forms of Expansion: Recent Long Poems by Women*, Lynn Keller analyzes eight contemporary women writers, including DuPlessis, who continue the long-poem tradition into the 1980s and 1990s.[30] In her study, Keller argues that the long poem has an expansive "formal and structural range," including formalist writing such as the sonnet sequence, originating in the fourteenth century, the classical epic that was remade into the "collage long poem" of the modernist epic, and the form of the lyric sequence, among others.[31] Her book helpfully contrasts formally dissimilar long poems written by an expansive list of writers who are not usually studied together. Keller, Susan Stanford Friedman, and other scholars also call into question "the prestige, the scale of achievement associated with the genre" of the "long," "big," or "epic" poem in part by removing assumed linkages between these kinds of poems and both whiteness and maleness.[32]

Another example that illustrates the diverse range of long poems is that which I have previously termed Afro-Modernist epics, important here because an emphasis on performativity prefigures Rankine's emphasis on the visual that leads to her video poem collaborations with Lucas.[33] These include long poems by Melvin B. Tolson and Langston Hughes. Tolson and Hughes's epics refuse to be contained by the page or even by written language. Tolson's *Harlem Gallery* (1965) is animated through the visual; he sets his epic in an art gallery to challenge discourses of race, aesthetics, and representation. Hughes's Afro-Modernist epic, *ASK YOUR MAMA: 12 MOODS FOR JAZZ* (1961) includes musical scores and performance instructions that suggest a performance always happening off the page. *ASK YOUR MAMA* is a visually experimental poem with, as the title indicates, twelve sections or "moods." Each of the twelve sections follows a two-column format, with the capitalized "poem" printed on the left side of the page and italicized musical instructions running in a column down the right. The book concludes with an additional section, a series of "Liner Notes," such as those printed on the sleeves of LP record albums or in accompanying booklets. Hughes's soundtrack is not mere marginalia; in fact, Hughes's attention to visual placement is so exact at this point, that the phrase "between verses" in the right-hand column is actually placed between the verses of the poem in the column on the left.[34] The poem is dedicated to Louis Armstrong, *"the greatest / horn blower / of them all,"*[35] and is meant to be performed. *ASK YOUR MAMA* was performed at Carnegie Hall in 2009.

While long poems present a variety of genres and hybrids, they do share a common, distinctive feature: their uncontainability. Walt Whitman's long free verse lines defy the form of the book to contain their length (without false line breaks and the resulting indentations), while DuPlessis's *Drafts* refuse to be contained by the form of a single book. *Surge: Drafts 96–114* (2013) is "the provocative, open-ended ending to DuPlessis's twenty-six year long poem project, *Drafts*."[36] While the poem may "end," it does not close.[37] Moreover, DuPlessis's collage poems move the practice of visual/verbal documentary forward, combining cut up images of what she calls "debris" (string, notation pads, newspaper clippings, a thread spool label) with her own text.[38] DuPlessis's contemporary Nathaniel Mackey has two multibook, multidecade long-poem projects: "Song of the Andoumboulou" and "Mu." The first was inspired by a recording of funeral chants from the Dogon people of Mali; the second began as a tribute to trumpeter Don Cherry. The preface to Mackey's *Splay Anthem* (2006), however, asserts that "Song of the Andoumboulou" and "Mu" are two parts of the same continuing project: "the two [are] now understood as two and the same, each the other's understudy. Each is the other, each is both."[39] Robin Tremblay-McGaw argues that Mackey's multibook projects are invested in "open seriality."[40] Again, though a book may "end," the poem does not close.

Rankine's *American Lyric* project shares the qualities of both uncontainability and performativity. Not only does the project extend beyond a single book, but it also reaches off the page with the "Situation" video poems. Based on *Citizen*'s poem scripts, but reaching beyond them, the video poems layer multiple soundtracks and images in palimpsestic fashion. This work begins in *Lonely*, which combines text and image in a paratactical arrangement, but *Citizen* moves the poem off the page into a multimodal performance. One of the aims of the video poems is to encourage viewers to enter the event, rather than acting as spectators who are outside, perhaps viewing the action as a kind of entertainment or diversion. Immanence, remaining within, the collective "you" that she employs in *Citizen*, requires being inside the frame. Crucially, this mode of viewing necessitates being with rather than looking at. The video collaborations between Rankine and Lucas thus deepen the conversations between not only language and thinking, but also seeing and thinking.

VIDEO POEMS

By insisting that the viewer look deeply into situations of the everyday, the video poems prompt the viewer to consider their own place in the social order and the history embedded in those encounters. "There are two worlds out there; two Americas out there," Rankine asserts. "If you're a white person, there's one way of being a citizen in our country; and if you're a brown or a black body, there's another way of being a citizen and that way is very close to death. It's very close to the loss of your life. It's very close to the loss of your liberties at any random moment."[41] In this essay, the scripts for the collaborative video poems published in *Citizen* are referred to as "poem scripts." But because the printed scripts in the book and the audio versions of the video poems (in the form of Rankine's voice-over) sometimes differ, a distinction will be made to denote which form is being quoted. Naming the videos "video poems" highlights the interaction between the poem script and the moving video footage. Rankine has also called the videos "video essays," highlighting how the videos draw on multiple generic categories.

Lauren Berlant calls the poem scripts one of the "embedded works" in *Citizen*. Other so-named works include photographs and reproductions of visual art. Asking Rankine about making the collaborative video poems with Lucas, Berlant inquires, "How did you (individually, together) conceive of this experiment in immanence, an experiment at being inside of an event rather than spectating it?" Rankine responds that "the 'Situation videos' came about because the use of video manipulation by John Lucas allowed me to slow down and enter the event, in moments, as if I were there in real time rather than as a spectator considering it in retrospect."[42] The ability to modulate the speed of the video, slowing it down, for example, in "Situation One" (poem script titled "October 10, 2006 / World Cup" in *Citizen*) allows for a moment-by-moment close looking and being with the subject.

In the video poem "Situation One," footage from the 2006 FIFA World Cup Final—a game won by Italy through a penalty kick shootout with France after extra time—is played in slow motion, frame by frame. In this now infamous instant replay, Italian player Marco Materazzi repeatedly taunts Zinedine Zidane from the French team and Zidane eventually turns and headbutts Materazzi in the chest, knocking him to the ground. Some said the insults were directed toward Zidane's mother or sister, while Rankine's text shows that Materazzi's taunts are aimed at Zidane's Arab and Algerian heritage. As the footage plays, we hear Rankine (off screen) reading from her poem script.[43] Rankine explains the choice of the freeze frame technique: "That kind of close looking, the ability to freeze the frame, challenges the language of the script to meet the moment literally second by second—in the Zidane World Cup piece, for example—to know as the moment knows, and not from outside."[44] The video poem thus allows viewers moments of indwelling. This is a form of the "absorption" that film theorist Richard Rushton argues can offer "the possibility of being another being."[45] In the book, the moment by moment, second by second, close looking is also represented visually by individual frames from the video recording of the 2006 World Cup incident that are printed across pages as if on a strip of film.

The video poems reflect some of the generic qualities of so-called Third Cinema that emerged during the 1960s. An early example, *La Hora de los Hornos* (Hour of the Furnaces, 1968) by filmmakers Fernando Solana and Octavio Getino, "is an essay film," according to Catherine L. Benamou, "incorporating documentary footage from a wide range of sources (including those antagonistic to the filmmakers' project), in which facts are presented and analyzed by way of intertitles and voice-over narration that often disrupt the spectator's immersion in the diegetic spaces of the images."[46] In the video poems, Rankine's nondiegetic recitation of the poem scripts acts as a voice-over for documentary materials shot by Lucas and taken from other sources, such as television. For example, the poem script "February 26, 2012 / In Memory of Trayvon Martin" does not narrate the action in what becomes the video poem called "Situation 5," but presents a simultaneous experience of listening and seeing that the viewer must then negotiate to discern the simultaneous meanings being presented.

In "Situation 5," the primary video consists of slowed-down images of individual Black men silently gazing out sometimes rainy windows as they are riding in cars or some other kind of vehicle, an ordinary experience of everyday life. That the men do not speak to the audience emphasizes their interiority. As the viewer listens to Rankine's voice-over, the camera remains intently focused on a Black man's face. The video poem's voice-over, which differs substantially from the text in *Citizen*,[47] begins: "My brothers are notorious. Though they have not been to prison, they have been imprisoned. But the prison is not a place you enter. It is no place." The voice-over thus suggests that while this "prison" is nowhere, no specific place, it is also everywhere, even inside of these "brothers." The voice-over goes on to note that "the hearts of my brothers are broken,"[48] emphasizing the importance of affect and Cvetkovich's "sensation and feeling" and creating an interior subjectivity for individual Black men who too often are represented as an indistinguishable group.

At the 02:01 mark of the video poem, still images are superimposed upon one another in a fast series while the video of the man in the car continues. Some of the images remain longer on the screen as other images continue to flash on top of them, creating a series of multilayered views difficult to discern simultaneously, raising questions about visibility and what remains unseen. These images include a hand-drawn historical map of bodies on a slave ship, upon which is layered a picture of Emmett Till, next a prison work gang, a "help wanted" sign that states "whites only," segregated buses, civil rights marchers, Rev. Dr. Martin Luther King Jr., a white cop bashing a Black man in the midsection of his torso with a billy club, a grotesque Jim Crow minstrel figure, Malcolm X, the Black Panthers, an empty factory, and others. The series ends with a photograph of a noose hanging from a tree. This series of photos is flashed within a mere fifteen seconds of the complete piece, which lasts four minutes and thirty-two seconds. Thereafter, additional video appears with the still-present footage of the man riding alone, including cell phone video of LAPD officers beating Black motorist Rodney King even as he lay on the ground.

The men riding in vehicles from the beginning of the video poem are in motion, yet they are trapped by repetitions of history: "the violence done to the body of a brown child and the time before this one."[49] The speaker recounts a long continuum of violence from the Middle Passage to slavery to the Great Migration to Jim Crow to the present: "Those years of and before me and my brothers, the years of passage, of plantation, of migration, Jim Crow segregation, poverty, of inner cities, profiling, of one in three, fast food, of two jobs, of boy, hey boy. Accumulate into the hours inside our childhood."[50]

The use of superimposition allows these historical photos to literally appear on the men's faces. This visually represents the embodied experience of history, while also obscuring each man's individual subjectivity, replacing the "self-self," in the language of *Citizen*, with the "historical self." Fractures of the social body occur in the space between these two selves. "A friend argues that Americans battle between the 'historical self' and the 'self-self.' By this she means you mostly interact as friends with mutual interest and, for the most part, compatible personalities; however, sometimes your historical selves, her white self and your black self, or your white self and her black self, arrive with the full force of your American positioning."[51]

History impacts the construction of the self even as one assumes herself to be a discrete individual having private experiences unrelated to a historical continuum. As *Citizen* demonstrates, however, the intimate attachments of the "self-self" become "fragile, tenuous" when transgressed within the social body made up of historical selves.[52] Rankine's invocations of the social, along with an attention to intimacy and affect, urge readers to contemplate how the social body might be redrawn in a way that fully appreciates the humanity of each person.

Yet, according to the ACLU, due to mass incarceration in the United States and the disproportionate violent policing of communities of color, "one out of every three Black boys born today can expect to go to prison in his lifetime, as can one of every six Latino boys—compared to one of every 17 white boys."[53] The speaker presents this statistic, "one in three," as part of the continuum of violence that continues through enforcement of contemporary policies, such as "Stop-and-Frisk." One of the phrases repeated in the poem script, "Stop-and-Frisk"—"And you were not the guy yet still you fit the description because there is only one guy who is always the guy fitting the description"[54]—emphasizes that despite their individual, unique physical features, Black and Latinx men are repeatedly subsumed into a picture of dangerous criminality. In one frame of the video, "Situation 5," a Black man appears to be looking at the camera from inside a prison cell.

Rankine demonstrates in *Citizen* that enduring this daily aggression and structural racism is not a fleeting experience, but is "stored" in the body: "The world is wrong. You can't put the past behind you. It's buried in you; it's turned your flesh into its own cupboard. Not everything remembered is useful but it all comes from the world to be stored in you."[55] The past also resides in the female speaker: "because I am a sister because I have brothers, it's as if I've always known."[56] Expanding the ethical relationship of self to other, as in *Lonely*, she is present for the men and speaks their story into the record. Whether or not she actually has a genetic relation has no bearing on this imperative: "Someone wrote I said he's my brother. I don't know why I would have said that. Maybe she knows the violence."[57] The speaker continues to address Black men tenderly as "brothers, each brother, my brother, dear brother, my dearest brothers, dear heart."[58] Drawing them to her with care, she addresses them finally as "dear heart" to stand with men whose hearts are broken.

Finally, a man speaks at the end of the video: "So I would change that, but as far as who I am, nah, I'm cool with me."[59] This quotation, which is nowhere in the poem script, plays off the repetition of the words "cool" and "cold": "Is it cold? Are you cold? It does get cool. Is it cool? Are you cool?"[60] What, here, is "cool"? In what circumstances must the man remain cool? The man is not present on the screen; we only heard his voice. Near the end of the video, a quote from poet Lyn Hejinian appears on the screen, giving us insight into these men and the title of the video series: "Nothing is isolated in history— / certain humans are situations."[61] By insisting that viewers look deeply into the situations of everyday life, the video prompts them to consider their own place in the social order and the history embedded in their encounters.

ACTIVE SPECTATORS

Much of film theory since the 1970s grounded in psychoanalysis (Sigmund Freud, Jacques Lacan) focuses on the distinction between passive and active spectators. Judith Mayne calls this dualism "complacent" versus "critical" spectatorship.[62] As Rushton explains: "Passive spectators were the products of mainstream, orthodox, Hollywood cinema, while active spectators were the hoped-for products of an avant-garde cinema."[63] Early feminist film theories rejected mainstream narrative films, for example, calling instead for "avant-garde work which made evident the working of those traditional [narrative] pleasures or created alternative modes of gratification for viewers."[64]

Likewise, Manthia Diawara highlights the importance of Black independent cinema, which he also names "contemporary oppositional film-making," to "increase awareness of the impossibility of an uncritical acceptance of Hollywood products." The aim of this resisting spectatorship is to transform "the problem of passive identification into active criticism which both informs and interrelates with contemporary oppositional film-making. [. . .] As more audiences discover such independent black films," Diawara argues, "spectatorial resistance to Hollywood's figuration of blacks will become increasingly focused and sharpened."[65] Third Cinema also challenges the construction of the passive spectator: "The form of the documentary should jolt the spectator out of passivity into action,"[66] precisely the hoped-for results of social documentary in the 1930s. Diawara presents the terms "resisting spectator" and "black spectator" as potentially interchangeable heuristic devices, suggesting that "black spectators may circumvent identification and resist the persuasive element of Hollywood narrative and spectacle."[67]

Stuart Hall, who posits the production of media texts as "encoding" and the reception of media texts to constitute "decoding," also opens the way for resistant readings of media texts, including a "negotiated" or an "oppositional reading."[68] In this discursive practice, the viewer decodes the message in a manner that Hall calls "globally contrary." Each of these theories presents methods for analyzing the relationship between the spectator and the work of art, but Rushton's theory of Deleuzian spectatorship comes closest to the concept of indwelling, or what it might mean to "switch out" one's body for another's. Built on an analysis of Gilles Deleuze's conception of "absorption" in his cinema books *Cinema 1: The Movement-Image* (1983) and *Cinema 2: The Time-Image* (1985), Rushton reads Deleuzian absorption not so much as a repudiation of the passive spectator, but as an intensification of this idea, though it accounts for the dangers of passive absorption as well. "This is one of the astonishing aspects of absorption: not merely that one can be looking in on another world, but also that one can have the sensation of bodily occupying that space in another world, the sensation of occupying the space of another being. To put it bluntly, one of the possibilities which absorption holds forth is the possibility of being another being."[69]

While passive spectatorship is something that feminist and Black filmmakers and others have sought to dismantle, through both avant-garde film techniques and presentation of content not available through mainstream films, this description by Rushton—"the sensation of occupying the space of another being"—reflects Rankine's stated goal of allowing viewers to "[switch] your body out with the body in the frame" and thus becomes a way actively to engage and challenge everyday experiences of racism and the forces of white privilege, rather than passively becoming entranced by or, in the language of spectator theory, absorbed into them. Rushton, through Deleuze, opens discursive techniques for transforming absorption into an active rather than passive form of viewing that can create the radical empathy of being with another being that Rankine demonstrates in her multimodal *American Lyric* project, which extends across two books and a series of video poems.

THE HISTORICAL PHOTOGRAPH

The placement of a historical photograph, "Public Lynching," at the end of the poem script written for Trayvon Martin underscores the ongoing precarity of African American life and suggests that George Zimmerman's killing of Martin is also a vigilante lynching.⁷⁰ Crucially, Rankine explains, "Historically, there is no quotidian without the enslaved, chained or dead black body to gaze upon or to hear about or to position a self against."⁷¹ "Public Lynching" is one among many photographs and other such items that not only document the history of lynching, but also were kept as grisly keepsakes by the white perpetrators of the violent murders and their communities: southern white mobs who killed at least 3,200 Black men between 1880 and 1940.⁷² White southerners "bought, sold, and circulated photographs and other souvenirs as consumer goods, and, in motion picture theaters, they watched scenes of lynching, projected as thrilling amusement."⁷³ Representations of lynching in photographs and films that re-created the spectacle of lynching "not only replicated, in starkly visual terms, the ideological force of pro-lynching rhetoric," Amy Louise Wood explains, "but also literally projected images that substantiated that rhetoric and allowed it to be continually reimagined."⁷⁴ Creating and then viewing the spectacle of Black death allowed (and continues to allow) whites to see themselves as pure, as powerful, and as the makers and enforcers of the law.

Rankine and Lucas's reproduction of this photograph, however, removes the hanging Black bodies, performing the extraordinary intervention of erasing the possibility of making a spectacle of Black death and instead "highlighting the excited faces of the white mob."⁷⁵ They had to obtain permission, in republishing the photograph, to alter it in this way. Studying the white spectators, rather than staring at the Black bodies and thus assuming the same role as the white spectators in the photograph, readers of *Citizen* are challenged to consider the role that spectatorship plays in the creation of Black death and Black suffering. The altered lynching photograph brings into sharp contrast the distinction between being with, rather than looking at, highlighting *Citizen*'s role in redefining the collective "you." Which "you" are you a part of? Who are you with in this scene?

> The opening, between you and you, occupied,
> zoned for an encounter,
>
> given the histories of you and you—
>
> And always, who is this you?⁷⁶

When the "opening" is occupied by the weight of the "historical self," the encounter careens "you" and "you" into a zone already designated for racist violence by eager spectators.

Through years of repetition, white audiences have become inured to images of Black death onscreen and in person. But being with the white perpetrators, as the altered photos requires, challenges the viewer to confront photographic evidence of the gratification of pleasure and desire that the white crowd experiences while taking part in and viewing ritualized murder. Wood notes, "mobs performed lynchings as *spectacles for other whites*."[77] Lynchings and visual representations of lynchings served not only as grotesque entertainment, but were also crucial in building and maintaining white supremacy, serving to unite white people across class, generation, and regional lines in order to assure racial dominance. As Wood's research shows, "[a] degree of political fluidity still existed after Reconstruction, when freedmen remained politically active and yeomen and poor whites flirted with interracial populism as a means to challenge planter and industrial power."[78] Thus, neither white solidarity nor white supremacy were certainties; instead, these ideologies "required constant replenishing and constant reenvisioning. That is, they needed to be performed and witnessed."[79]

Considering lynching historically as "ritualized murder" and a remarkably uniform ritualized theater, Koritha Mitchell argues that the "predictable steps, and their standardization across the country, reflected white agreement with mainstream declarations that African Americans were immoral and bestial, that they were not citizens and perhaps not fully human."[80] Wood concurs, arguing that "the melodramatic tone of prolynching rhetoric, with its tropes of helpless white women and villainous black men, itself pronounced lynching as theater."[81] Thus, rather than being drawn into the "theater" of ritualized murder and the spectacle of it, Rankine stresses the need to "redirect our gaze" to the white spectators.[82]

Several of the spectators turn toward the camera and two men smile, as if posing for a family portrait. One of the men facing the camera simultaneously points toward where the Black bodies are in the original photograph, emphasizing the purpose of the gathering. Rankine and Lucas are not the first to employ lynching photographs to direct attention to the violence of white spectatorship. For example, the NAACP printed a ghastly photograph in an antilynching circular with the caption: "Do not look at the Negro. His earthly problems are ended. Instead, look at the seven WHITE children who gaze at this gruesome spectacle."[83] Rankine argues, "Though the white liberal imagination likes to feel temporarily bad about black suffering, there really is no mode of empathy that can replicate the daily strain of knowing that as a black person you can be killed for simply being black."[84] Some contemporary responses to viewing the original photo may include sympathy for the victims (temporarily feeling bad) and revulsion toward the heinous violence. Indwelling with the lynch mob in the photo, however, forces readers (white readers in particular) to confront the grotesque, murderous delight that can historically, and into the present, attach itself to expressions of whiteness.

Citizen also explores what it may mean for a Black subject to inhabit the "I," to be the subject instead of the object:

> Sometimes "I" is supposed to hold what is not there until it is. Then *what is* comes apart the closer you are to it.
>
> This makes the first person a symbol for something.
>
> The pronoun barely holding the person together.[85]

The lyric "I" is supposed to "hold what is not there until it is" making it a symbol for a whole subject or person, but here the pronoun can barely hold the person together. Rankine explains, "I also wanted to put a little bit of pressure on the sense of who has power, who can stand in that 'I' versus who can't, and, talking specifically about African-Americans, on the notion that we started as property. The notion that personhood came *after* objecthood, that the move into the 'I' was actually—insanely—a step that had to be taken legally."[86] Rankine's "I" in this section, however, holds a space, fighting for Black subjectivity, while also demonstrating the contradictions a Black poet may encounter in the use of the lyric poetic form that presupposes a universal, transcendent subject that does not include them.

As Kamran Javadizadeh asks, "Once the idea of a transcendent lyric subject—the end result of a century and a half of lyricization—has been exposed as a form of white innocence, how can a poet retain the intimacy allowed by the lyric tradition without replicating its pernicious political effects?"[87] The dislocation of Black subjectivity is at times so laden with trauma that the body disintegrates into its parts. This idea is explored in the "Landscape at Dawn" from Rankine's first book, *Nothing in Nature Is Private*:

> Within
> you locate all defined parts of yourself,
> > the lungs,
> > the brain,
> > the heart,
> > and so on,
> to place on rocks like markers to exist[88]

Although the "you" addressed in the poem knows "most intimately / this landscape" she remains unsteady because she feels it disowns her. All history is present—not past—and "you" cannot feel connected to "yourself" or the land, even in the landscape at dawn. Thus, "each step taken / becomes all bruised time / in the overdone spring" and "another start to a dubious end" as the speaker tries to identify her "parts" to confirm her own existence.[89]

JUST US

Just Us (2020) builds upon Rankine's aim of inviting public conversation about race, shifting from "An American Lyric" to "An American Conversation," while incorporating an even wider array of visual and collaged materials than the previous two books, such as multiple redacted facsimile pages from Thomas Jefferson's *Notes on the State of Virginia*, including the portion about the impossibility of a Black poet (which he wrote in reference to Phillis Wheatley); tweets and other social media postings; and the "Usage-Advisory Safety Warnings" from a package of "Natural Blonde" hair dye.[90] The content is consistent with some of Rankine's previous work, as well as with other collaborations she has undertaken with Lucas. The couple has collaborated on art installations and collage art including "Stamped" and "whiteness, inc." In "Stamped," which investigates the relationship between blondness and whiteness, "the artists take a dual approach to their subject: photographs and videos of blond hair, sometimes printed on stamps, and audio snippets of Ms. Rankine asking people about their fair hair."[91] "whiteness, inc.," published in *Artforum* in 2016, presents photographs with collaged texts from advertisements to explore the relationship between whiteness and consumer capitalism.[92]

Currently, discussion is emerging suggesting that *Just Us* marks the end of an "American Lyric" trilogy.[93] *Don't Let Me Be Lonely* and *Citizen*, however, make up a two-part social documentary. Social documentary, as capacious a genre as it is, cannot hold *Just Us*. In form, rather, *Just Us* most resembles a textbook and is highly didactic. Gone is the parataxis and ensuing readerly invitation to make meaning in the "gaps" of social documentary. This interactivity, the making of connections between seeing photographs and reproductions of contemporary art and reading the text on the page, is necessary to the production of the two-step of affective and intellectual response that the genre inspires. Instead, *Just Us* addresses Rankine's anxiety about students' lack of historical knowledge when she was teaching her class on whiteness at Yale. This book thus instructs the reader to ensure that she is familiar with the Shirley Cards or where the term "white privilege" and other concepts come from, illustrating what Jackson calls the volume's "pedagogical intentions."[94] In *Just Us*, red dots connect to a "Fact Check" and "Notes and Sources" that ensure that the reader will make the correct connections, rather than being required to do the work themselves.

This form is radically different from that of *Citizen*, in which the first photograph, combined with the seemingly unconnected text above it, enacts Rukeyser's "third meaning" and illustrates the interaction between word and image enabled by social documentary poems. Again, this arrangement is strikingly different from *Just Us*, which instructs the reader in what kinds of meanings to form. Though taken in color, the photograph emphasizes the contrast of black and white: big white houses with black shutters, a white car with black tires. All is very ordinary, even bland, in this suburban landscape, except for the name of the street on the sign in the foreground: "JIM CROW RD."[95] Despite the brutal segregationist policies in the Jim Crow era and the grotesque blackface minstrel character from which the name derives, there is more than one location in the United States that has had a street bearing this name, including Flowery Branch, Georgia, where this photo was taken.

The juxtaposition of text and photo creates a meaning greater than either element individually, as the "interruption," the pause between them, creates the opportunity for opening perception: In a country where municipalities fail to see a problem with giving a street a name synonymous with the degradation of its Black citizens, Black women and girls will remain unseen. The photograph is placed in section I of *Citizen* with an account concerning two twelve-year-old girls in Catholic school, showing that African Americans' experiences of erasure and hypervisibility begin in childhood: "The girl sitting behind you asks you to lean to the right during exams so she can copy what you have written." The reader learns: "You never really speak except for the time she makes her request and later when she tells you you smell good and have features more like a white person. You assume she thinks she is thanking you for letting her cheat and feels better cheating from an almost white person."[96] The Black girl is invisible to the white girl as an individual: The white girl can only apply white standards of beauty to judge her as both looking and smelling "white," in a supposed compliment that degrades the Black child.

Above the photo of Jim Crow Road, the vignette about the two schoolgirls concludes: "Sister Evelyn never figures out your arrangement perhaps because you never turn around to copy Mary Catherine's answer. Sister Evelyn must think these two girls think a lot alike or she cares less about cheating and more about humiliation or she never actually saw you sitting there."[97] Sister Evelyn fails to see Black girls and women as individuals, or fails to see them at all.[98] This paratactical arrangement of text and image—the seemingly unconnected photograph and the conclusion of the vignette on the same page—continues the form of documentary poetry seen in Rukeyser's "The Book of the Dead" and other long poems from the 1930s. In contrast, the red dots in *Just Us* suggest the urgency (Stop! Red Alert!) of the need to make specific connections that may, finally, move white people and institutions to radically redo the forms that cast Black lives in America as "afterlives of slavery" that deny Black citizens freedoms, or life itself.[99]

The *American Lyric* sequence works to expose, but also to repair, the ruptures between both "I and I" and "I and you," first by emphasizing the power of connection in *Lonely*, second by addressing "you" in *Citizen* to take responsibility for your place in the social order, and third by recasting conventional modes of spectatorship in the video poems. This two-book-long poem employs the multimodal possibilities of social documentary, but expands it to include a greater variety of images to emphasize the ethics of media consumption in twentieth-century depictions of social inequality and racialized violence. While Rukeyser had intended to include Nancy Naumberg's photographs of their journey in "The Book of the Dead" and attempted to write a movie script version of the poem, Rankine achieves what Rukeyser could not, while broadening the possibilities of still and moving images in the long poem. Rankine's video poems create a cinematic version of the long poem that emphasizes the importance of being with, rather than looking at, a resistance to spectatorship that reforms the social body and the role of the citizen within it.

NOTES

1. Portions of this essay appeared in an earlier form in Kathy Lou Schultz, *Introduction to Claudia Rankine* (Lake Forest, IL: Lake Forest College Press, 2023). The author gratefully acknowledges permission from the publisher.
2. Claudia Rankine, *Don't Let Me Be Lonely: An American Lyric* (Minneapolis, MN: Graywolf Press, 2004), 6.
3. William Stott, *Documentary Expression and Thirties America* (Chicago: University of Chicago Press, 1986), 26.
4. Eric Westervelt, "In 'Citizen,' Poet Strips Bare the Realities of Everyday Racism," *NPR.org*, January 3, 2015, https://www.npr.org/2015/01/03/374574142/in-citizen-poet-strips-bare-the-realities-of-everyday-racism.
5. Claudia Rankine, *Citizen: An American Lyric* (Minneapolis, MN: Graywolf Press, 2014), 152.
6. Muriel Rukeyser, *The Life of Poetry* (Williamsburg, MA: Paris Press, 1996), 8.
7. Rukeyser, *The Life of Poetry*, 137.
8. Muriel Rukeyser, *The Collected Poems of Muriel Rukeyser*, ed. Janet Kaufman (Pittsburgh: University of Pittsburgh Press, 2006), 110.
9. Muriel Rukeyser, "'We Aren't Sure . . . We're Wondering': Review of *Land of the Free* by Archibald MacLeish," *New Masses* 27, no. 5 (1938): 27.
10. Lauren Berlant, "Claudia Rankine by Lauren Berlant," *BOMB Magazine* 129 (2014): n.p., https://bombmagazine.org/articles/claudia-rankine/.
11. Dominick LaCapra, *Writing History, Writing Trauma* (Baltimore: Johns Hopkins University Press, 2001), 78.
12. Cynthia Hogue, "'The Fact of Her Witness': Kathleen Fraser and the Poetics of Empathic Witness," *Jacket2* (2022): n.p., https://jacket2.org/article/fact-her-witness.
13. Rankine, *Don't Let Me Be Lonely*, 130; the correct spelling of the poet/translator's first name is Rosmarie.
14. Rankine, *Don't Let Me Be Lonely*, 130.

15. Rankine, *Don't Let Me Be Lonely*, 131.
16. William Franke, "Poetics of Silence in the Post-Holocaust Poetry of Paul Celan," *Journal of Literature and Trauma Studies* 2, no. 1–2 (2013): 144.
17. Franke, "Poetics of Silence," 139.
18. Rankine, *Don't Let Me Be Lonely*, n.p.
19. Frantz Fanon, *The Wretched of the Earth* (New York: Grove Atlantic, 2007), 140.
20. Susan Sontag, *On Photography* (New York: Farrar, Straus and Giroux, 1977), 14.
21. Ann Cvetkovich, *Depression: A Public Feeling* (Durham, NC: Duke University Press, 2012), 11.
22. Rankine, *Don't Let Me Be Lonely*, 17.
23. Rankine, *Don't Let Me Be Lonely*, 17.
24. Rankine, *Don't Let Me Be Lonely*, 18.
25. Rankine, *Don't Let Me Be Lonely*, 17.
26. Rebecca Macmillan, "The Archival Poetics of Claudia Rankine's *Don't Let Me Be Lonely: An American Lyric*," *Contemporary Literature* 58, no. 2 (2017): 189.
27. Cvetkovich, *Depression*, 11.
28. Annie Finch, "Female Tradition as Feminist Innovation," *Poetry Foundation*, August 2, 2010 [2005], https://www.poetryfoundation.org/articles/69567/female-tradition-as-feminist-innovation.
29. Finch, "Female Tradition as Feminist Innovation," n.p.
30. Keller's study discusses long poems by Sharon Doubiago, Judy Grahn, Rita Dove, Brenda Marie Osbey, Marilyn Hacker, Susan Howe, Dahlen, and DuPlessis. Other innovators of the long-poem tradition include Theresa Hak Kyung Cha and Myung Mi Kim.
31. Lynn Keller, *Forms of Expansion: Recent Long Poems by Women* (Chicago: University of Chicago Press, 1997), 1, 5, 155.
32. Keller, *Forms of Expansion*, 4–5.
33. Kathy Lou Schultz, *The Afro-Modernist Epic and Literary History: Tolson, Hughes, Baraka* (New York: Palgrave Macmillan, 2013).
34. Schultz, *The Afro-Modernist Epic and Literary History*, 130.
35. Langston Hughes, *ASK YOUR MAMA: 12 MOODS FOR JAZZ* (New York: Alfred A. Knopf, 2009), xvii.
36. "Home," *Rachel Blau DuPlessis*, n.d. https://rachelblauduplessis.com.
37. For DuPlessis's own thoughts on this conundrum in terms of "assemblage" and the notion of Gesamtkunstwerk, see her contribution to this volume;

on the structural "incompleteness" of long poems, see Nathan Brown's contribution.
38. Andrew Mossin, "Collage and Poetry as Social Document," *Hyperallergic*, October 17, 2020, http://hyperallergic.com/576635/rachel-blau-duplessis-poetry-collage/.
39. Nathaniel Mackey, *Splay Anthem* (New York: New Directions Book, 2006), ix.
40. Robin Tremblay-McGaw, "Sounding Out: Nathaniel Mackey's Ontological Archive in Fugitive Run," *Journal of Narrative Theory* 51, no. 3 (2021): 329.
41. Westervelt, "In 'Citizen,' Poet Strips Bare the Realities of Everyday Racism," n.p.
42. Berlant, "Claudia Rankine by Lauren Berlant," n.p.
43. On the Academy of American Poets site, the title was "Video: Situation One," whereas on Lucas's Vimeo page it appeared as "Situation 1." In *Citizen*, the script is titled "October 10, 2006 / World Cup."
44. Berlant, "Claudia Rankine by Lauren Berlant," n.p.
45. Richard Rushton, "Deleuzian Spectatorship," *Screen* 50, no. 1 (2009): 50.
46. Catherine L. Benamou, "Third Cinema," in *Schirmer Encyclopedia of Film Volume 4: Romantic Comedy–Yugoslavia*, ed. Barry Grant (Farmington Hills, MI: Schirmer Reference, 2006), 250.
47. Rankine, *Citizen*, 89–90.
48. Claudia Rankine and John Lucas, "Situation 5, by Claudia Rankine and John Lucas," *YouTube*, July 27, 2011, https://www.youtube.com/watch?v=0xx1dwFxAv0.
49. Rankine and Lucas, "Situation 5."
50. Rankine and Lucas, "Situation 5."
51. Rankine, *Citizen*, 14.
52. Rankine, *Citizen*, 14.
53. American Civil Liberties Union, "Mass Incarceration," *ACLU.org*, https://www.aclu.org/issues/smart-justice/mass-incarceration.
54. Rankine, *Citizen*, 108, 109.
55. Rankine, *Citizen*, 63.
56. Rankine and Lucas, "Situation 5."
57. Rankine and Lucas, "Situation 5."
58. Rankine and Lucas, "Situation 5."
59. Rankine and Lucas, "Situation 5."
60. Rankine and Lucas, "Situation 5."

61. Rankine and Lucas, "Situation 5."
62. Judith Mayne, *Cinema and Spectatorship* (London: Routledge, 1993), 4.
63. Rushton, "Deleuzian Spectatorship," 47.
64. E. Deidre Pribram, "Spectatorship and Subjectivity," in *A Companion to Film Theory*, ed. Toby Miller and Robert Stam (Oxford: Blackwell, 2003), 151.
65. Manthia Diawara, "Black Spectatorship: Problems of Identification and Resistance," *Screen* 29, no. 4 (1988): 76.
66. Benamou, "Third Cinema," 252.
67. Diawara, "Black Spectatorship," 66.
68. Stuart Hall, "Encoding, Decoding," in *The Cultural Studies Reader*, ed. Simon During (London: Routledge, 1993), 516, 517.
69. Rushton, "Deleuzian Spectatorship," 50.
70. Rankine, *Citizen*, 91.
71. Claudia Rankine, "The Condition of Black Life Is One of Mourning," *New York Times*, June 22, 2015, https://www.nytimes.com/2015/06/22/magazine/the-condition-of-black-life-is-one-of-mourning.html.
72. Amy Louise Wood, *Lynching and Spectacle: Witnessing Racial Violence in America, 1890–1940* (Chapel Hill: University of North Carolina Press, 2009), 3.
73. Wood, *Lynching and Spectacle*, 10.
74. Wood, *Lynching and Spectacle*, 10.
75. Felicia R. Lee, "A Poetry Personal and Political," *New York Times*, November 28, 2014, https://www.nytimes.com/2014/11/29/books/claudia-rankine-on-citizen-and-racial-politics.html.
76. Rankine, *Citizen*, 140.
77. Wood, *Lynching and Spectacle*, 2 (emphasis added).
78. Wood, *Lynching and Spectacle*, 8.
79. Wood, *Lynching and Spectacle*, 13.
80. Koritha Mitchell, *Living with Lynching: African American Lynching Plays, Performance, and Citizenship, 1890–1930* (Urbana: University of Illinois Press, 2012), 24.
81. Wood, *Lynching and Spectacle*, 10.
82. Lee, "A Poetry Personal and Political," n.p.
83. Courtney Baker, "The E-Snuff of Alton Sterling and Philando Castile," *Avidly*, July 8, 2016, http://avidly.lareviewofbooks.org/2016/07/08/the-e-snuff-of-alton-sterling-and-philando-castile/.
84. Rankine, "The Condition of Black Life Is One of Mourning," n.p.
85. Rankine, *Citizen*, 71.

86. Alexandra Schwartz, "On Being Seen: An Interview with Claudia Rankine from Ferguson," *The New Yorker*, August 22, 2014, https://www.newyorker.com/books/page-turner/seen-interview-claudia-rankine-ferguson.
87. Kamran Javadizadeh, "The Atlantic Ocean Breaking on Our Heads: Claudia Rankine, Robert Lowell, and the Whiteness of the Lyric Subject," *PMLA* 134, no. 3 (2019): 477.
88. Claudia Rankine, *Nothing in Nature Is Private* (Cleveland: Cleveland Poetry Center at Cleveland State University, 1994), 72.
89. Rankine, *Nothing in Nature Is Private*, 73.
90. Claudia Rankine, *Just Us: An American Conversation* (Minneapolis, MN: Graywolf Press, 2020), 34, 108–17, 296.
91. Martha Schwendener, Jillian Steinhauer, and Will Heinrich, "What to See in New York Art Galleries This Week," *New York Times*, August 8, 2018, https://www.nytimes.com/2018/08/08/arts/design/what-to-see-in-new-york-art-galleries-this-week.html.
92. Claudia Rankine and John Lucas, "whiteness, inc.," *Artforum International* 54, no. 10 (2016): 368–69.
93. Virginia Jackson, for example, argues in her review of *Just Us*: "*Citizen* was the second book in a trilogy that started with *Don't Let Me Be Lonely: An American Lyric* in 2004 and that has now concluded with *Just Us: An American Conversation* in 2020. The difference between the subtitles of the first two books in the trilogy and the subtitle of the last one tells you everything you really need to know, but I will spend this review trying to explain why I think the sequence *American Lyric, American Lyric, American Conversation* is such an important chord progression, why it makes this trilogy such a timely contribution to lyric theory as well as to American public discourse. The fact that you may think that those are two different things is an indication of how far Rankine's trilogy has to go to convince you otherwise." Virginia Jackson, "How Does It Feel to Be a Problem?" *Georgia Review* (Spring 2021): n.p., https://thegeorgiareview.com/posts/how-does-it-feel-to-be-a-problem/.
94. Jackson, "How Does It Feel to Be a Problem?" n.p.
95. Rankine, *Citizen*, 6.
96. Rankine, *Citizen*, 5.
97. Rankine, *Citizen*, 6.
98. Rankine, *Citizen*, 5.
99. This formulation, from Saidya Hartman's *Lose Your Mother: A Journey Along the Atlantic Slave Route*, is quoted in Rankine, *Just Us*, 102.

BIBLIOGRAPHY

American Civil Liberties Union. "Mass Incarceration." *ACLU.org*., n.d. https://www.aclu.org/issues/smart-justice/mass-incarceration.

Baker, Courtney. "The E-Snuff of Alton Sterling and Philando Castile." *Avidly*, July 8, 2016. http://avidly.lareviewofbooks.org/2016/07/08/the-e-snuff-of-alton-sterling-and-philando-castile/.

Benamou, Catherine L. "Third Cinema." In *Schirmer Encyclopedia of Film Volume 4: Romantic Comedy–Yugoslavia*, edited by Barry Grant, 249–25. Farmington Hills, MI: Schirmer Reference, 2006.

Berlant, Lauren. "Claudia Rankine by Lauren Berlant." *BOMB Magazine* 129 (2014): n.p. https://bombmagazine.org/articles/claudia-rankine/.

Cvetkovich, Ann. *Depression: A Public Feeling*. Durham, NC: Duke University Press, 2012.

Diawara, Manthia. "Black Spectatorship: Problems of Identification and Resistance." *Screen* 29, no. 4 (1988): 66–79.

Fanon, Frantz. *The Wretched of the Earth*. New York: Grove Atlantic, 2007.

Finch, Annie. "Female Tradition as Feminist Innovation." *Poetry Foundation*, August 2, 2010 [2005]. https://www.poetryfoundation.org/articles/69567/female-tradition-as-feminist-innovation.

Franke, William. "Poetics of Silence in the Post-Holocaust Poetry of Paul Celan." *Journal of Literature and Trauma Studies* 2, no. 1–2 (2013): 137–58.

Hall, Stuart. "Encoding, Decoding." In *The Cultural Studies Reader*, edited by Simon During, 507–17. London: Routledge, 1993.

Hogue, Cynthia. "'The Fact of Her Witness': Kathleen Fraser and the Poetics of Empathic Witness." *Jacket2* (2022): n.p. https://jacket2.org/article/fact-her-witness.

"Home." *Rachel Blau DuPlessis*, n.d. https://rachelblauduplessis.com/.

Hughes, Langston. *ASK YOUR MAMA: 12 MOODS FOR JAZZ*. New York: Alfred A. Knopf, 2009.

Jackson, Virginia. "How Does It Feel to Be a Problem?" *Georgia Review* (Spring 2021): n.p., https://thegeorgiareview.com/posts/how-does-it-feel-to-be-a-problem/.

Javadizadeh, Kamran. "The Atlantic Ocean Breaking on Our Heads: Claudia Rankine, Robert Lowell, and the Whiteness of the Lyric Subject." *PMLA* 134, no. 3 (2019): 475–90.

Keller, Lynn. *Forms of Expansion: Recent Long Poems by Women*. Chicago: University of Chicago Press, 1997.

LaCapra, Dominick. *Writing History, Writing Trauma*. Baltimore: Johns Hopkins University Press, 2001.
Lee, Felicia R. "A Poetry Personal and Political." *New York Times*, November 28, 2014. https://www.nytimes.com/2014/11/29/books/claudia-rankine-on-citizen-and-racial-politics.html.
Mackey, Nathaniel. *Splay Anthem*. New York: New Directions Book, 2006.
Macmillan, Rebecca. "The Archival Poetics of Claudia Rankine's *Don't Let Me Be Lonely: An American Lyric*." *Contemporary Literature* 58, no. 2 (2017): 173–203.
Mayne, Judith. *Cinema and Spectatorship*. London: Routledge, 1993.
Mitchell, Koritha. *Living with Lynching: African American Lynching Plays, Performance, and Citizenship, 1890–1930*. Urbana: University of Illinois Press, 2012.
Mossin, Andrew. "Collage and Poetry as Social Document." *Hyperallergic*, October 17, 2020. http://hyperallergic.com/576635/rachel-blau-duplessis-poetry-collage/.
Pribram, E. Deidre. "Spectatorship and Subjectivity." In *A Companion to Film Theory*, edited by Toby Miller and Robert Stam, 146–64. Oxford: Blackwell, 2003.
Rankine, Claudia. *Citizen: An American Lyric*. Minneapolis, MN: Graywolf Press, 2014.
Rankine, Claudia. "The Condition of Black Life Is One of Mourning." *New York Times*, June 22, 2015. https://www.nytimes.com/2015/06/22/magazine/the-condition-of-black-life-is-one-of-mourning.html.
Rankine, Claudia. *Don't Let Me Be Lonely: An American Lyric*. Minneapolis, MN: Graywolf Press, 2004.
Rankine, Claudia. *Just Us: An American Conversation*. Minneapolis, MN: Graywolf Press, 2020.
Rankine, Claudia. *Nothing in Nature Is Private*. Cleveland: Cleveland Poetry Center at Cleveland State University, 1994.
Rankine, Claudia, and John Lucas. "Situation 5, by Claudia Rankine and John Lucas." *YouTube*, July 27, 2011. https://www.youtube.com/watch?v=0xx1dwFxAv0.
Rankine, Claudia, and John Lucas. "Video: Situation One." Academy of American Poets, Oct. 26, 2010. https://poets.org/text/video-situation-one.
Rankine, Claudia, and John Lucas. "whiteness, inc." *Artforum International* 54, no. 10 (2016): 368–69.
Rukeyser, Muriel. *The Collected Poems of Muriel Rukeyser*. Edited by Janet Kaufman. Pittsburgh: University of Pittsburgh Press, 2006.

Rukeyser, Muriel. *The Life of Poetry*. Williamsburg, MA: Paris Press, 1996.
Rukeyser, Muriel. "'We Aren't Sure . . . We're Wondering': Review of *Land of the Free* by Archibald MacLeish." *New Masses* 27, no. 5 (1938): 26–28.
Rushton, Richard. "Deleuzian Spectatorship." *Screen* 50, no. 1 (2009): 45–53.
Schultz, Kathy Lou. *The Afro-Modernist Epic and Literary History: Tolson, Hughes, Baraka*. New York: Palgrave Macmillan, 2013.
Schultz, Kathy Lou. *Introduction to Claudia Rankine*. Lake Forest, IL: Lake Forest College Press, 2023.
Schwartz, Alexandra. "On Being Seen: An Interview with Claudia Rankine from Ferguson." *The New Yorker*, August 22, 2014. https://www.newyorker.com/books/page-turner/seen-interview-claudia-rankine-ferguson.
Schwendener, Martha, Jillian Steinhauer, and Will Heinrich. "What to See in New York Art Galleries This Week." *New York Times*, August 8, 2018. https://www.nytimes.com/2018/08/08/arts/design/what-to-see-in-new-york-art-galleries-this-week.html.
Sontag, Susan. *On Photography*. New York: Farrar, Straus and Giroux, 1977.
Stott, William. *Documentary Expression and Thirties America*. Chicago: University of Chicago Press, 1986.
Tremblay-McGaw, Robin. "Sounding Out: Nathaniel Mackey's Ontological Archive in Fugitive Run." *Journal of Narrative Theory* 51, no. 3 (2021): 326–54.
Westervelt, Eric. "In 'Citizen,' Poet Strips Bare the Realities of Everyday Racism." *NPR.org*, January 3, 2015. https://www.npr.org/2015/01/03/374574142/in-citizen-poet-strips-bare-the-realities-of-everyday-racism.
Wood, Amy Louise. *Lynching and Spectacle: Witnessing Racial Violence in America, 1890–1940*. Chapel Hill: University of North Carolina Press, 2009.

PART III

Experiment

Chapter Seven

The Paradise of *Rock-Drill*

Far-Right Politics in the Late Cantos of Ezra Pound

Josephine Nock-Hee Park

This chapter explores the relevance of Ezra Pound's late cantos in a post-Trump era of American nativism. It is my contention that *The Cantos* have stayed news because of their vituperations and not in spite of them. My reading builds on presently deepening inquiries into the aesthetic force and continuing reception of Pound's far-right views to reread the poetry he composed amid the furious output of writing and correspondence during his postwar detention. The contemporary surge of white terrorism has changed how I read Pound's epic, and my reading will explore Pound's direct engagement with the cultural and political fringe evident in the cantos of the 1950s.

In reconsidering Pound's treasonous views, I am venturing back to some familiar questions about Pound's work. This inquiry into Pound's postwar politics belongs to an examination of the Cold War resurgence of an American race war whose throughline extends from the nation's origins to the present. The terms of this race war are a grounding condition of every major work of the American imagination, and the products of Pound's American captivity are shot through with this darkness. And yet, in this period of indefinite detention for Pound, he finally attained the yearned-for paradise of his epic, before an audience of acolytes who newly turned his ideas into action.

Pound wrote a lot, and very quickly at St. Elizabeths: In addition to two blocks of cantos, he completed a set of Confucian translations and masterminded a dizzying number of publications, all while sending out emphatic letters to an astonishing array of personalities. My inquiry returns to *Rock-Drill*, the first book of cantos composed and published in this period. Pound explained the plan of this series in a 1954 letter: "There are three different kinds of Cantos: 3 chinese / 2 american / 6 paradise."[1] *Rock-Drill*'s structure reproduces the larger arc from the Chinese history to the Adams Cantos that Pound fashioned in the 1930s, and the achievement of this later series is the final approach into paradise after the "enormous tragedy" of *The Pisan Cantos*. These late cantos are newly schematic, and their intent is spelled out in a "draft press-release (of all things) published by New Directions in 1956" cited by Michael Kindellan: "the 'Rock-Drill' of the title refers to the purpose of this part of the poem in which 'the lies of history must be exposed to the truth hammered home by reiteration, with the insistence of the rock-drill.'"[2] There has been a fair amount of hammering in *The Cantos* before this point, but the particular force of reiteration is striking here.

It goes without saying that these truths are absolute and impervious to context; there is no evolution in Pound—and indeed he pitched himself against such theories—and he never comprehended the movement of history. All ages are simultaneous to Pound, who imagines history spread out on a single plane; he plucks exempla from this vast scape to cobble together a civilization that is vitiated from the start because it cannot exist in time. The paradise Pound fashioned out of the rubble of the postwar, however, notably belonged to his time and place: in America, at the frontier of racial segregation.

Massimo Bacigalupo, the finest reader of Pound's late cantos, lays bare their ambitions: "In fact the difficulties of *Rock-Drill*, as always in Pound but unlike most modern poetry, are only of the surface—indeed his writing is so nakedly transparent that too hard a look will evaporate the poetry."[3] Bacigalupo's seminal 1980 study of the later cantos opens with a very hard look, which bears quoting at length:

> In many ways the *Cantos* belong in those shops that sell swastikas and recordings of Mussolini's speeches, for they are, among other things, the sacred poem of the Nazi-Fascist millennium which mercifully never eventuated.
>
> The only connection I see between Pound's stature as a poet and his political aberrations is precisely the abnormalities of both. (Which is not to say that his poetics and his politics are not of one piece.) A conventional mind in many ways, Pound broke off malgré

lui from the travelled roads of Western culture, which he was not even equipped to understand, and dreamed up—for he had that power of energy—another world, which, the West having come to where it is and seeking its antithesis (if that is how Yeats puts it), turned out to be very attractive to all who in the arts were intentionally and for better reason severing themselves from the old tree. Pound, on the other hand, was never even aware that his writing was different, he just did not know any other way to go about his job. For all he consciously knew, he was aiming at the effects of Rossetti and Swinburne. Like Columbus, he was seeking the old and he found the new.[4]

The Cantos were prominently featured in "those shops" in America, tended by the young adherents of the far right that Pound gathered around him at St. Elizabeths. What Bacigalupo terms Pound's "political aberrations" were attractive to these American militants: From the poetic revolution launched by Pound's aesthetic renewals in the 1910s, Pound pitched himself within an American frenzy in the 1950s. The fevered work that constructed "another world" of Nazism-fascism clicked into place in Cold War America. Anderson Araujo's recent account of Pound's fascism underscores that "he was nothing if not explicit." Araujo identifies Pound as "very much a creature of his own time. His downfall, then, might owe less to his initial support for Italian fascism than to his stubborn refusal to shun it once its racial policies took hold after 1938." It is this shift, from seeking a politico-economic middle ground between "bourgeois liberal capitalism and the tyranny of Communism,"[5] to racial policy, that is newly significant in Pound's Washington period.

In what follows, I will consider Pound's "downfall" into racism by turning to a recent cluster of scholarship on Pound's postwar commitments that details the extent of this fall, demonstrated by the reach of Pound's writings into far-right America at midcentury and the persistence of his celebrity among this group into the present. From this dark terrain, I will turn to the *paradiso terrestre* of Cantos 90 to 95 as an exhibit of both Pound's direct engagement with an acolyte at St. Elizabeths as well as a reckoning with this contact in conjunction with his epic ambitions. The chapter concludes with the duties entailed in reading Pound's poetry, and it closes by seeking out an alternative to his art.

BRINGING IT HOME

Speaking in the 1990s, Charles Bernstein decried "the degree to which fascist ideas have rooted themselves so deeply in mainstream American life": "Pound's most fascist polemics resonate in an eerie way with the current wave of attacks on the arts, gays, the disenfranchised poor, immigrants, feminism, and the cities. I say this because there is often a tendency among Americans to exoticize fascism. Pound did his best to bring it home."[6]

It is eerier now, after the 2017 showcase of white supremacy in Charlottesville and the insurgent attacks of January 6, 2021. Bernstein's emphasis on the repercussions of Pound's political inculcation—in Bernstein's words, Pound's work "insists that it be read, form and content, for its politics and ideas"[7]—cuts against prevailing reasoning within Pound scholarship that analyzes the genealogy of Pound's economic and political thinking to conclude, as Peter Nicholls does, that Pound "was blind to the ideological entailments of his own writing."[8] Nicholls's landmark 1984 study reads the premium on practical knowledge and methodology throughout Pound's oeuvre against a missing and mistaken comprehension of ideology in Pound's thought. Tim Redman's 1991 *Ezra Pound and Italian Fascism* echoes Nicholls in judging Pound "a political naïf,"[9] and both studies present exegeses of what Pound failed to understand in his encounters with the extremist political ideologies of the 1930s that would break out into the Second World War.

Between Nicholls and Redman, however, appeared Robert Casillo's *The Genealogy of Demons: Anti-Semitism, Fascism, and the Myths of Ezra Pound*, which stepped into the breach of what Pound knew to "weigh Pound the poet, and Pound the anti-Semite and fascist, in a single balance."[10] Bacigalupo's readings of the late cantos are seeded through Casillo's study, and from these accounts to Bernstein, we can trace a line of indictment. Nicholls dispensed with Bacigalupo's judgment as an "extreme instance" of the camp of Pound critics inflamed by moral outrage,[11] but Pound's ideological activism has increasingly come to be understood by scholars beyond Pound studies as inseparable from the terrorist acts of white supremacists and neofascists.

Alex Houen's 2002 study of terrorism and modern literature features "Pound's call for violence," explicitly reading against the long-standing "elision of Pound's agency" to ask: "What is the relation of his aesthetic practice to the specific acts of terrorism that Pound later came to be associated with?"¹² The terrorist acts in question are those of John Kasper, a violent segregationist whose open worship of Pound contributed to delaying Pound's release from St. Elizabeths. Houen recounts the response of Attorney General William P. Rogers to Harry Meacham, who advocated for Pound's release: Rogers "felt that if he were released Pound might join Kasper in the South and people would be killed."¹³ That Pound's teaching has threatened lives is a cornerstone of Matthew Feldman's 2012 presentation of archival evidence for Pound's "ideological activism" on the part of Mussolini's regime,¹⁴ as well as his more recent, collaborative effort to trace Pound's "unusually diverse legacy amongst the post-war extreme right."¹⁵ Together with Andrea Rinaldi, Feldman traces the "heavy use of Pound's writing" in numerous extremist publications, including a 1980 republication of portions of Canto XXX in *The National Socialist*, an American neo-Nazi journal, as well as a 1995 special issue devoted to Ezra Pound in *The Barnes Review*, which Rinaldi and Feldman explain "has remained the most influential publishing outlet for the transnational extreme right for decades."¹⁶ This movement of ideas into action has been accumulating in plain sight, and the perennial question of the implications of this activity for Pound and his epic has come back to Poundian scholarship.

To Houen's point that "there has been no extensive analysis of the letters or the friendship" between Kasper and Pound despite their availability,¹⁷ the recent scholarship of Alec Marsh grapples with these archives to weave the strand of moral outrage against Pound's politics back into Pound studies proper. In the acknowledgments to his 2021 *Ezra Pound's Washington Cantos and the Struggle for Light*, the second study devoted to this period of Pound's writing, Marsh positions himself: "Somewhat to my own surprise, in this book I find myself walking down a dissident path of Pound scholarship first blazed by Massimo Bacigalupo in *The Forméd Trace* (1980), followed a few years later by Robert Casillo's courageous *The Genealogy of Demons* (1988)."¹⁸ Marsh's walk along this dissident path is an American inquiry: Delving into Pound's infamous postwar turn to segregationists during the Washington years, Marsh finds himself contending with what Pound brought home after the war, to an American political scene mired in its foundations in racist tyranny.

Marsh examines the coterie of far-right bohemians who learned at Pound's feet in the gardens of St. Elizabeths. Before the war, in Rapallo, the Ezuversity inculcated remarkable students: Louis Zukofsky, Basil Bunting, and James Laughlin, who created New Directions Press at Pound's urging.

But over the course of the war, Bacigalupo writes, Pound "had become a bad teacher, imparting *idées fixes* of the worst sort with ever-increasing insistence,"[19] and after the war, he found terrifyingly earnest new students in America who yearned for an ideological fix.

Marsh's first study of Pound's Washington period is devoted to Kasper, and in exposing Pound's relationship with the infamous segregationist, Marsh notes that "Pound has often been studied as a racist, but not much as an American racist."[20] *John Kasper and Ezra Pound: Saving the Republic* (2015) traces the "transformation of Kasper from young anti-Semite to arch-segregationist after 1956 as he fought against the integration of public schools trying to comply with the two Brown v. Board of Education decisions of 1954 and 1955" alongside what he identifies in Pound's thinking as a "persistent 'southern' orientation" that ultimately led him to underwrite Kasper's cross-burning terrorism.[21]

Writing against the general view among Pound scholars who file Kasper away as "a near-mental case rather than taking him seriously as an American extremist of a well-known type," Marsh argues that Kasper "was a serious student of Pound; indeed he was one of his most astute and committed readers."[22] Marsh spells out the implications of his findings: "It is uncomfortable to imagine Kasper a well-informed, close student of the poet, listening, reading, and distributing the latest scholarship on him, to say nothing of their own intense correspondence. We are supposed to believe that Kasper misunderstood both poem and poet. But the evidence suggests that Kasper understands Pound all too well; that is, he knows that Pound is a man putting his ideas into action."[23]

Marsh's claim is far-reaching: "All in all Kasper was Pound's most perspicacious reader, seeing through the elaborate and recondite surface of the poem to its radical, and therefore simple intent: to 'save the republic.' In curious ways, some literary, some political and historical, he was Pound's most important reader in the 1950s."[24] This terrifying young man, a star pupil of the Ezuversity of the 1950s, is Pound's ideal reader. Kasper never possessed Laughlin's means, but he created a whole venue for Pound's *paideuma*: the Make It New bookstore in Greenwich Village, which he relocated to DC. Kasper made up for his lack of wealth and standing by his obeisance to his master, as evidenced in the hundreds of letters from Kasper that Marsh waded through for his study, filled with expressions of fealty, as in these lines from a 1956 letter: "If I'm doing wrong, going down the wrong road, getting corrupt in character, acting unConfucian, am in a rut or stupid, please so say. I would quit Citizens Councils today if you asked me to. I will do anything you ask me to. Sire, you're my real Grampop sure."[25]

Kasper sent this particular letter to Pound from Charlottesville, where he was arrested for distributing handbills for the chapter of the White Citizens' Council he launched, whose motto was "Honor-Pride-Fight: Save the White." Kasper targeted Charlottesville for a raid after the city schools were ordered to desegregate in July, and he peddled a pamphlet "written by the St Elizabeths circle called *Virginians on Guard!*, pushing legislation to reinforce segregation" and inciting terrorist action against the Supreme Court.[26]

Marsh is at pains to point out that "Pound was well aware of *Virginians on Guard!* because he wrote part of it and vetted the rest." The pamphlet featured "52 increasingly strident proposed laws," and Marsh readily identifies Pound's contributions, which include a lecture on usury and a plan to issue stamp-scrip, and he underscores Pound's editorial allowance on "detailed prohibitions in #47 that excluded Negroes [sic] from higher education, and even from many professions such as dish-washer and bell hop, maid, waiter, and waitress, long-sanctioned under Jim Crow, without a personal license won by passing a written exam and a high-school diploma." Marsh concludes, "As editor Pound signed off on the SWCC vision of racial apartheid."[27] Kasper's plea to Pound as he whips himself up for violent action in the Charlottesville letter recalls the brainwashing scare of the early Cold War: Programmed by Pound, he appeals to his master for confirmation. Pound was his arbiter of wrong and right, and Pound had the power to switch off this cold warrior.

It is a straight shot from Kasper's Charlottesville raid to the Unite the Right rally of 2017. Considering the frenzy of Kasper's organizing efforts then, Houen writes, "The army was indeed gathering"[28]; programmed by Pound, Kasper disseminated his writings to a mob who relit their torches under Trump's reign. In detailing a far-right continuum that enshrines Pound's thought, Feldman cites journalist Christopher Hitchens's encounter with Willis Carto, a publisher notorious "as the main disseminator of Holocaust 'revisionism'": "'Ezra Pound!' exclaimed Mr. Carto. 'Why, I love that man's work. Except for all that goddam poetry!' I thought then that if one ever needed a working definition of an anti-Semite, it might perhaps be an individual who esteemed everything about Ezra Pound except his Cantos."[29]

But Kasper "esteemed everything about Ezra Pound," including his Cantos. Marsh's portrait is remarkable for demonstrating Kasper's comprehension: This ideal reader unnervingly cuts to the chase of *The Cantos*. Bacigalupo's piercing judgment of Pound's "conventional mind," "not even equipped to understand" the aesthetic cultures he revered echoes with the pleas of Kasper, the aspirant who longs to be set on Pound's path. Between the master and pupil, the poetry "evaporates"—to cite Bacigalupo again—to reveal Pound's "nakedly transparent" design.[30] The distinction between Pound's poetry and politics retained by Hitchens in his remembered exchange with Carto does not hold for Pound's 1950s adherents, who read all of Pound's writings as direct correspondence, and Pound in turn communicated with them in his cantos of the period.

MARSHMALLOWS IN PARADISE

Marsh's study of Kasper overflowed into his second book on Pound in Washington, a critical sequel that features Sheri Martinelli, a long-standing curiosity among Pound scholars whom Marsh unveils as the true subject of *Rock-Drill*. The paradisal light of Pound's epic took living form at St. Elizabeths in the person of Martinelli, "a *Vogue* model, painter, and Greenwich Village eccentric."[31] By the time she captivated Pound, Martinelli had been named a muse by Anaïs Nin and captured in William Gaddis's fiction, and recent scholarship on Pound's late cantos and the Washington period has shone a new light on her presence. Kindellan traces Pound's annotations on Martinelli's typescript copies of *Rock-Drill* into the published cantos, and he demonstrates that explanations Pound wrote out for her benefit made their way into the final text: "These cantos were written both for and about her."[32]

Kindellan explains that Martinelli is the amalgam of "Sybilla-Beatrice, Kuthera (Aphrodite), Kwanon, Ra-set, and Leucothea, among other idealized female figures" that glimmers throughout *Rock-Drill*, and in reading her presence, he identifies "a new kind of exclusivity" to these cantos to explain that "this verse is *really* about him and Martinelli."[33] Marsh expands upon Kindellan's archival study to state definitively that Pound and Martinelli were lovers—against long-standing doubt cast on the probability of a physical relationship between the aged poet and the ingenue, in an institutional space that guarded against privacy—to argue for "the thoroughly erotic nature of Pound's paradise."[34] Marsh is adamant about her primacy: "We must now understand that these cantos were inspired by her, written for her, *specifically for her to read*."[35] If, as Bacigalupo states, the *Rock-Drill* poems are all surface difficulty, Martinelli is the naked figure that lies beneath.

To read this living muse as the key to these cantos is to posit an order of interpretation distinct from earlier portions of the epic. The difficulty of the postwar poems lies in the situation of Pound's detention, first at Pisa and then in Washington. *The Pisan Cantos* are celebrated for their effort to preserve "what thou lov'st well"; by contrast, Cantos 90 to 95, the paradise sequence of *Rock-Drill*, as Marsh explains, is a record of a "human situation, the lovers' drama," which "is well concealed in a thicket of private allusions, foreign languages, and inspired blather." Marsh adds that these poems "have a didactic purpose: they are to educate Martinelli as well."[36] And so, if Kasper was the most important reader of Pound's work in this period, Martinelli was the most intimate, and Pound's relationships with both of these fervent young disciples were disguised yet blatant: Though Pound strove to conceal the most explicit elements of his inculcation of these pupils, their bond with him was in plain sight.

Marsh underscores the significance of Martinelli by naming this series the "Sheri Cantos," sealing them within the gauzy erotics of the Bohemian muse. Canto 90 presents the ascent into paradise:

> Sybilla,
> from under the rubble heap
> m'elevasti
> from the dulled edge beyond pain,
> m'elevasti[37]

The lines continue in this alternation, and these cantos preserve an airy space for a host of goddesses and seeresses—Kuthera and Sybilla, Beatrice and Kuanon—who come to the grounds of St. Elizabeths, all channeled into the figure of Martinelli: "Grove hath its altar / under elms, in that temple, in silence / a lone nymph by the pool."[38] These cantos are about both seeing this lone nymph and what this figure can see—Canto 91 opens by urging "That your eyes come forth from their caves"[39]—but the clarity and crystal that run through this series are cast as a minor mysticism. Bacigalupo's reading of Canto 91 expresses what is missing from this transparency: "We miss not a little, in this somewhat excessive clarity, a sense of tragedy."[40]

We find a faint sea-change in Canto 92:

> And from far
> > il tremolar della marina
> chh chh
> > the pebbles turn with the wave
> chh   ch'u
> > "fui chiamat'
> > > e qui refulgo"[41]

The noise of the waves morphs into a more human utterance, "ch'u," bringing forth Dante's Cunizza, whose line we hear: "I was called and here I glow."[42] It is worth noting that Cunizza appeared in *The Pisan Cantos*, brought in with the sun that entered Pound's cell; her appearance here, however, is rendered in sonic and not visual terms. Her fugitive glow is largely unseen; no hieroglyphs or ideograms light the way in this passage. Instead, the elemental movement of the wave churns the rubble.

The lines that follow in this passage echo the ascension of "m'elevasti" in Canto 90, but their stepped form cuts against paradise:

> Le Paradis n'est pas artificiel
> > but is jagged,
> For a flash,
> > for an hour.
> Then agony,
> > then an hour,
> > > then agony[43]

Martinelli explicated these lines for Charles Bukowski, claiming they were written "when cruel Miz Martinelli was his beloved & she was out... down in Spade-town... turning on... and sweet gramps was locked up inside St. Liz ... longing to protect his fragile butterfly."[44] Martinelli's interpretation is entirely viable: The allusion to Baudelaire resonates with Pound's distress at Martinelli's drug use, and Marsh notes the butterflies just above this passage: "farfalle in tempesta."[45] Martinelli's "sweet gramps"—a telling echo of Kasper's "Grampop"—reduces Pound to his confinement, and her tell-all localizes the broader desensitization that Pound decries in Canto 92 onto her own act of "turning on." In casting herself as the subject of these lines, however, Martinelli dramatically constricts the poem.

To decode the poem in this manner is to evaporate its art. Reading the jagged flashes of paradise as Martinelli "turning on" falsifies paradise. In Martinelli's reading, Le paradis est artificiel. Canto 92 presents periodic illuminations within a continuous dark age; what light there is here describes a failed connection on several fronts: between maestro and muse, and, more significantly, between Martinelli's delight in locating herself and the poetic diminishment entailed in this recognition. Her interpretation lays bare the travesty of this paradise, in which the light that jags into agony is an extinguishing advance, and the movements of wave and lightning are self-canceling actions.

Canto 93, the centerpiece of the series, seeks out a more durable illumination. Mussolini reappears: "'Perché' said the Boss / 'vuol mettere le sue idee in ordine?' / 'Pel mio poema.'" Pound is recalling his single interview with Mussolini in 1933, and the passage gestures toward the poetics of Pound's political order, citing "distributive justice"[46] but then pauses to acknowledge his didacticism:

> All ov which may be a little slow for the reader
> or seem platitudinous[47]

We can read this passage as a direct address to Martinelli, whose "mental velocity" Pound praised. Perhaps she drifted away during these rehearsals, but her master pounded on nevertheless, arriving at his Make It New ideograms: "'Renew' / as on the T'ang tub: / Renew."[48] But whether this muse can comprehend this illumination is an open question:

> Shall two know the same in their knowing?
>   You who dare Persephone's threshold,
>   Beloved, do not fall apart in my hands.[49]

These lines register the perils of the "carnal paradise"[50] of these Cantos: In questioning whether two can "know the same in their knowing," Pound detaches carnal from political knowledge. The exhortation not to fall apart: this is the weakness of paradise cast in human form.

The closing lines of Canto 93 lament the beloved's softness:

> You are tender as a marshmallow, my Love,
> I cannot use you as a fulcrum.

> You have stirred my mind out of dust.
> Flora Castalia, your petals drift thru the air,
> the wind is 1/2 lighted with pollen
> > diafana,
> e Monna Vanna ... tu mi fai rimembrar.[51]

The tenderness of Martinelli's breast, which she claimed to have felt, instinctively, at the moment Pound composed the marshmallow line, is useless. The diaphanous cluster—Flora Castalia, Pound's made-up nymph, in a flight of petals; a recollection of Cavalcanti's beloved; a Dantescan recollection poised in a vision of earthly paradise—is a tribute to Martinelli, for stirring the mind. But this gratitude belongs to an attenuation of Pound's paradise: No fulcrum means Martinelli is inessential.

Marsh's study of Kasper demonstrated that this disciple did "know the same in their knowing," and perhaps we can align Kasper and Martinelli to two modes of knowing, worldly and otherworldly. But Pound himself did not settle for such divisions; the paradisal is political for Pound. Canto 94 spells out a political duty: After a coy mention of himself as "fuss-cat," Martinelli's endearment for Pound, he exhorts his heroes to "maintain antisepsis / let the light pour."[52] And then, in Canto 95, the last of the paradisal series, Pound dispenses with his muse:

> "My bikini is worth yr/raft". Said Leucothea
> And if I see her not
> No sight is worth the beauty of my thought.[53]

Throughout the series, Martinelli is Leucothea, the sea nymph who rescued Odysseus; the bikini line, a postwar transposition of her magic cloth, is repeated from Canto 91. In this reprise, Pound chooses his own beauty over the nymph, devaluing her arguments for her worth: "My bikini is worth yr/raft," Pound has written in the end of his dalliance with Martinelli—she would be replaced by Marcella Spann, a more practical muse—by reducing her to mere distraction, marshmallows, and bikinis. Instead of the little light they offer, Pound elects his own, significantly darker, thoughts, and so *Rock-Drill* ends, to be followed by *Thrones*.

There is little beauty to Pound's thought in the Washington period. The ugliness of his segregationist diatribes, which activated a cross-burning fanatic, also fashioned his muse. Marsh cites Martinelli's different lovers as indications of a lack of racist conviction, and he concludes that "Martinelli's paradisal spirit was polluted with Pound's right-wing, racialist outlook." We cannot know whether it was entirely Pound's influence that led Martinelli to make proclamations like "one IS WHITE & not to feel any guilt for it,"⁵⁴ but her apotheosis in *The Cantos* is inseparable from Pound's ascendant white supremacy during this period. In the pallor of her light, we can register the dimensions of Pound's paradise, which was finally a racist ordering. But Martinelli's seductions were ultimately insufficient to bear what Pound knew and thought.

A nonparadisal passage from Canto 91 demonstrates the proximity of heaven to hell in Pound's cosmology: "*Democracies electing their sewage / till there is no clear thought about holiness / a dung flow from 1913 / and, in this, their kikery functioned, Marx, Freud / and the american beaneries.*"⁵⁵ In the present climate of white terrorism in America, we know all too well that what Pound sought was no paradise. And so the problem is not that Martinelli was a marshmallow; it is that paradise had to be a fulcrum. In tracing the debasement of Pound's paradise, from its embodiment in a postwar bikini to the blind eye Pound finally turns to it, the light goes out, leaving a vast darkness.

THE DUTY TO POUND

In an early argument for *The Cantos* as a fascist epic, John Lauber showcases Pound's totalitarian longing, demonstrating that his "way of thinking" exemplifies "the paranoid style," characterized by a "leap from facts to conclusion."⁵⁶ Peter Dale Scott's 1990 reading of the late cantos, too, underscores a paranoiac thinking that exceeds the poet: Identifying Pound's "relentless pursuit of those of his personal obsessions, or pathologies, which are not trivial but rooted in the pathology of his culture," Scott argues, "Precisely because our culture is to some degree pathological, Pound's poetic *ira*, like Dante's, deserves understanding as a response to it."⁵⁷ Scott qualifies this understanding, however: "If Pound's poetry could be shown to have instigated anyone like Crommelin or Kasper in their terrorism, the case for teaching it would be tenuous."⁵⁸ John G. Crommelin was a perpetual political candidate of the far right in midcentury, and he appears in *Thrones* with a fellow aspirant, Pedro Del Valle: "With a Crommelyn at the breech-block / or a dell Valle, / This is what the swine haven't got."⁵⁹ Houen notes "Kasper's letter in which he thanks Pound for the Crommelin and Del Valle references"[60] to demonstrate the dialogue Pound conducted with the American far right, whose pathological thinking he wrote into his epic.

Considering the repercussions of Pound's interlocking aesthetic and political visions for American poetry, Redman writes, "the combination that we find in Pound of undoubted poetic mastery and questionable political beliefs has contributed to the widespread retreat of American poets from political engagement." For Redman, this "turn to the lyrical and away from the political" has resulted in the "radical loss of bardic consequence."[61] Yet the crisis of Pound is, in fact, his bardic consequence, and it is no surprise that the young poet who made a pact with Walt Whitman in an effort to take over the mantle of American bard should sound his barbaric yawp back home, where his unshakably American tones could be received as direct communiqués. In Washington, DC, in the roiling aftermath of *Brown v. Board of Education*, the revived Ezuversity activated a new generation of Americans to identify and attack the scourges that Pound deemed threats to his art. Redman pitches his reading as an effort to reassert poetry's "claim to cultural consequence,"[62] all the while acutely aware of the cultural consequences of *The Cantos*. The pathological thinking enshrined in Pound's epic has overrun America, now awash in conspiracy theories.

Marsh grapples with what he has uncovered in his study of Pound's Washington activities:

> The fact that Pound was an anti-Semite, a fascist, and a white racist bothers me a lot as an American and a human being and the fact that he could have stopped Kasper, who worshipped the poet as a father, teacher, and Master, at any time had he thought that his young protégé had gone too far is hard to bear. But to scholars of Pound, the duty to Pound is to understand him.[63]

Like Marsh, I believe that we must be able to read reprehensible texts, and our duty to this work involves an understanding of its grounding political assumptions. The significance of reception is one lesson of Marsh's study, which details how Kasper did in fact extend Pound's oeuvre. Kasper's actions are not a distortion but a desired outcome of Pound's aesthetic works. This is the fate of the Tale of the Tribe, which requires the horizon of the reader because the epic binds the bard to the folk. Pound has stayed current because of his extraordinary enmity: That *The Cantos*, a tome deemed unreadable, can be received as an active communication vouchsafes its epic force while, again, evaporating its poetry.

It is worth recalling Donald Davie's declaration that "Pound has made it impossible for anyone any longer to exalt the poet into a seer."[64] The darkest aspect of Pound's legacy, however, is that there remain armies who exalt Pound into a seer, and we are living in an era in which these forces have overtaken the seats of government. It is little consolation that a notorious Holocaust denier could not love Pound's "goddam poetry," but in Pound's recognition of the inutility of Martinelli for his paradise, I register the narrowed straits of illumination in St. Elizabeths. Marsh's reading of the "Sheri Cantos" as a private conversation is a constriction of Pound's epic light, in which natural and prophetic forces are drawn down, into a plaintive, white softness. The nymph's veil for a bikini: This is the bargain Pound struck to get to paradise, but by the end of Canto 95 he returned to the scene of Odysseus's rescue by the nymph to get to dry land. Achieving paradise did not end the epic; instead, Pound moved on.

Against the little light of the Washington Cantos, the celebrated *Pisan Cantos* secured broad recognition. Marjorie Perloff's 2004 reassessment of the Bollingen controversy, when *The Pisan Cantos* were awarded the inaugural prize in 1948, insists upon their value: "most critics would agree that, whatever else the sequence was or wasn't, it was certainly the best book of poems published in 1948 and hence well deserved the much disputed prize."[65] Yet *The Pisan Cantos* was deemed the best book of poems in significant part because the prize was much disputed, and Pound remains a live topic because of the disputes he occasions. For his nonfascist adherents, the enormous tragedy in the series is the welcome failure of an annihilating vision; the punishment Pound endured for his political agitation lent an aesthetic value to the verse he composed, in significant part because it could be read as atonement. Thus it is not that *The Pisan Cantos* are beautiful despite the DTC cage but because of it, and the growing significance of Pound's time in the "bughouse" in Washington, DC, is presently remaking our understanding of the cantos that appeared after the Bollingen award, when Pound peddled his obsessions to a new order of American faithful, scaling paradise down to their pleas.

I would like to conclude with the poetry that was not deemed the best book of poetry in 1948, Muriel Rukeyser's *The Green Wave*, a finalist for the Bollingen. It seems to me that we would now live in a different world if this understanding had been prized:

Then I Saw What the Calling Was

All the voices of the wood called "Muriel!"
but it was soon solved;   it was nothing, it was not for me.
The words were a little like Mortal and More and Endure
and a word like Real, a sound like Health or Hell.
Then I saw what the calling was   :   it was the road I traveled,
  the clear
time and these colors of orchards, gold behind gold and the full
shadow behind each tree and behind each slope.   Not to me
the calling, but to anyone, and at last I saw   :   where
the road lay through sunlight and many voices and the marvel
orchards, not for me, not for me, not for me.
I came into my clear being;   uncalled, alive, and sure.
Nothing was speaking to me, but I offered and all was well.
And then I arrived at the powerful green hill.[66]

Rukeyser presents a natural world that entices but does not offer itself; instead, "I offered." The clarity here is a sense of assured being that does not feed on the orchard fruit. This is a paradise without the snake, in which the calling words resolve into gold, shadow, tree, hill. No one is calling, and there is no danger.

What would we be like now, having learned that we are not called? That the voices of the wood are not solely for us? And that we could arrive at a source of power and all could be well? But this is fantasy; the past is done. We can move forward differently, though, and we can choose what we will carry into the future. It is up to us to decide what calls to us and to take those roads where anyone—everyone—can travel.

NOTES

1. As quoted in Massimo Bacigalupo, *The Forméd Trace: The Later Poetry of Ezra Pound* (New York: Columbia University Press, 1980), 232.
2. Michael Kindellan, *The Late Cantos of Ezra Pound: Composition, Revision, Publication* (New York: Bloomsbury Academic, 2017), 74.
3. Bacigalupo, *The Forméd Trace*, 260.
4. Bacigalupo, *The Forméd Trace*, x.

5. Anderson Araujo, "Italian Fascism," in *The New Ezra Pound Studies*, ed. Mark Byron (Cambridge: Cambridge University Press, 2019), 209, 217, 220
6. Charles Bernstein, "Pound and the Poetry of Today," in *My Way: Speeches and Poems* (Chicago: University of Chicago Press, 1998), 158.
7. Bernstein, "Pound and the Poetry of Today," 158.
8. Peter Nicholls, *Ezra Pound: Politics, Economics, and Writing* (Atlantic Highlands, NJ: Humanities Press, 1984), 94.
9. Timothy Redman, *Ezra Pound and Italian Fascism* (New York: Cambridge University Press, 1991), 9.
10. Robert Casillo, *The Genealogy of Demons: Anti-Semitism, Fascism, and the Myths of Ezra Pound* (Evanston, IL: Northwestern University Press, 1988), 3.
11. Nicholls, *Ezra Pound*, 87.
12. Alex Houen, *Terrorism and Modern Literature from Joseph Conrad to Ciaran Carson* (New York: Oxford University Press, 2003), 145, 146, 158.
13. Houen, *Terrorism and Modern Literature from Joseph Conrad to Ciaran Carson*, 182.
14. Matthew Feldman, "The 'Pound Case' in Historical Perspective: An Archival Overview," *Journal of Modern Literature* 35, no. 2 (2012): 92.
15. Andrea Rinaldi and Matthew Feldman, "'Penny-wise . . .': Ezra Pound's Posthumous Legacy to Fascism," *Sanglap: Journal of Literary and Cultural Inquiry* 1, no. 2 (2015): 31.
16. Rinaldi and Feldman, "Penny-wise . . . ," 39, 43.
17. Houen, *Terrorism and Modern Literature from Joseph Conrad to Ciaran Carson*, 173.
18. Alec Marsh, *Ezra Pound's Washington Cantos and the Struggle for Light* (London: Bloomsbury Academic, 2021), xiii.
19. Bacigalupo, *The Forméd Trace*, 192.
20. Alec Marsh, *John Kasper and Ezra Pound: Saving the Republic* (London: Bloomsbury Academic, 2015), 10.
21. Marsh, *John Kasper and Ezra Pound*, xi.
22. Marsh, *John Kasper and Ezra Pound*, xii.
23. Marsh, *John Kasper and Ezra Pound*, 58.
24. Marsh, *John Kasper and Ezra Pound*, xvi.
25. Marsh, *John Kasper and Ezra Pound*, 144.
26. Marsh, *John Kasper and Ezra Pound*, 136, 139.
27. Marsh, *John Kasper and Ezra Pound*, 139, 140, 141–42.
28. Houen, *Terrorism and Modern Literature from Joseph Conrad to Ciaran Carson*, 178.

29. Rinaldi and Feldman, "Penny-wise . . . ," 38.
30. Bacigalupo, *The Forméd Trace*, x, 260.
31. Kindellan, *The Late Cantos of Ezra Pound*, 102.
32. Kindellan, *The Late Cantos of Ezra Pound*, 102.
33. Kindellan, *The Late Cantos of Ezra Pound*, 102, 103.
34. Marsh, *Ezra Pound's Washington Cantos*, 121.
35. Marsh, *Ezra Pound's Washington Cantos*, 113 (emphasis in original).
36. Marsh, *Ezra Pound's Washington Cantos*, 123.
37. Ezra Pound, *The Cantos of Ezra Pound* (New York: New Directions, 1993), 90/626.
38. Pound, *The Cantos*, 90/627.
39. Pound, *The Cantos*, 91/630.
40. Bacigalupo, *The Forméd Trace*, 291.
41. Pound, *The Cantos*, 92/640.
42. Ezra Pound, *New Selected Poems and Translations*, ed. Richard Sieburth (New York: New Directions, 2010), 341.
43. Pound, *The Cantos*, 92/640.
44. Marsh, *Ezra Pound's Washington Cantos*, 137.
45. Pound, *The Cantos*, 92/639.
46. Pound, *The Cantos*, 93/646, 647.
47. Pound, *The Cantos*, 93/647.
48. Pound, *The Cantos*, 93/648.
49. Pound, *The Cantos*, 93/651.
50. Marsh, *Ezra Pound's Washington Cantos*, 128.
51. Pound, *The Cantos*, 93/652.
52. Pound, *The Cantos*, 94/655.
53. Pound, *The Cantos*, 95/665.
54. Marsh, *Ezra Pound's Washington Cantos*, 139.
55. Pound, *The Cantos*, 91/634.
56. John Lauber, "Pound's Cantos: A Fascist Epic," *Journal of American Studies* 12, no. 1 (1978): 15, 16.
57. Peter Dale Scott, "Anger in Paradise: The Poetic Voicing of Disorder in Pound's Later Cantos," *Paideuma* 19, no. 3 (1990): 56.
58. Scott, "Anger in Paradise," 58.
59. Pound, *The Cantos*, 105/771.
60. Houen, *Terrorism and Modern Literature from Joseph Conrad to Ciaran Carson*, 190.

61. Redman, *Ezra Pound and Italian Fascism*, 13.
62. Redman, *Ezra Pound and Italian Fascism*, 14.
63. Marsh, *John Kasper and Ezra Pound*, xv.
64. Donald Davie, *Ezra Pound: Poet as Sculptor* (New York: Oxford University Press, 1964), 243.
65. Quoted in Carrie J. Preston, "Pound, Gender, Sexuality," in *The New Ezra Pound Studies*, ed. Mark Byron (Cambridge: Cambridge University Press, 2020), 198.
66. Muriel Rukeyser, *The Collected Poems of Muriel Rukeyser* (Pittsburgh: University of Pittsburgh Press, 2006), 267. Copyright © Muriel Rukeyser, 1948. Reprinted by permission of the Estate of Muriel Rukeyser.

BIBLIOGRAPHY

Araujo, Anderson. "Italian Fascism." In *The New Ezra Pound Studies*, edited by Mark Byron, 208–26. Cambridge: Cambridge University Press, 2019.

Bacigalupo, Massimo. *The Forméd Trace: The Later Poetry of Ezra Pound*. New York: Columbia University Press, 1980.

Bernstein, Charles. "Pound and the Poetry of Today." In *My Way: Speeches and Poems*, 155–65. Chicago: University of Chicago Press, 1998.

Casillo, Robert. *The Genealogy of Demons: Anti-Semitism, Fascism, and the Myths of Ezra Pound*. Evanston, IL: Northwestern University Press, 1988.

Davie, Donald. *Ezra Pound: Poet as Sculptor*. New York: Oxford University Press, 1964.

Feldman, Matthew. "The 'Pound Case' in Historical Perspective: An Archival Overview." *Journal of Modern Literature* 35, no. 2 (2012): 83–97.

Houen, Alex. *Terrorism and Modern Literature from Joseph Conrad to Ciaran Carson*. New York: Oxford University Press, 2003.

Kindellan, Michael. *The Late Cantos of Ezra Pound: Composition, Revision, Publication*. New York: Bloomsbury Academic, 2017.

Lauber, John. "Pound's Cantos: A Fascist Epic." *Journal of American Studies* 12, no. 1 (1978): 3–21.

Marsh, Alec. *Ezra Pound's Washington Cantos and the Struggle for Light*. London: Bloomsbury Academic, 2021.

Marsh, Alec. *John Kasper and Ezra Pound: Saving the Republic*. London: Bloomsbury Academic, 2015.

Nicholls, Peter. *Ezra Pound: Politics, Economics, and Writing*. Atlantic Highlands, NJ: Humanities Press, 1984.

Pound, Ezra. *The Cantos of Ezra Pound*. New York: New Directions, 1993.
Pound, Ezra. *New Selected Poems and Translations*. Edited by Richard Sieburth. New York: New Directions, 2010.
Preston, Carrie J. "Pound, Gender, Sexuality." In *The New Ezra Pound Studies*, edited by Mark Byron, 196–207. Cambridge: Cambridge University Press, 2020.
Redman, Tim. *Ezra Pound and Italian Fascism*. New York: Cambridge University Press, 1991.
Rinaldi, Andrea, and Matthew Feldman. "'Penny-wise . . .': Ezra Pound's Posthumous Legacy to Fascism." *Sanglap: Journal of Literary and Cultural Inquiry* 1, no. 2 (2015): 27–70.
Rukeyser, Muriel. *The Collected Poems of Muriel Rukeyser*. Pittsburgh: University of Pittsburgh Press, 2006.
Scott, Peter Dale. "Anger in Paradise: The Poetic Voicing of Disorder in Pound's Later Cantos." *Paideuma* 19, no. 3 (1990): 47–63.

Chapter   Eight

Petitionary Long Poems

Layli Long Soldier, Juliana Spahr, and Srikanth Reddy

Peter Middleton

PETITIONS

It is tempting to begin a chapter about the contemporary North American long poem with a flyover view of the continent of poetry today. Remembering that the extremely heterogeneous North American long poem cannot be a genre category nor a set of conventions, features, styles, or traditions, not even a congeries of family resemblances, any critical consensus about them can only ever be open ended. We might back away and still try to exercise our inner philologist on the terms *North*, and *America*, and *long*, and *poetry*, checking the wiring behind such word devices. But is not discussing something as vast, incompletely archived, and rapidly changing as recent North American poetry like trying to audit a hyperobject?[1] What would be the boundaries of this American long poem: conceptual art, folk ballads, visual art, and poetry paratexts? And what is a poem anyway, when poems in the magazines and books of traditional formats are also now resituated across the internet? How long is long? Rachel Blau DuPlessis's major work *Drafts* runs to over nine hundred pages; Claudia Rankine's *Citizen* to around two hundred pages; and Layli Long Soldier's "Whereas" to a little less than fifty pages. And what does it mean for a text to be described as "American" given the global reach of the US economy, its cultural capital, and its military control? Where does the adjacent anglophone (and partially francophone) nation of Canada fit in?[2] The adjective "American" has had enormous cultural reach across the world and has often been defined in a manner that might seem strange to US citizens, while in the United States, the term "American" has been prismatically opened up to many colors of race, sexuality, and disability, a dazzling intersectionality that has led to entire new fields of research into identity.

Enough rhetorical foreplay. Exhausted at the thought of such encyclopedic possibilities, while wanting to insist that they remain there in the background of this chapter, I bring myself back to earth from such an Olympian altitude by recalling what for me is an iconic image of America, the urban American highway from my childhood in mid-1960s Washington, DC, with its distinctive mix of stale hot air, gas fumes, overheated car vinyl, and gum, full of finned automobiles and lined with neon in daylight. But this iconic image is only helpful as metaphor. The automobile is no longer the primary vehicle of American freedoms today; it is computer devices that drive the information highway (already a faded cliché), dominated by what we now call social media. This is where I plan to start, investigating the intersection between poems, American technology, and new forms of readership, a dynamic cultural economy that is now commonly called digital, although this seemingly neutral allusion to electronic code obscures the interdependence of other more expansive forms of social power, including weaponry, space exploration, and environmental engineering. I will discuss longer poems within the changing conditions of reading and circulation created by the rapid establishment of the digital institutions and managed commons that are providing new affordances to poets. It is easy to forget that reading itself has a history still unfolding, that it has to be learned, that it is not an instinctive ability, and that the reading skills required by long poems are necessarily complex and always changing.

My contention here will be that we can understand the condition of the North American long poem today by examining how poems at the short end of the long poem spectrum are responding to the social relations of language constructed within the digital spaces of our time. Over the past three decades this scale of poem that can extend from a dozen pages to an entire book has become an increasingly prominent form, to the extent that in the introduction to their incisive showing of how poets and critics understand this recent development in avant-garde poetics, *The Fate of Difficulty in Our Time*, Charles Altieri and Nicholas Nace can make the large claim that "for many poets who approach issues of authorship, difficulty takes place less in short lyric or anti-lyric forms than in longer book-length works."[3] I take "difficulty" to be a mark of the demands for updated reading skills required by cultural change.

In this chapter I shall concentrate on three such poems that use documents as means of activating a potentially radical public discourse: Layli Long Soldier's "Whereas" (2017), Juliana Spahr's *That Winter the Wolf Came* (2015), and Srikanth Reddy's *Voyager* (2011). The choice of these titles is not intended to stand in for my discarded overview; they can however help us think about what poets now consider a credible aesthetic for internet America. Long Soldier is an American Indian activist, artist, and poet who has found a new means to write for the First Nations as a poet, by exposing the oppressive pragmatics of a seemingly well-intentioned US government initiative, a congressional apology to all American Indians. Ann Vickery provides a useful introduction to this work:

> While another would say "at least there was an Apology," she draws attention to its inadequacy as an occupied body on occupied land: "Whereas I have spent my life in unholding." Long Soldier notes the challenges of being a dual citizen of the United States and the Oglala Sioux Tribe, framing the collection with the imperative: "I must work, I must eat, I must art, I must mother, I must friend, I must listen, I must observe, constantly I must live."[4]

Spahr is a versatile writer, variously a blogger, educationalist, memoirist, historian, polemicist, poet, performer, and editor. I shall take cues from her questioning of what she sees as a necessary yet flawed radicalism of avant-garde poetics in relation to ecology, queer politics, political activism, literature in the academy, anglophone hegemony, and the continuing challenge of reshaping sociality. Having grown up in a working-class town with no history of interest in the arts, studied on the Poetics Program at Buffalo, lived in New York, Hawaii, and California, worked in several universities, and helped set up poetry presses, she has intersected with many of the institutions that support poetry, notably the university, small press publishing, communitarian politics, and digital media. Reddy has become known as an erasure poet for his extraordinary book-length poem *Voyager*, though he deserves to be known also for his highly original work in a subsequent book, *Underworld Lit*, which takes on the whole issue of the global reach of American culture by slyly concentrating on an extended would-be comp lit exploration of literary representations of the afterlife.

Each of these books is "documental," to use Michael Leong's term, "grounded in the empirically and ontologically identifiable units of cultural memory called documents," engaging respectively with a congressional resolution, oil industry reports, and a self-serving memoir by an ex-Nazi who became secretary-general of the United Nations.[5] These poems look tiny in the scale of their public agency, especially alongside the institutions represented by their documentary foundations, and they each pose a tacit question: How can the poet reach past futile rhetorical engagement with the public world? Leong argues that reproducing, reframing, and opening up official documents from the archive to poetic scrutiny can be an effective political strategy, insisting that our questions about poetry's deployment of archival documents ought to be expressed in terms of labor.[6] Documental poetry may sound like an earnest project. Lisa Robertson captures the spirit at work in these three long poems when she writes, "You worked with painstaking fidelity to the documents . . . Your face was pure query."[7] Such pure query can be found in the communicative labor active in each of these poems.

"Whereas" exists in fragments on the Poetry Foundation website where you can hear Long Soldier read "Whereas a string-bean blue-eyed man," and if you listen closely you can notice her making subtle adjustments to the printed text.[8] Most readers will also want visual access on screen to the US Congress website page for "S.J. Res.14—111th Congress (2009–2010)," a resolution apologizing to Native Americans, which provides the textual background to her poem.[9] Spahr's collection from Commune Editions, *That Winter the Wolf Came*, acknowledges that her poetry "is full of debts and thefts," including "language from 'The Rise and Fall of the Oakland Commune,'" a website, and a report on the Deepwater Horizon disaster.[10] Her book takes its title not from folk tale or legend but from a social media event, the online tracking of a wolf that strayed into California, and the entire book is "hashing," to use her own trope, with internet material. In her poem "Turnt," a friend comments on the poet's reliance on the internet, saying "your feed is all riots, plants, picnics, and poets / . . . And I said, my son, my son is in my feed too."[11] The poet activist is alert to the felicitous semantic ambiguities of describing social media as "feed." Reddy's *Voyager* extends well beyond the page to extensive online materials, exposing in considerable detail the stages of the compositional process of erasure, including reproductions of many pages from a memoir by Kurt Waldheim. Most readers will also want to find images and text about the Voyager space program, and perhaps listen to the golden record that carried the music and voices of our planet, including Waldheim's strangely compromised message of peace, out to the galaxy.

As we can see, to understand the innovative strategies of these poets we should think about the communicative ontology of the internet itself. A twentieth-century invention, it has been transformed in the twenty-first century by the arrival of social media institutions controlled by oligarchs with massive banking sector support, notably Facebook, Twitter, and Google, surrounded by a penumbra of lesser organizations. Although the word revolution is overworked, this surely qualifies as a revolution of both language and communication. Writing, not voice, has been at the heart of this process, in text that is endlessly repeated, distorted, illustrated, erased and inflated, split into its component atoms, and harvested by AI language models. As cultural theorists have argued since the 1970s, it is an error to think of users of such services, whether poets or readers, as passive consumers. The work of my three poets demonstrates that it is also a mistake to conceptualize the internet solely as an attention economy, a corporate business strategy of surveillance. Some users of these platforms wrench them to their own ends, creatively and destructively, in acts of what cultural theorists once called cultural dissidence, the opportunistic repurposing of popular culture, often at the social margins, for their countercorporate and political ends. One consequence has been the growth of a petitionary political culture, a culture especially evident in "Whereas."

Let me explain. A petition is a collective request to an authority, often a political institution, asking them to address a wrong. In its simple form it will consist of a statement, the appeal, followed by many signatures, making it easy to lose sight of how this appeal works by repeating the appeal over and over. Each signature endorses the appeal and tacitly repeats it, giving the signer's voice to it, while dispensing with the need actually to repeat the writing each time. Petitions by their nature differ.[12] The internet has altered the pragmatics or social relations of many forms of utterance, including the petition, making explicit petitions appear much easier to launch. In the words of a group of political theorists:

> A growing number of scholars argue that the availability of internet-based platforms challenges long-standing conventional wisdom about the limits and barriers to mass political participation [...] particularly through the facilitation of huge online gatherings of

people who do not know each other, and who have carried out small participatory actions, such as signing an e-petition or raising the profile of a demonstration through endorsement or notification on a social media site.[13]

On the social media pages provided by platforms made available by corporations with the economic power of small countries, corporations that call themselves platforms rather than the more accurate term publishers in order to sidestep responsibility for the content, individuals can put into print their ideas, opinions, criticisms, and aspirations for potentially global circulation. In talking of a petitionary internet culture, I am thinking of the tumultuous waves of loosely delineated, collective public requests for action and change, sometimes manifest as trending, followers, downloads, comments, Twitter storms, trolling, and going viral. This is a messy form of democracy.[14] Endorsements of calls for action, praise, denunciation, social and cultural change, are repeated on an unprecedented scale. The result is a deep change in our collective social relations of communication, a shift to petitionary groundswells and outbursts often only tenuously or not at all connected to existing political institutions.

Digital media sites crucially retain a key feature of other traditional publishers. When a film review appears in the *New York Times*, it is customary to speak of the opinion of the film as that of the newspaper itself, not just the named reviewer, because the *Times* confers its warrant, its authority, on what it prints under its name. Likewise, a text that we write on Twitter carries the imprimatur of Twitter itself, and we say that it is "on" Twitter, using a misleading preposition that relates to our screen experience rather than the complex corporate, internet, and electronic actualities, including control, of its publication. From this point the tweet is copied, multiplied, and distributed according to algorithms and user choices in an extensive process of replication and response, similar to the traditional paper-based petition, which is also a means of enabling a large number of people to copy a statement requesting action from some power. By signing their name to a single token of it, each signatory can be said to have repeated what the others are also petitioning for, which gives the one text great force. A petition is a clamor. And the similarities are not just a matter of replication. They also extend to the form of the petitionary appeal, a call for recognition, for a response that addresses the concerns of the petition. For poets this new digital media structure of verbal exchange offers many possibilities. The documental poet copies an existing text with some public status relocating it into their own pragmatics, their own act of saying it, so that the poem becomes a palimpsest of speech acts.

LAYLI LONG SOLDIER REDELIVERS A GOVERNMENT APOLOGY

The most obviously petitionary poem of my three is Long Soldier's "Whereas," which cleverly inverts a government message aimed at Indigenous peoples into a petitionary response to it. In Canada in 2008, Prime Minister Stephen Harper stood in the House of Commons and delivered a "Statement of Apology—To Former Students of Indian Residential Schools" to legislators and a special audience of Indian chiefs accompanied by several of those students themselves. In the United States a year later, Sen. Sam Brownback introduced in Congress "A joint resolution to acknowledge a long history of official depredations and ill-conceived policies by the Federal Government regarding Indian tribes and offer an apology to all Native Peoples on behalf of the United States." The Canadian apology is composed in an accessible, friendly style, and includes gestures such as this: "I stand before you, in this chamber so central to our life as a country, to apologize to aboriginal peoples."[15] The United States apology was drafted by lawyers, and its initial enactment did not require anybody to stand up and be seen by the nation to apologize. Its legalese continues with a whole series of whereas clauses, just as if this was a contract. Here are a few sample clauses from the twenty in the full text:

> Whereas the ancestors of today's Native Peoples inhabited the land of the present-day United States since time immemorial and for thousands of years before the arrival of people of European descent;
>
> Whereas Native Peoples are spiritual people with a deep and abiding belief in the Creator, and for millennia Native Peoples have maintained a powerful spiritual connection to this land, as evidenced by their customs and legends;
>
> Whereas the arrival of Europeans in North America opened a new chapter in the history of Native Peoples;

Whereas Native Peoples and non-Native settlers engaged in numerous armed conflicts in which unfortunately, both took innocent lives, including those of women and children;

Whereas the Federal Government violated many of the treaties ratified by Congress and other diplomatic agreements with Indian tribes;

The second half of the document asks the president to "acknowledge the wrongs of the United States against Indian tribes in the history of the United States in order to bring healing to this land; and [. . .] commends the State governments that have begun reconciliation efforts with recognized Indian tribes." Then a sting in the tail: "Nothing in this Joint Resolution authorizes or supports any claim against the United States" nor does it serve as a "settlement of any claim against the United States."[16] This official apology was signed into law as an appendage to a large defense spending bill by President Obama and was almost hidden there. Only the following year was it "delivered," by Senator Brownback, who actually spoke its words to a tiny audience of Native Americans.[17] By contrast, the Canadian apology was televised as it was spoken directly by the prime minister to tearful Indian representatives. Not surprisingly the American apology went almost unnoticed. Long Soldier only heard about the apology the following year, 2010, and was immediately disappointed by its furtive arrival in the public sphere, dismayed by its legalistic discourse, especially its use of the all-purpose listing device, whereas, and by its egregious misrepresentations of the history of Native Americans. She comments in an interview that describing the arrival of Europeans in North America as having "opened a new chapter for Native People" is "crazy. It wasn't 'opening a new chapter,'" a claim made even more preposterous by the refusal to use the term "genocide."[18] As an Oglala Lakota woman, a member of a nation that was pulverized by European settlers, Long Soldier was especially aware of this history.[19] She also discerned that the language of the apology was far from casual. It was so "carefully crafted" it made her exclaim, "I mean, my goodness, these guys are poets."[20] Could a Native American poet transform its rhetoric into a politically active intervention?

Long Soldier felt impelled to respond to the apology because of its "nondelivery," by which I assume she means its lack of pragmatics, acts of communication that would recruit listeners capable of hearing and acting upon what is asserted in the apology. The question then was how as a poet she might help "deliver" it, ensure its greater circulation, and generate responsive challenges to its feeble atonement. After all, the apology was there on the internet for anyone to read. What was missing was the social practice of address, its performative dissemination that I have been calling petitionary. By constructing a series of poems whose form simulates the tripartite structure of the apology, its separation into whereas statements, resolutions, and that disclaimer that the apology cannot be the basis for any claims against the US government, she performs an extensive rhetorical analysis of the apology, employing several different modes, including the type of erasure poetics that Reddy is identified with. She pivots on the strangeness of using the standard legal term "whereas" in an apology for violent crimes, saying that she is "a child of that Whereas." "Whereas" is normally used with the force of "nevertheless," to prefigure a statement that contrasts with the main clause, but legal discourse also uses "whereas" in another manner as what the *OED* calls an "illative or adversative conjunction," a convenient, specialist preamble that means something like "that being the case" or "considering that."[21] Illative is derived from the Latin word for inference, *illativus*, and still signifies this idea of introducing an inference. "Whereas" clauses are widely used in legal documents where they are known as "contract recitals," explanations of the who, the what, and the why of the contract. It was precisely this performative dimension of the apology, its failure to announce the who, the what, and the why, that enraged Long Soldier. In the concluding section, "Disclaimer," she parodies the congressional apology's final words: "Nothing in this book—(1) authorizes or supports any claim against Layli Long Soldier by the United States; or / (2) serves as a settlement of any claim against Layli Long Soldier by the United States, here in   the grassesgrassesgrasses."[22] This merging of three iterations of the word grasses powerfully echoes Walt Whitman. It also alludes to the prairie home of the Dakota and to a catastrophic time in their history, earlier recounted in the poem "38," when her predecessors were reduced to starvation because their land tenure as agreed in treaties with the US government was stolen from them and they could neither hunt nor buy food. A local trader called Andrew Myrick notoriously said, "If they are hungry, let them eat grass."[23]

As part of the process of delivery (which I am including in the concept of the "petitionary") the poem includes autobiographical moments, introduced each time by "whereas," that have helped define her, making her "a child of that Whereas"[24]: A teacher bullying Layli; a father who was mentally ill when she was a girl; the moment of noticing that her own daughter tries to hide her upset when she falls and scrapes her knees; and occasions when Long Soldier smashes hard into linguistic denial of her right to exist. "Whereas I once attended a summer writing program and while there a lecture by a poet on Native American myths. As a student I wanted to stand up at the mic during Q and A to challenge the terms under which one applies the term *myth* not to mention *legend*."[25] Sometimes these moments have the tenor of the micro-aggressions in Claudia Rankine's *Citizen*:

> Whereas a woman I know says she watched a news program a reporter detailed the fire a house in which five children burned perhaps their father too she doesn't recall exactly but remembers the camera on the mother's face the mother's blubbering [. . .] I let her finish wanting someone to say it but she hated saying it or so she said admitting how she never knew until then they could feel.[26]

These moments are not only personal, they exemplify the missing who, what, and why of the progenitive "whereas."

Her onslaught on the US government rhetoric identifies misleading categorizing and objectifying labels applied to Indians. In one passage, she erases key words from two sections of the apology using square brackets and a space, deleting for instance the words spiritual, belief, Creator, customs, from this clause: "Whereas Native Peoples are [   ] people with a deep and abiding [   ] in the [   ], and for millennia Native Peoples have maintained a powerful [   ] connection to this land, as evidenced by their [   ] and legends."[27] A little later the missing words indicated by square brackets are printed as an erasure poem, a page with just twelve words on it, each enclosed in square brackets, most of them categories imported by the colonists (spiritual, belief, customs) that would replace and sometimes discredit the validity of Native American concepts.[28] Colonial knowledge would replace Indigenous belief.

A text in "Resolutions" begins: "I too urge the President to acknowledge the wrongs of the United States against Indian tribes."[29] Long Soldier's poem effectively claims that in order for her to speak publicly in her poems she has to do so within the space of communications governed by the political and legal language of statements such as the apology. A credible poem representing the Lakota lifeworld may only be possible if it acknowledges the documented power relations of the United States.

JULIANA SPAHR IDENTIFIES FORCES THAT SHAPE LITERARY PRODUCTION

What does Long Soldier's bold interruption of the careful government muting of the apology to Indians tell us about the current conditions of credibility in poetry? Spahr's *That Winter the Wolf Came* can help us answer this question. In her study of "Literary Resistance and State Containment," she shows how "literary production is shaped by forces external to it," notably in North America government agencies such as the CIA, and much more broadly the entire enterprise of colonialism.[30] She has moved away from her earlier full commitment to the politics and poetics of language writing, a transformation of poetic identity signaled in her remarkable memoir *Transformation*. In a long passage about her early life, education, and growth as a writer, she recalls the reassuring affects elicited by difficult "writing that used fragmentation, quotation, disruption, disjunction, agrammatical syntax, and so on."[31] In Steinian fashion, this long phrase is repeated word for word several times across a section of the book to the point where its semantic value starts to empty out and it becomes pure form, a formalist allegory of her increasing skepticism about the political values claimed for language writing. This for Spahr is an awkward aesthetic distancing from the poetic forms into which she was inducted at university, a withdrawal that invites a question: How have other poets instigated their own exit from expiring, once vital dogmas about difficulty of an earlier avant-garde? Spahr believes that a key step toward an adequate response to the times is to recognize that "literature has been sequestered into irrelevance" by postwar American governments, making it hard to imagine a radical political value for twenty-first-century poetry.[32]

Spahr works out some of the implications for the poet in conjunction with two activist collaborators, Jasper Bernes and Joshua Clover, in a recent, brash informal talk published in 2020 on their Commune Editions website. They playfully parody Theodor W. Adorno's essay on late style, arguing that last-century poetic techniques that relied on formalist disruption are now politically inert; poets have created instead a "late period style" merging three cultural turbulences: theory, pop, and riot. Theory, pop, riot: This is an odd conjunction. They claim that each of these elements needs the others to create a workable poetics that "brings into relief that world's contours" and to sketch these abstract contours of the world of the contemporary poet in the following terms: It is "bounded by the academy, the internet, and the social movement. By earth, wind, and fire."[33] Let me paraphrase this list:

the research and teaching located in universities, digital communication, political activism, environment, the oxygen of survival and the carbon dioxide of climate change, and energy both potential (as in oil) and in action (as in our machines for living). Although this is a particular sector of the poetry world they are describing, one that might not be recognizable to some writers outside it, I think it helps us see more clearly how we might understand the petitionary character of the poetry of my three poets when we consider two of these concepts, theory and riot.

Firstly, *theory*. I argue in my recent book *Expanding Authorship* that as powerful a tool as theory has been for analyzing power, colonialism, sexuality, gender, and texts, theory has sometimes been hampered by a restrictive model of language as a system of differences, a code, and as a closed system of writing.[34] The poets I am discussing are part of a much wider pushback that recognizes that all utterances, including both speech and writing, are embodied actions taking place in a spatial and temporal world, that words are not fully reducible to a combination of signifier and signified, and that all utterances, however citational, are also expressive directed commitments. This could be called a neopragmatist position.[35] Whether spoken or written, an utterance is always an action, directed from one person or group to another person or group, located geographically and in time. Iterations, copying, repetition, are social forms of interaction by which we amplify utterances, co-opting affirmation and stirring transformative debate.

Secondly, *riot*, a term that may seem flatly confrontational. In his new book *The Quiet Before: On the Unexpected Origins of Radical Ideas*, journalist Gal Beckerman discusses the role of new media in social movements for change, the connection between riot and theory, arguing that intense, local conversation away from the pressure of public events is a necessary precursor to social action: "The incubation of radical new ideas is a very distinct process with certain conditions: a tight space, lots of heat, passionate whispering, and a degree of freedom to work toward a common, focused aim."[36] Beckerman is concerned that too much credence is given to social media sites as wellsprings of social change, not simply because they are corporately managed platforms, but also because they are too like riots, online riots, because they do not allow time for strategic reflection and planning. On the other hand, we cannot go back to typed samizdats and zines, or the eighteenth-century coffee house that according to Jürgen Habermas helped create the public sphere; the internet, Beckerman says, perhaps too sweepingly, "has almost completely annihilated all those other modes of communication."[37] Yet his prescription for improvement sounds oddly like the character of many little magazines, printed as well as digital. What is needed, according to Beckerman, are inventive versions of systems such as Discord, platforms that are local, have a well-defined "governance model" (meaning active moderators), an ideology of mutuality and shared control, and helpful design features that promote constructive engagement, often in the form of a slower reception (he gives the example of a system on which each post is fixed and has to be read in its entirety). Beckerman is not denying the need for street activism, the need for occupations and demonstrations; he is pointing to a role for sites of precursor deliberation. I want to suggest that these poems by Long Soldier, Spahr, and Reddy coexist with the social movements that Spahr identifies, and these volumes of poetry provide shared work-tops for planning, analysis, and thoughtful disagreement because of the imaginative manner in which they link their poems with the petitionary character of parts of the internet, with contemporary activisms, and with new theories and ideas.

Spahr is probably best known for two collections, *This Connection of Everyone With Lungs* (2005) and *Well Then There Now* (2011), which include several climate change poems, including "Unnamed Dragonfly Species," "Gentle Now, Don't Add to Heartache," and "The Incinerator," poems I have discussed elsewhere.[38] In 2015 her press Commune Editions published *That Winter the Wolf Came*, consisting of nine sections of poems and prose poems that together form one integral work, a long poem that deliberately stretches the boundaries of the genre. She draws on her experience of the Occupy movement, where we are introduced to the many "new muses of innovation" that can be found inspiring the "common vocabulary" of groups ranging from oil engineers to field zoologists.[39] Overhearing a woman talking in a café, Spahr believes she is listening to a discourse imposed on this woman: "This is the language she has, a language given to her by multinational corporations. A language of idealized family."[40] The question for Spahr is how to give such people other, more enfranchising discourses.

One way to do this is to strike sparks from the clash of dissonant registers. As she says in the prose poem "Brent Crude," "I start writing a poem about oil extraction in iambic pentameter because Cara emails me and asks me this: 'how can we, as poets, take care of ourselves, our creative work, and the larger planetary body on which we depend?'"[41] One outcome is an oil poem, "Dynamic Positioning," written in syllabic verse of ten syllables and varying meter set out in two-line stanzas. Its graceful, poetic form is polluted by discursive material taken from reports and eyewitness accounts of the Deepwater Horizon catastrophe (the explosion of an oil drilling rig in the Gulf of Mexico).[42] Here is an extract from partway through the poem, showing how Spahr pressurizes the report text into couplets and lineation that distort the language, a formalist representation of the terrible destructive pressures of the well.

> It is almost at ten o'clock when mud
> Then shoots up through the derrick. It is almost
>
> At ten o'clock, diverter shut so that
> The gas and drilling fluid could be routed
>
> To the baffle plates, the poorboy degass-
> Er, then the lower annual prev-
>
> Enter is activated. The drill press-
> Ure, the volumes of gases, fluids, drill-
>
> Ing mud, seawater, then is steadily in-
> Creasing. And it begins again. Or be-
>
> Gins some more. First as mud. A mud that roar-
> Ing, rained. Then the gas as it discharge-
>
> Ing, hissing, the poorboy degasser fill-
> Ing. Next the first gas alarm then the oth-[43]

One result of her compositional procedure is the conjuring up of semantic ghosts in the text, as in the line: "Ing, hissing, the poorboy degasser fill-" where "ing" becomes a threatening entity, a "hissing ing," and the technical term "poorboy" comes to stand for the men who are about to die. Spahr writes earlier in the poem, "I could go on and on here calling the / New muses of innovation, common // Vocabulary, that covers over the / Elaborate simplicity of this."[44] But will the muses answer these calls? One type of call is conveyed by the sometimes drastic enjambment that cracks open words to see what emerges, dross or phantoms with messages from the underworld of this environmentally dangerous drilling enterprise that covers itself in deceptively simple rhetoric.

That Winter the Wolf Came includes a section that we might call a "riot poem," "It's All Good, It's All Fucked," a free-flowing, first-person prose poem where Spahr traces the affects elicited by active, exhilarating participation in the Occupy movement, permeated by reflections on the obsessive use of social media to keep up with what is happening in the protest movement.[45] An extended conversation with a friend about activism, childbirth, and poetry ends with some uncertainty: "I can tell that it is puzzling my friend that I have held onto every possible turn of phrase ever said by a poet and read it as critique, as mattering in some way."[46] And this is one of the strong questions Spahr's book leaves us with: Does poetry like "Dynamic Positioning" matter, and if so, how and why?

SRIKANTH REDDY DESCENDS INTO THE UNDERWORLD

Spahr's intensive questioning of the values of protest (the "incubation" that Beckerman describes) is a reminder that this petitionary culture, the massive changes brought about by digital culture, bring with them senses of loss, of threat to the commons. In a study of the relevance of Georg Wilhelm Friedrich Hegel's theories of practical reason for today, the philosopher Robert Pippin argues that "any given social world is also a nexus of common significances, saliences, taboos, and a general shared orientation that can also either be sustained or can fail. Indeed, one of the most interesting aspects of such a social condition, shared meaningfulness, or intelligibility, is that it can fail, go dead, lose its grip."[47]

This is the context in which we might read Reddy's questioning of prior models of poetic credibility in *Voyager*. His poem is the least explicitly petitionary long poem of the three, not because it is not a long poem or because it does not have a public document at its core and relies on a subtle form of repetition, but because of the transformations to which it subjects this document. *Voyager*, we should remember, was written just before the emergence of the world of social media that we know today (Facebook began 2004, Reddit in 2005, and Twitter in 2006). I said earlier that my selected poets transform their source documents by employing acts of repetition that simulate those already widely active on the internet and relocate these acts into their own pragmatics, so that the poem becomes a palimpsest of speech acts. My final example of a petitionary poet does not conceive of a public address in quite the same form; it conceives of a public that shapes itself around repeated imitation without articulating explicit demands (it would be possible to think of Reddy's poem as influenced by the communal model represented by Wikipedia, though I shall not pursue this idea here, not least because of the difficulty of reconstructing what Wikipedia would have looked like at the time of composition of the poem). Reddy transforms his source text into three different iconic poetic forms that each presuppose an aesthetic pragmatics: aphorism, confession, narrative. Reddy's poem evokes the tessellated quality of screen internet in the first decade of the twenty-first century, as he cleverly captures the not-quite-right quality of so much of that internet traffic, its ever-present tendency to skew slightly into absurdity. It is in this type of act of repetition of source material that the petitionary character of Reddy's poetic transformations can be felt, in what has been a groundbreaking intervention in contemporary poetics.

Reddy's book-length poem *Voyager* is permeated with a sense that a shared orientation that has made poetry possible has begun to fall apart, that authenticity is impossible, and any statement is contaminated by intertextual failures. The poem is constituted of three sections titled "books," each of them exemplifying a different mode of poetic thinking from the past half-century: aphoristic poems in which each line is strongly propositional; a series of confessional prose poems; and an allegorical descent into the underworld in the triadic mode used by William Carlos Williams. The available lexicon is highly constrained. All the words used in the poem are taken in the order they occur from what Reddy calls the "ghastly bureaucratic language" of a whitewashing memoir, *In the Eye of the Storm*, by the former Nazi Kurt Waldheim, later secretary-general of the United Nations and president of Austria.[48] In the foreword to his memoir, Waldheim says in his characteristically confident manner, "I have been granted an unparalleled opportunity to observe – and to some extent influence – the attempts of nations to cope, through collective action, with violence, terror and human suffering." Although he concludes with a seemingly modest plea, saying, "I trust this book will explain why, in certain cases, I acted as I did; what objectives I had in mind; and where I succeeded or failed,"[49] most readers have concluded that he hid or misrepresented his Nazi past in an act of dissimulation that further discredited his words. It would be hard to think of a more complete example of a text that demonstrates the loss of meaningfulness Pippin describes. Reddy was prompted to write his poem because this temporizing politician became by chance a spokesman for the whole of humanity, indeed the entire planet Earth and all its life, while he was secretary-general. He recorded a brief message of peace on what is known as the golden record, a compilation of music, images, and speeches by people from across our planet that was sent out into the galaxy in 1975 on two US spacecraft named Voyager. This was part of a mission to search for alien civilizations, the Search for Extraterrestrial Intelligence or SETI project, led by Carl Sagan.

Waldheim trusts that he can explain his actions; Reddy's poem trusts that it can explain why he acted as he did by employing a tricky procedural constraint. Using Waldheim's words has several disturbing effects. We can read Reddy's poem and try to pretend that the source of the words does not matter, that the recent usage of words in a toxic context does not matter, that each new employment of these words rinses away earlier contamination, as happens with cash, which we use without regard to its recent former owners. However much we try to ignore the contextual traces clinging to the words of Reddy's poems, Waldheim's own history and self-justifications tend to insist on themselves. Think of the genre of paintings that create recognizable, realistic images out of jarringly inappropriate tesserae, such as bus tickets, vegetables, and more. Reddy's poem keeps the reader off-balance, unable to tell what is serious, what is a joke, and, above all, who is accountable for what is said: Reddy, Waldheim, a fusion of the two, a supernatural power, or chance. Another consequence of this uneasy relation with Waldheim's discourse is that Reddy's text asks whether its three main poetic forms, all of them current in the poetry world, retain aesthetic credibility if they are composed of words of self-exoneration of genocidal crimes or international technocratic overriding of humane values. The first book echoes a widespread epigrammatic tendency in nonconfessional poetry, employing endstopped lines, sentences ringing with finality that tend toward cheap aphorisms with intimations that this is Friedrich Nietzsche or Ludwig Wittgenstein. From the very first line we are nudged by a meaningless tautology, "The world is the world," toward skepticism about any semblance of philosophical and psychological profundity.[50] Although this opening line echoes Wittgenstein's opening gambit in his *Tractatus*, "The world is everything that is the case," it enacts the equivalent of a shrug; in a widely used fashionable phrase often used to fend off criticism of institutional decisions, "it is what it is." A later line, "Fact is the script of the unknown,"[51] is emptily sententious, obviously wrong in many instances, yet its allusion to the unknown is resonant here, since it is the truth of Waldheim's career as an organizer of state killings, that much of what he did is unknown. By no means are all the lines in this first section emulating philosophy. Dante shows up: "He shall be placed in the first circle."[52] The first circle is Limbo, the destination of those who were never baptized, born before the revelation of Christ, including the classical poets, Homer, Horace, Ovid, Lucretius, and, of course, Virgil, poets without religious authorization.

The second book of *Voyager* is a sequence of confessional poems that sound convincingly like Reddy's own thoughts about academic tenure, about SETI, about his half-formed wish to join protesters in the streets, and recurrently about the very labors of writing such a complex procedural text. "In November last year, I became interested in the fate of a machine which had been launched into creation and disappeared from sight during my boyhood ... Every morning, I would visit the library to dig out information for my dissertation on the principles of writing, and in the night, overhead, sought refuge in the parallel journey."[53]

Reddy calls attention to the traces of Waldheim. "His story cast a shadow of unreality over everything."[54] If these are Reddy's own thoughts, then what does it mean that he has expressed them using a selection of Waldheim's words? Or is this poetic self, this "I," an alien assemblage, a Frankenstein author botched together from parts of the subjectivities of Waldheim and Reddy? In this section particularly, Reddy hints that Waldheim still casts a shadow over poetry: "I had to cross his world out anew. This history is the effect of that curious process."[55] In these lines there is a powerful tension between what is said, which appears to be entirely Reddy's sentiments, and the words he uses. Does Waldheim's intrusion signify that the personal lyric is no longer tenable because its supposedly authentic, personal subjectivity is infected by powerful, ethically compromised voices?

Book three of *Voyager* visually resembles Williams's late poems such as "Asphodel, That Greeny Flower." "I was cheered," writes Williams, "when I first came to know / that there were flowers also / in hell."[56] Williams's poem stays outside hell. Reddy goes much further; he leaves behind the flowers as he descends into a dreary, second-rate underworld composed of fragments from the long Western literary and religious tradition of visits to the underworld. This will be a phantasmagoric journey that openly borrows from Homer, Dante, William Shakespeare's *Hamlet* (a play hinting that the events take place in a castle already half in hell), John Milton, Jean Cocteau, T. S. Eliot, and Robert Duncan (especially in the Dantean sections of "Passages").[57] Part five of the poem opens with the bathos of this allusion to the *Inferno*: "Lost in the middle of life / we continued. / It seemed essential // to build a house."[58] The following short passage is strongly reminiscent of the blackly comic punishments imposed in the circles of hell: "I saw him quiet / those who refused him— / their heads in a privy."[59] Later in the same section is an allusion to *The Waste Land*: "I could not accept // that there were so many / and was overcome / on the banks of the canal,"[60] though the immediate context in Reddy's poem is Dante, since everything is unsteadily allegorical: house, privy, canal.

The first person narrator in Book three is part Waldheim (at certain points the text gives his name with a line canceling it), part Reddy, and part "innumerable I," a composite subject whose selves we readers will struggle to keep separate. The narrator has a godlike view of their domain, casting an ironic glance across great spans of history ("It was happy hour / for the next thousand years"),[61] and repeatedly gesturing at vast geographical areas, the "East" and the "West." Who the underworld's rulers might be is never made explicit, though several characters, including Un, Silence, Archbishop A, and the mysterious figure of the Minister, play leading roles. Their abstract names make them sound bland by refusing the ultimately consolatory religious mythologies that might make them morally intelligible. The Minister may be a minister but he is far from benign; he reads as a composite of Waldheim's political contemporaries, a government official mediating with the spirit world, who challenges the narrator for not believing "in his extraordinary world," threatens crudely to stuff the narrator's head in a privy, and eats former congressmen as if they were beef.[62]

However much Reddy's narrative of a trip to the underworld tries to qualify for membership in the great literary tradition, it appears to fall short repeatedly. It does not cohere, it breaks up, it is too kitschy, it is often out of focus, disconnected, both its narrative sequence and its images alike disjunctive. As a whole it is almost pastiche, almost self-parody, yet not quite. "This all seemed to me / to have a distinct / Alice in Wonderland quality. // Nevertheless the Ambassador / outlined the plan / of a public performance. // White was his wing / working in the dark / as I listened with increasing doubt," says the narrator.[63] Is this white wing a sign of angelic qualities that have survived the Fall, or a devilish whitewash? Doubt permeates the narrator's outlook: "I was troubled / by the quiet / river of illusion."[64] This river of illusion runs through the whole of Book three, yet despite the phantasmagoria, Book three is also a realist text. It might sound like a long poem by John Ashbery, who commends *Voyager* in an endorsement on the cover, saying it is "A work unlike any other, deeply moving, disturbing, and ultimately fulfilling." We should heed Ashbery. *Voyager* is not an homage to Ashbery, not a text shaped by brilliant self-consuming verbal inventions in which there is rarely any structural diegesis, usually no actual scene being represented, just a verbal space that calls attention to its constructedness at every turn.[65] Book three does give its phantoms realist treatment, and it even ends with a kind of closure, that though it may teeter on the edge of parody, does not succumb to self-referentiality: "And my search / for peace underground / now come to an end / —constraints accepted / in spirit as well as in letter [. . .] I viewed the balances / more clearly than ever before."[66]

The failings, the imperfections, the disjointedness of the narrative, are its point. Reddy knows perfectly well that this story of a visit to the underworld is repeatedly failing to emulate the classic accounts of the underworld; indeed that it is not working to redeem Waldheim or reassure us that good wins over evil.[67] Instead Reddy's artistry creates an awareness of the impossibility of imagining a redemption for Waldheim and the world he represents, at the same time insisting that we recognize the strength of this desire, which might better and more devastatingly be called hope.

We might be tempted to justify the disorder of the story of the descent into the underworld by saying that it is the nature of dreams to be incoherent, an alibi that does not quite work because the traditional underworld journey relies on several principles of belief, two of which are crucial here. First, the underworld of hell was believed to be a real place, despite being inaccessible to the everyday senses, a place existing within a religious cosmos. The challenge of Book three is that the descent into the underworld retains features of the hell narrative tradition, and strives for credibility. The Minister tells the narrator, "We don't believe / we're making believe," admitting that this is "our little joke."[68] Second, a trip to the underworld made sense not only as a warning of what might befall those who anger the gods, God, or moral law, it was also a form of penitence; indeed of potential, if dangerous, redemption. The underworld visitor might not make it back to the upper worlds.

What then does it mean to use only words from Waldheim? Reddy signals that he is aware that this is a thought experiment when in Book two he exposes the prose debris from which he has lifted the underside of Waldheim's message. Reddy gives an explicit example of what happens when words are made to disappear from a text: "to cross out a figure such as *to carry out programmes they approve the various regional economic commissions and inter-governmental bodies* sometimes increases the implications."[69] Carry out bodies; this feels like the ghost text haunting Waldheim's memoir. Reddy wants an easily glimpsed example of how, for the reader inclined to make them fully conscious, the prose does contain what Roman Jakobson calls "subliminal" patterns.[70] Under the camouflage of the bureaucratic language Reddy spies a concealed phrase that perfectly captures Waldheim's guilt: "carry out bodies."

In everyday practical usage, proximity and syntax dominate the reading of a text; in poems, however, words at a distance can also stick together, as rhyme words, or through phonetic semblance, etymological resonance, semantic adhesion, or what Wallace Stevens wonderfully called "ghostlier demarcations."[71] While Reddy himself describes his working method as an erasure procedure, I think this categorization can distract us from the significance of its source materials, their selection, and the effect on the reader.[72] He raises the possibility that our impression of any text, like our impression of a painting in which we concentrate on a few details, might be shaped by connecting words that are some distance apart yet shine with exceptional brightness in our subliminal recollection.[73] Reddy makes salient to the reader what without his poetic treatment would have been subliminal patterns in the text, turning us into dyspraxic readers who focus on intermittent, often distant words, to elicit syntactically connected sequences over such distances, whose verbal connections would normatively be treated as semantic noise.

THE OUTER SPACES OF THE LONG POEM

The twenty-first-century North American long poem can create space for the petitionary use of documents by employing pragmatics developed from the tumultuous development of internet discourse over the past two decades. In the poems discussed here the poets work with documents that carry political weight: a contentious government apology, official reports on an environmental disaster, or an autobiography charting the writer's involvement in setting up the United Nations. Both Long Soldier and Spahr work in a petitionary mode by selectively retweeting and splicing their documentary source texts into poetic passages that express resistances to the authority vested in these documents. Digital media endlessly recycle the content of their communications, frequently petitioning for recognition of a belief, an attitude, a hope, an aspiration. Petitionary form does not have to entail a direct request for a specific social transformation. It can also take the shape of a bold transformative appropriation of an official text, so that it is the act of seizure itself, and sometimes in aesthetic frameworks, its allegorical implication, that becomes the petitionary act.

Writing in the years when Twitter and Facebook were in their early stages of development, when social media were only just beginning to be a major sociopolitical phenomenon, Reddy does something rather different from the other poets. He sets up a textual framework in which Waldheim and the historical forces he represents are translated first into doxa, then into statements that mold a recognizable subjectivity, then into a dream narrative of a trip to the underside of the Western imaginary, to a hell where the powers that carried out genocide and massive violence against human populations are placed in Dantean circles. Although Reddy's poem is not composed in the explicit form of a collective request, a plea for a wrong to be addressed, or a change in governing frameworks, he too is building upon the collective intersubjectivities of petition and repetition. Reddy is open about the seeming futility of a poem challenging the apologetic discourses of modern war, and he does not give way to despair. He chooses poetic forms that will allegorize the need to confront the collaboration between poetry and the rationalizations of "violence, terror and human suffering," and he makes good use of the many implications of Waldheim's association with the golden record.[74] Like the other poets, he strives to find meaning in the social impact of the long poem. He shows that within the most unpromising documents possibilities can be found. Each of these poems opens up dissident possibilities for working through the new digital communications to create spaces for poetry, and for creating opportunities for political reform.

NOTES

1. Exemplary hyperobjects include radiation, global warming, and hydrocarbons. Timothy Morton offers interleaved definitions of a hyperobject that emphasize the elusive sublimity due to its vast spatiotemporal scale and its insistent ubiquity: The rain falling on one's head both is and is not climate change. "Hyperobjects are so huge and so long-lasting, compared with humans, that they obviously seem both vivid and slightly unreal." He hints that poetry too might qualify as a hyperobject, "since all entities are chameleon poets." Timothy Morton, *Hyperobjects: Philosophy and Ecology after the End of the World* (Minneapolis: University of Minnesota Press, 2013), 129, 199.
2. For an astute summary of the issue, see the discussion of the editorial policy of *HOW(ever)*, and its tendency to "recontextualize" Canadian poems that they published in Heather Milne, *Poetry Matters: Neoliberalism, Affect, and the Posthuman in Twenty-First Century North American Feminist Poetics* (Iowa City: University of Iowa Press, 2018), 21, passim. There is now a large literature on Chicanx and Latinx poetry and its connections to the southern American nations.
3. Charles Altieri and Nicholas D. Nace, "Introduction," in *The Fate of Difficulty in the Poetry of Our Time*, ed. Charles Altieri and Nicholas D. Nace (Evanston, IL: Northwestern University Press, 2018), 3.
4. Ann Vickery, "Changing Topographies, New Feminisms, and Women Poets," in *The Cambridge Companion to Twenty-First-Century American Poetry*, ed. Timothy Yu (Cambridge: Cambridge University Press, 2021), 77.
5. Michael Leong, *Contested Records: The Turn to Documents in Contemporary North American Poetry* (Iowa City: University of Iowa Press, 2020), 55.
6. Leong writes, "A new aesthetic of the twenty-first century must surely take into account a series of questions: what is the *work* of poetry within a socio-cultural arena, what *kinds* of work go into the making and presenting of poetry, and how does poetry relate to nonpoetic labour?" Leong, *Contested Records*, 107.
7. Lisa Robertson, *Cinema of the Present* (Toronto: Coach House Books, 2014), 11.

8. Layli Long Soldier, "Whereas," *Poetry Foundation*, n.d., https://www.poetryfoundation.org/poetrymagazine/poems/91697/from-whereas.
9. The full title of the resolution is revealing: "S.J.Res.14 – A joint resolution to acknowledge a long history of official depredations and ill-conceived policies by the Federal Government regarding Indian tribes and offer an apology to all Native Peoples on behalf of the United States." US Government, "S.J.Res.14—111th Congress (2009–2010)," Congress.gov, April 30, 2009, https://www.congress.gov/bill/111th-congress/senate-joint-resolution/14/text.
10. Juliana Spahr, Acknowledgements, in *That Winter the Wolf Came* (Oakland: Commune Editions, 2015), n.p. For a history of the Oakland Commune, see Some Oakland Antagonists, "After the Crest, Part II: The Rise and Fall of the Oakland Commune," *CrimethInc.*, August 2013, https://crimethinc.com/2013/09/10/after-the-crest-part-ii-the-rise-and-fall-of-the-oakland-commune.
11. Spahr, *That Winter the Wolf Came*, 85.
12. In a wide-ranging history of petitions from the nineteenth and early twentieth centuries as "hybrid form of political representation," the authors Richard Huzzey and Henry Miller show that the petition was a creatively diverse instrument, and that the meaning of petitions was always a matter of debate, as much as their content. Richard Huzzey and Henry Miller, "Petitions, Parliament and Political Culture: Petitioning the House of Commons, 1780–1918," *Past and Present* 248, no. 1 (2020): 163.
13. Helen Z. Margets, Peter John, Scott A. Hale, and Stéphane Reissfelder, "Leadership without Leaders? Starters and Followers in Online Collective Action," *Political Studies* 63, no. 2 (2015): 278. Petitionary culture is as profligate as an oak tree scattering acorns: "most online mobilizations do not succeed." Margets et al., "Leadership without Leaders?," 294.
14. In an article primarily about the democratic role of parliamentary petitions, the authors point out that the internet is expanding these democratic processes: "Online platforms offer alternatives for political participation and mobilisation and are increasingly used." Sieglinde Rosenberger, Benedikt Seisl, Jeremias Stadlmair, and Elio Dapra, "What Are Petitions Good For? Institutional Design and Democratic Functions," *Parliamentary Affairs* 75, no. 1 (2022): 220.
15. "Statement of Apology to Former Students of Indian Residential Schools," Government of Canada / Gouvernement du Canada, June 11, 2008, https://www.rcaanc-cirnac.gc.ca/eng/1100100015644/1571589171655.
16. U.S. Government, "S.J.Res.14—111th Congress (2009–2010)," n.p.

17. He was a curious messenger to choose, a religious right-wing Republican (and member of Opus Dei) opposed to same-sex marriage and abortion, author of a massive cut in Kansas state spending that shifted the tax burden from the wealthy to the poor.
18. Krista Tippett, "Layli Long Soldier: The Freedom of Real Apologies," *On Being*, April 22, 2021 [March 30, 2017], https://onbeing.org/programs/layli-long-soldier-the-freedom-of-real-apologies/.
19. Barry Lopez describes Lakota people along with other devastated Indigenous people from around the world as *hibakusha*, the Japanese word for Hiroshima survivors, "explosion-affected people," because they have been disoriented, numbed by their fate. Lopez specifically mentions the Lakota people in the reservation at Pine Ridge, South Dakota. Barry Lopez, *Horizon* (London: Penguin, 2019), 44.
20. Tippett, "Layli Long Soldier," n.p.
21. "whereas, *adv.* and *conj.* (and *n.*)," OED Online, https://www.oed.com/view/Entry/228215.
22. Layli Long Soldier, *Whereas* (Minneapolis, MN: Graywolf Press, 2017), 101 (spacing in the original).
23. Long Soldier, *Whereas*, 53.
24. Long Soldier, *Whereas*, 74.
25. Long Soldier, *Whereas*, 67–68.
26. Long Soldier, *Whereas*, 78.
27. Long Soldier, *Whereas*, 83.
28. Long Soldier, *Whereas*, 85.
29. Long Soldier, *Whereas*, 94.
30. Juliana Spahr, *Du Bois's Telegram: Literary Resistance and State Containment* (Cambridge, MA: Harvard University Press, 2018), 26.
31. Juliana Spahr, *The Transformation* (Berkeley: Atelos, 2007), 63.
32. Spahr, *Du Bois's Telegram*, 184.
33. Jasper Bernes, Joshua Clover, and Juliana Spahr, "Period Style and the Art of the Present (Presented at Annual Meeting of the *Association for the Study of the Arts of the Present*, October 26–29, Oakland CA)," *Commune Editions*, n.d. https://communeeditions.com/period-style-and-the-art-of-the-present/.
34. Peter Middleton, *Expanding Authorship: Transformations in American Poetry Since 1950* (Albuquerque: University of New Mexico Press, 2021).
35. For an account of late-twentieth-century pragmatism see Robert Brandom, *Reason in Philosophy: Animating Ideas* (Cambridge, MA: Harvard University Press, 2009).

36. Gal Beckerman, *The Quiet Before: On the Unexpected Origins of Radical Ideas* (London: Penguin, 2022), 3–4. "We think about the dark corners of the internet as places of danger and radicalization, where the absence of shame allows terrible notions to fester. And it's true. But there is another way of conceiving of what happens when a self-selecting group retreats to a quieter, slower, more private, and less performative space to have conversation: it breeds imagination." Beckerman, *The Quiet Before*, 201. One of Beckerman's historical examples is the exchange of manifestos amongst the futurists, including Mina Loy's *Feminist Manifesto*. Beckerman's argument can be illuminated from an unexpected direction, the Jewish tradition of theological debate or midrash, as explained by Gerald Bruns. "The idea is that Torah speaks to a public, communal situation, not to the solitary, single-minded private reader. Under these conditions—which are very different from those produced by the printing press, and which led Luther to restructure hermeneutics around the individual reading subject—interpretation is bound to be many-sided and open-ended." Gerald Bruns, *Hermeneutics Ancient and Modern* (New Haven, CT: Yale University Press, 2009), 107.
37. Beckerman, *The Quiet Before*, 217.
38. Middleton, *Expanding Authorship*, 7–9.
39. Spahr, *That Winter the Wolf Came*, 44.
40. Spahr, *That Winter the Wolf Came*, 73.
41. Spahr, *That Winter the Wolf Came*, 20.
42. A BP report contains diagrams, chronologies, detailed highly technical accounts of the engineering, presented in a style that minimizes human agency as well as political and cultural issues, a style captured in the very first brief summary of what happened: "On the evening of April 20, 2010, a well control event allowed hydrocarbons to escape from the Macondo well onto Transocean's Deepwater Horizon, resulting in explosions and fire on the rig. Eleven people lost their lives, and 17 others were injured. [. . .] Hydrocarbons continued to flow from the reservoir through the wellbore and the blowout preventer (BOP) for 87 days, causing a spill of national significance." BP, Deepwater Horizon: Accident Investigation Report, September 8, 2010, 9. https://www.bp.com/content/dam/bp/business-sites/en/global/corporate/pdfs/sustainability/issue-briefings/deepwater-horizon-accident-investigation-report.pdf.
43. Spahr, *That Winter the Wolf Came*, 47–48.
44. Spahr, *That Winter the Wolf Came*, 44.

45. Spahr, *That Winter the Wolf Came*, 67.
46. Spahr, *That Winter the Wolf Came*, 76.
47. Robert Pippin, *Hegel's Practical Philosophy: Rational Agency as Ethical Life* (Cambridge: Cambridge University Press, 2008), 6.
48. Waldheim composed the memoir to defend himself from the increasing evidence of his wartime past and to prepare for his campaign for the presidency of Austria, inventing a youthful anti-Nazi, cosmopolitan self out of a partially erased biography. Waldheim's signature is on documents authorizing mass deportations of Jews from Banja Luka and several Greek islands, assigning prisoners to slave labor, deporting civilians to death camps, and executing partisans. In 1987, the American Office of Special Investigations (OSI) issued a report concluding that between 1942 and 1945 Waldheim had "assisted, or otherwise participated in the persecution of . . . person[s] because of race, religion, national origin or political opinion" (ellipses in original). Office of Special Investigations, In the Matter of Kurt Waldheim, April 9, 1987, 3, https://nsarchive2.gwu.edu/NSAEBB/NSAEBB331/04-09-87waldheim-rpt.pdf. There is a helpful summary of the history of the OSI's investigation of Waldheim, and its consequences, in a later report: Judy Feigin, The Office of Special Investigations: Striving for Accountability in the Aftermath of the Holocaust, December 2008, https://www.justice.gov/sites/default/files/criminal/legacy/2011/03/14/12-2008osu-accountability.pdf.
49. Kurt Waldheim, *In the Eye of the Storm: The Memoirs of Kurt Waldheim* (London: Weidenfeld and Nicolson, 1986), vii.
50. Srikanth Reddy, *Voyager* (Berkeley: University of California Press, 2011), 3.
51. Reddy, *Voyager*, 8.
52. Reddy, *Voyager*, 5.
53. Reddy, *Voyager*, 19.
54. Reddy, *Voyager*, 22.
55. Reddy, *Voyager*, 25.
56. William Carlos Williams, *The Collected Poems of William Carlos Williams Volume II*, ed. Christopher MacGowan (Manchester: Carcanet, 1988), 310–11.
57. See, for example, Robert Duncan, "Passages 35: Before the Judgment," where he pictures the poet Dante having to be warned by Virgil not to be drawn into the Malebolge. I would guess that this poem was a strong influence on Reddy. Robert Duncan, *The Collected Later Poems and Plays*, ed. Peter Quartermain (Berkeley: University of California Press, 2014), 461–69.

58. Reddy, *Voyager*, 52.
59. Reddy, *Voyager*, 52.
60. Reddy, *Voyager*, 52.
61. Reddy, *Voyager*, 106.
62. Reddy, *Voyager*, 52.
63. Reddy, *Voyager*, 75.
64. Reddy, *Voyager*, 83.
65. Mary Kinzie describes Ashbery's practice as "a new kind of contemporary poem that takes grammar far more seriously than it takes the kind of organization of experience grammar has traditionally served. Ashbery does not use the details of experience as the details of his poems." Mary Kinzie, "'Irreference': The Poetic Diction of John Ashbery, Part I: Styles of Avoidance," *Modern Philology* 84, no. 3 (1987): 268.
66. Reddy, *Voyager*, 114.
67. Reddy's next book, *Underworld Lit*, a memoir of illness woven into imaginative reinventions of myths of the underworld from around the world, makes amply clear how familiar he is with these traditions. "One would not write 'Virgil wrote,' but rather, 'Virgil writes of two ways to exit the realm of the dead,' in a formal study of underworld closure. Just so, every writer, living or dead, is forever suspended in a crepuscular present indicative." Srikanth Reddy, *Underworld Lit* (Seattle: Wave Books, 2020), 163.
68. Reddy, *Voyager*, 49.
69. Reddy, *Voyager*, 31.
70. In "Subliminal Verbal Patterning in Poetry," Jakobson argues that poems often present intricate weaves of phonemes and recurrent letters that their authors and readers are not normally conscious of. His discussion takes for granted that these patterns extend well beyond the linear syntactical connections to much larger spaces of the text. "Intuition may act as the main or, not seldom, even sole designer of the complicated phonological and grammatical structures in the writings of individual poets. Such structures, particularly powerful on the subliminal level, can function without any assistance of logical judgment and patent knowledge both in the poet's creative work and in its perception by the sensitive reader." Roman Jakobson, *Language in Literature*, ed. Krystyna Pomorska and Stephen Rudy (Cambridge, MA: Harvard University Press, 1987), 261.
71. Wallace Stevens, *The Collected Poems of Wallace Stevens* (New York: Vintage, 1990), 130.

72. See Peter Middleton, "Parrots and Paragrams: AI Language Models and Erasure Poetry," *Modern Philology* 121, no. 3 (February 2024): 352–74.
73. Michel de Certeau has a name for this sort of reading: poaching. He describes reading a text as a process of "detours, drifts across the page, metamorphoses and anamorphoses of the text produced by the travelling eye, imaginary or meditative flights taking off from a few words, overlapping of spaces on the militarily organized surfaces of the text, and ephemeral dances." Michel de Certeau, "Reading as Poaching," in *The Practice of Everyday Life* (Berkeley: University of California Press, 1984), 170.
74. Waldheim, *In the Eye of the Storm*, vii.

BIBLIOGRAPHY

Altieri, Charles, and Nicholas D. Nace. "Introduction." In *The Fate of Difficulty in the Poetry of Our Time*, edited by Charles Altieri and Nicholas D. Nace, 1–26. Evanston, IL: Northwestern University Press, 2018.

Beckerman, Gal. *The Quiet Before: On the Unexpected Origins of Radical Ideas*. London: Penguin, 2022.

Bernes, Jasper, Joshua Clover, and Juliana Spahr. "Period Style and the Art of the Present (Presented at Annual Meeting of the *Association for the Study of the Arts of the Present*, October 26–29, Oakland CA)." *Commune Editions*, n.d., https://communeeditions.com/period-style-and-the-art-of-the-present/.

BP. Deepwater Horizon: Accident Investigation Report, September 8, 2010. https://www.bp.com/content/dam/bp/business-sites/en/global/corporate/pdfs/sustainability/issue-briefings/deepwater-horizon-accident-investigation-report.pdf.

Brandom, Robert. *Reason in Philosophy: Animating Ideas*. Cambridge, MA: Harvard University Press, 2009.

Bruns, Gerald. *Hermeneutics Ancient and Modern*. New Haven, CT: Yale University Press, 2009.

de Certeau, Michel. *The Practice of Everyday Life*. Berkeley: University of California Press, 1984.

Duncan, Robert. *The Collected Later Poems and Plays*. Edited by Peter Quartermain. Berkeley: University of California Press, 2014.

Feigin, Judy. The Office of Special Investigations: Striving for Accountability in the Aftermath of the Holocaust, December 2008. https://www.justice.gov/sites/default/files/criminal/legacy/2011/03/14/12-2008osi-accountability.pdf.

Huzzey, Richard, and Henry Miller. "Petitions, Parliament and Political Culture: Petitioning the House of Commons, 1780–1918." *Past and Present* 248, no. 1 (2020): 123–64.

Jakobson, Roman. *Language in Literature*. Edited by Krystyna Pomorska and Stephen Rudy. Cambridge, MA: Harvard University Press, 1987

Kinzie, Mary. "'Irreference': The Poetic Diction of John Ashbery, Part I: Styles of Avoidance." *Modern Philology* 84, no. 3 (1987): 267–81.

Leong, Michael. *Contested Records: The Turn to Documents in Contemporary North American Poetry*. Iowa City: University of Iowa Press, 2020.

Long Soldier, Layli. *Whereas*. Minneapolis, MN: Graywolf Press, 2017.

Lopez, Barry. *Horizon*. London: Penguin, 2019.

Margets, Helen Z., Peter John, Scott A. Hale, and Stéphane Reissfelder. "Leadership without Leaders? Starters and Followers in Online Collective Action." *Political Studies* 63, no. 2 (2015): 278–99.

Middleton, Peter. *Expanding Authorship: Transformations in American Poetry Since 1950*. Albuquerque: University of New Mexico Press, 2021.

Middleton, Peter. "Parrots and Paragrams: AI Language Models and Erasure Poetry." *Modern Philology* 121, no. 3 (February 2024): 352–74.

Milne, Heather. *Poetry Matters: Neoliberalism, Affect, and the Posthuman in Twenty-First Century North American Feminist Poetics*. Iowa City: University of Iowa Press, 2018.

Morton, Timothy. *Hyperobjects: Philosophy and Ecology after the End of the World*. Minneapolis: University of Minnesota Press, 2013.

Office of Special Investigations. "In the Matter of Kurt Waldheim." April 9, 1987. https://nsarchive2.gwu.edu/NSAEBB/NSAEBB331/04-09-87waldheim-rpt.pdf.

Pippin, Robert. *Hegel's Practical Philosophy: Rational Agency as Ethical Life*. Cambridge: Cambridge University Press, 2008.

Reddy, Srikanth. *Underworld Lit*. Seattle: Wave Books, 2020.

Reddy, Srikanth. *Voyager*. Berkeley: University of California Press, 2011.

Robertson, Lisa. *Cinema of the Present*. Toronto: Coach House Books, 2014.

Rosenberger, Sieglinde, Benedikt Seisl, Jeremias Stadlmair, and Elio Dapra. "What Are Petitions Good For? Institutional Design and Democratic Functions." *Parliamentary Affairs* 75, no. 1 (2022): 217–37.

Some Oakland Antagonists. "After the Crest, Part II: The Rise and Fall of the Oakland Commune." *CrimethInc.*, August 2013. https://crimethinc.com/2013/09/10/after-the-crest-part-ii-the-rise-and-fall-of-the-oakland-commune.

Spahr, Juliana. *Du Bois's Telegram: Literary Resistance and State Containment*. Cambridge, MA: Harvard University Press, 2018.

Spahr, Juliana. *That Winter the Wolf Came*. Oakland: Commune Editions, 2015.

Spahr, Juliana. *The Transformation*. Berkeley: Atelos, 2007.

"Statement of Apology to Former Students of Indian Residential Schools." Government of Canada / Gouvernement du Canada. June 11, 2008. https://www.rcaanc-cirnac.gc.ca/eng/1100100015644/1571589171655.

Stevens, Wallace. *The Collected Poems of Wallace Stevens*. New York: Vintage, 1990.

Tippett, Krista. "Layli Long Soldier: The Freedom of Real Apologies." *On Being*, April 22, 2021 [March 30, 2017]. https://onbeing.org/programs/layli-long-soldier-the-freedom-of-real-apologies/.

U.S. Government. "S.J.Res.14 – A joint resolution to acknowledge a long history of official depredations and ill-conceived policies by the Federal Government regarding Indian tribes and offer an apology to all Native Peoples on behalf of the United States." Congress.gov, April 30, 2009. https://www.congress.gov/bill/111th-congress/senate-joint-resolution/14/text.

Vickery, Ann. "Changing Topographies, New Feminisms, and Women Poets." In *The Cambridge Companion to Twenty-First-Century American Poetry*, edited by Timothy Yu, 71–89. Cambridge: Cambridge University Press, 2021.

Waldheim, Kurt. *In the Eye of the Storm: The Memoirs of Kurt Waldheim*. London: Weidenfeld and Nicolson, 1986.

"whereas, *adv.* and *conj.* (and *n.*)." OED Online. https://www.oed.com/view/Entry/228215.

Williams, William Carlos. *The Collected Poems of William Carlos Williams Volume II*. Edited by Christopher MacGowan. Manchester: Carcanet, 1988.

Chapter Nine

Whitman's Long, Long Poem

Sascha Pöhlmann

THE LONG POEM AND THE LONG, LONG POEM

Like the short story, the long poem is a mode of writing defined by what seems like the most arbitrary, subjective, and flexible property, as their material length is both a definite given and an entirely indefinite criterion. Edgar Allan Poe famously engages with both genres in his "Philosophy of Composition" (1846), which is often considered a theoretical treatise on the aesthetics of the short story although it really outlines a poetics. More precisely, it posits the effective brevity of the poem as the model shorter forms of prose may aspire to but, presumably, never attain, or at least as long as they aspire to the goal of "unity" Poe delineates. Poe determines the "proper length" for his poem "The Raven" at around one hundred lines, but he remains vague on what the length of "one sitting" might be;[1] in his review of Nathaniel Hawthorne's *Twice-Told Tales* (1842) he suggested that "the short prose narrative require[s] from a half-hour to one or two hours in its perusal."[2] Notwithstanding the very real possibility that "Philosophy of Composition" is a hoax and not the dead serious writing manual it purports to be,[3] what I am interested in here is Poe's focus on time. While he does translate the temporal aspect of readerly investment into a concrete number of lines and textual length, first and foremost his notion of brevity is based on duration. This is the aspect on which I want to build the following considerations on the long poem, and perhaps this is somewhat of a recovery of temporality, as the long poem in the twentieth and twenty-first century is mainly considered in terms of spatial and not temporal length.

This does not mean that critics of the long poem would not see the obvious and trivial connection between these two categories, and some address the issue of temporal scope directly without pursuing it much further (and this says more about the poems they deal with than about their critical approach). For example, Susan Stanford Friedman includes this aspect in her conceptualization of the long poem:

> A long poem is a "big poem," that is, a poem that situates itself within a long tradition of poems that ask very big questions in a very long way—historical, metaphysical, religious, and aesthetic questions. As a "big" poem, a "long" poem has volume—it is a many-sided figure that swells up to take space. As a long sequence, it also takes up time—literally, lots of time to read. In this horizontal-vertical discourse, vast space and cosmic time are the narrative coordinates within which lyric moments occur, the coordinates as well of reality, history. Big long poems go far, tunnel deep, and fly high. They have scope. They are "potent, important."[4]

For her, this is mainly the groundwork for a consideration of how these parameters have served tacitly to mark the genre as male: "Rooted in epic tradition, the twentieth-century long poem is an overdetermined discourse whose size, scope, and authority to define history, metaphysics, religion, and aesthetics still erect a wall to keep women outside."[5] Yet the "cosmic time" she mentions earlier quickly becomes "history" in her particular project, so that it does not include a further consideration of other temporal modes because the long poems she considers do not operate in them. In a different but even more precise way, Margaret Dickie in *On the Modernist Long Poem* is interested mainly in "the long process of composition through which these poets moved to find the form."[6] Brian McHale, in a related way, draws attention to the "long poem in the American tradition of lifelong poems [. . .], literally interminable except by the poet's death."[7] Undoubtedly, temporality does play a role in critical considerations of the long poem, but this role is often that of an extra without even a line to speak.

How can we put temporality center stage then? There are surely many ways in which this could be achieved, and I want to focus on what I consider to be a particularly salient one in the following. I want to propose a productive reconsideration of the poetics of the long poem from a temporal perspective so that the long poem is not that of arbitrary but sufficient textual length but rather a poem that projects a sufficient temporal scope from the present into the future (and in doing so may well incorporate the past as well). In order to avoid a confusion of terminology and to distinguish this kind of temporal long poem from the long poem that is vaguely defined by textual length, I will draw on one of Walt Whitman's late poems from 1891, which also happens to suggest some major aspects of his temporal poetics I will focus on in this chapter:

Long, Long Hence

After a long, long course, hundreds of years, denials,
Accumulations, rous'd love and joy and thought,
Hopes, wishes, aspirations, ponderings, victories, myriads of readers,
Coating, compassing, covering—after ages' and ages' encrustations,
Then only may these songs reach fruition.[8]

I will thus call the poem that projects a sufficient temporal scope from the present into the future a "long, long poem." In building my argument on a pun, I am admittedly also emulating Poe's playful mode, and yet I do seriously believe that this temporal imagination can provide a fruitful take on a poetic mode that has not yet been extensively discussed in this regard. At the same time, this is decidedly not an attempt to define the long poem in any precise way; I quite happily subscribe to Smaro Kamboureli's memorable quip that the long poem is "a genre without a genre,"[9] while being mindful of Lynn Keller's suggestion that such generic indeterminacy should not detract from the fact that models and conventions *have* emerged and done their work in various ways at various times, and that these explicit and tacit norms and their ideological values merit critique.[10]

I will not unearth a history of the long, long poem from our contemporary moment throughout the major developments in the "genre-that-is-not-one"[11] in American poetry, and I cannot proffer a narrative of a continuum or even a tradition that I could then retrace to a single origin from which such a poetics would spring. Instead, I will single out Whitman as the strongest beginning of this poetic practice in US-American literature, even though mentioning him as a model by now borders on cliché: Whitman has so often been hailed as a foundational American poet, and especially "as the inaugural figure of the long poem in America,"[12] that repeating this gesture risks reinforcing an empty stereotype instead of making a useful statement, and it also risks reinforcing his canonicity (and once more the problematic status of the long poem as a male-dominated genre) without sufficient justification. I am keenly aware of this, and so I hope to provide precisely such justification in arguing for the exemplary role Whitman has in this particular respect, as his poetry genuinely is unparalleled when it comes to a temporal imagination, both in scope and variety; at the same time, this uniqueness also makes it a problematic rather than a straightforward model for later long poems.

In fact, I want to challenge rather than affirm just what kind of a model he is, and for what canon. A focus on Whitman's particular temporalities actually suggests to me that his work is not an influential precursor for the long poems of male-dominated modernism, and that, in fact, this difference may be one way in which these modernists sought to reinvent the tradition Whitman began without adhering to it too much. If his long, long poem is not a model for that kind of long poem at all—the one that has become illustrative, if not definitive of the genre—then this shift in parameters may enable us to describe a different kind of long-poem continuum outside the lineage of canonical male modernism.[13] (At the same time, it naturally also suggests a continuum of long, long poetry that includes poems that textually are not long at all.)

There is nothing new about pointing out this exceptional rather than exemplary quality of Whitman's long poetry, although the original argument went largely unnoticed when it was made: Klaus Heinrich Köhring's 1967 study *Die Formen des „long poem" in der modernen amerikanischen Literatur* has a brief subchapter on temporal continuity, in which he convincingly argues that "for the other writers of the long poem, with the exception of Whitman, the construction of a continuity means preparing for making sense of the modern human condition with the help of the past."[14] In other words, Whitman differs from the canonical male modernist tradition of American long poems precisely in not merely constructing a continuity between past and present, and in not merely extending this continuity to include the future, but especially in shifting this framework to focus mainly on the present and the future and neglecting the past.[15]

I wrote above that a long, long poem is one that projects a sufficient temporal scope from the present into the future, yet I could not provide a clear definition of this sufficiency any more than Poe could say how long that one sitting should be, and any precision would be ridiculous rather than useful. But there is one temporal marker I want to use in order to proffer at least a tentative understanding of the scope I have in mind when describing long, long poetry: It is a scope that exceeds what could be called the phenomenological five-generation model of "the contemporary," in which we usually have a close relation and concrete imagination of a past that reaches back to include our grandparents and a future that includes our grandchildren (even though usually only three to four generations are actually contemporaries). Of course, such a scope is subject to a number of social, cultural, and historical variables (not to mention a few others), and I do not seek to propose an anthropological constant here. Instead, I want to use this modern, Western imagination of the past and future as the basic normative conception from which Whitman's long, long poetry deviates,[16] and I want to argue that a deviation from this arbitrary but strong norm is what defines a long, long poem in this particular context (and it would be highly desirable to see what would count as a long, long poem in other contexts that do not adhere to this Western model of the contemporary).

This deviation, however, needs to occur in a decidedly future-oriented way, or otherwise the long, long poem would be too general a term without much to distinguish it from the long poem, since that form routinely includes "a greater sweep of historical time,"[17] or what McHale discusses as the modernist "master trope of archaeological depth."[18] While such a historical focus may well reach beyond the generational scope I suggested, it is best understood in terms of what Jan Assmann describes as "communicative memory" and "collective memory," two "registers of the past [Vergangenheitsregister]."[19] The former denotes contemporary memories that exist and vanish along with those three to four generations who communicate them, while the latter transcends the contemporary generations as a matter of "institutional mnemonic device [institutioneller Mnemotechnik]."[20] Historical long poems are invested in collective rather than communicative memory, but they lack what the long, long poem is invested in: a register of the future. There is no neat opposite of "memory" that would allow for the easy adaptation of Assmann's concepts for future-oriented thinking, and Eliot's "Memory and Desire"[21] from *The Waste Land* is not quite enough; perhaps Ernst Bloch's notion of "hope" comes closest as an equivalent. Different from the common use of the term, this hope is not merely a kind of wishful thinking or optimism. "The work of this emotion requires people who throw themselves actively into what is becoming, to which they themselves belong,"[22] so that such hope denotes an interdependence between present and future that maintains the openness of both, and the future is not just something to come but rather something the subject is actively involved in generating. Fusing Bloch's concept with Assmann's, we could argue that long, long poems address collective hope rather than communicative hope, in the sense that they do not merely imagine a future of contemporaries but a future that exceeds this limit, while nevertheless insisting that it is their future with a connection to their present. One could adapt Matthew Carbery's suggestion that long poems work through "acts of extension" by saying that the long, long poem is a particular kind of such an act of reaching from the present into the future.[23]

Most recently, we have seen such a temporal expansion toward the noncontemporary future in environmentalist discourses, in poetry or otherwise, as our self-inflicted ecological predicament demands that we rethink Western temporality as a framework for social justice, ethical agency, and concrete policy. On the one hand, the next generations within the five-generation model have provided a very strong rhetorical trope, perhaps best exemplified by the phrase "we do not inherit the earth from our ancestors; we borrow it from our children"[24]; this trope, however, also reinforces a heteronormative valorization of "the child" as an imaginary entity that can be mobilized for all sorts of political goals.[25] On the other hand, ecological thought also pointed out that the realities created by human "progress" demand an imagination of the future that massively exceeds these limits, as, for example, the plutonium we produce in our nuclear power plants has a half-life of 24,100 years (whereas fossil fuels probably will not last us much longer than the two generations we usually imagine and care about). Philosophers such as Hans Jonas, in *The Imperative of Responsibility* (1979), have addressed this concept of futurity, summarized in the double dictum: "'Do not compromise the conditions for an indefinite continuation of humanity on earth'; or, again turned positive: 'In your present choices, include the future wholeness of Man among the objects of your will.'"[26] Since this future is indefinite, we may well ask how far into the future we can and may think to assess the morality of our choices in the present, and there is no reason to assume any particular cutoff point to this future-oriented ethics. This requires a radically different conception of society and democracy, as it includes those who are not born yet among those who, to adopt Karl Marx's phrase, cannot represent themselves and thus must be represented.[27] Notably, these future generations can only be imagined, and this makes literature and other modes of artistic representation not just privileged sites for their conception but really the only sites where they gain some form of existence, and definitely the sites where we can and need to practice imagining what we did not bother to imagine before. In poetic terms, it was Allen Ginsberg who engaged with this imagination of futurity most extensively from an ecological perspective, not only in such prominent poems as his "Plutonian Ode" (1978),[28] but really in a profoundly environmentalist body of work that is still too often neglected for the sake of his much briefer Beat period.

Whitman speaks to such an environmentalist focus to some extent, but mainly because he provides the poetic model for the necessary temporal scope this imagination needs, and not because he would in any way have anticipated the ecological necessity of imagining such extended futures. His poetry surely speaks of a deep-ecological sense of equality not only between humans and nonhuman beings but between the animate and the inanimate world itself, and his romantic take on nature lends itself to ecocritical readings.[29] Given that it is informed by a nineteenth-century belief in plenitude, which was particularly prominent in the United States, rather than our contemporary notions of scarcity, I do not want to focus on this particular environmentalist aspect but wish to indicate more broadly how Whitman's long, long poetry exceeds the five-generation model, and how this temporal imagination of noncontemporary futures is conveyed by poetic means, whatever purpose it is then put to.

I will discuss the most prominent aesthetic strategies of doing that in reference to a few select poems instead of Whitman's whole oeuvre. These poems are genuinely exemplary in that they are the most prominent instances of more abstract modes that characterize numerous other poems as well, although not necessarily with any overlap between those modes in the same poems. This choice is just based on preference and not on necessity or argument; it would be no less relevant to consider Whitman's poetry as a whole and consider it more broadly in quantitative terms. Its various editions make *Leaves of Grass* a unique example of McHale's "lifelong poems,"[30] and it is a long poem in itself that started out with a first edition in 1855 where the twelve poems did not have individual titles but were all headed "Leaves of Grass." Yet for the argumentative purposes of this chapter, it seems best to concentrate on the most salient examples of Whitman's long, long poems without concern for how *Leaves of Grass* changed across its editions, and so I will discuss what I consider to be the two major aspects of his poetry that transcend the five-generation model of the contemporary and expand from the present to the future.

This has the added benefit that I can actually focus on a long poem to discuss the long, long poem; or rather, I can draw on *the* American long poem, "Song of Myself" (1855), to show how it is also a model for the long, long poem (and I will use the 1855 version as it is the most radical in its formal openness, even though it is probably the deathbed edition of 1892 that defined "Whitman" for the modernists and even later writers of long poetry). My reading will begin with a focus on the poem's imagination of a vast temporal scope across past, present, and future, and then move to a particular consideration of how the future is not just alluded to or represented but actually addressed in the form of the concrete reader, and how Whitman employs a distinctly deictic mode to achieve this cross-generational conflation to make his poetry not timeless but always timely in any possible future in which it is being read. I will supplement this argument with references to the shorter poems "Crossing Brooklyn Ferry" (1856) and "So Long!" (1860) as significant examples or varieties of this deictic mode, now using the deathbed edition.

"SONG OF MYSELF" AND THE AMPLITUDE OF TIME

It seems redundant to point out that this will be a selective reading even within "Song of Myself," as the poem is notoriously abundant; after all, it is basically about everything. I hope my selection represents the more general underlying theme of a temporal imagination that transcends the contemporary and that could be illustrated in reference to far more examples than I can include here. The first significant instance of the poem's massive temporal scope is actually prepared for by contrast, as "Song of Myself" opens in a way that highlights the local, immediate experience of the present, and it seems like "the song of me rising from bed and meeting the sun."[31] Yet this line is immediately followed by questions of scale: "Have you reckoned a thousand acres much? Have you reckoned the earth much?," and the distinctly spatial imagery turns temporal just a few lines later: "You shall possess the good of the earth and sun . . . there are millions of suns left."[32] This is a reference to temporal plenitude, as it does not state that there are millions of suns but that they are left, and this indicates an imagination of futurity that exceeds not just the framework of the contemporary but also that of the human. At this point this may still seem poetic hyperbole, a casual metaphor, but it is modified and repeated and becomes part of a more profound imagination of longevity and futurity in which large numbers are decisive and not offhand at all. In his essay on

"Whitman's Engagement with Large Numbers," Ed Folsom not only shows how Whitman introduced the names for large numbers into poetic discourse, but also how these large numbers "allowed Whitman to articulate a very early version of what, in the second half of the twentieth century, came to be called 'deep time' and 'deep space,' concepts necessitated by the vast geological and astronomical expansions of the limits of human perception and conception that have opened the realms of the posthuman."[33] Notably, this is universal deep time, not the anthropological deep time that Wai Chee Dimock used to trace *American Literature across Deep Time*, as the title of her 2006 study has it. Dimock's deep time is a strong imagination of what transcends the contemporary, and yet it is historical in the sense that it only relates to the human and to documents of the past qua human history; Whitman's deep time, in contrast, leaves the human framework behind as easily as that of the contemporary, and not just in the direction of the past but also that of the future.

We can trace this imagination as we read through the poem, and it includes minor references as much as fully developed sections that coexist with much more immediate senses of past, present, and future. There are microscopic lines about "how we lay in June, such a transparent summer morning,"[34] just like there are also numerous references to contemporary generations, procreation, and parenthood; yet there are also macroscopic expansions of the past that go far beyond any personal experience, involvement, or memory, all related to that fundamental ontological "puzzle of puzzles, / [...] that we call Being"[35]:

> Before I was born out of my mother generations guided me,
> My embryo has never been torpid.... nothing could overlay it;
> For it the nebula cohered to an orb.... the long slow strata piled to rest it on.... vast vegetables gave it sustenance,
> Monstrous sauroids transported it in their mouths and deposited it with care.
>
> All forces have been steadily employed to complete and delight me,
> Now I stand on this spot with my soul.[36]

Note that even this immense time span leads up to the present moment, so that "Song of Myself" is not so much a meditation on the insignificance of human lives but rather an expression of wonder at their accidental constitution, which means that individual lives are significant precisely because the odds are overwhelmingly stacked against them. Whitman's philosophy of compost—"All goes onward and outward. . . . and nothing collapses, / And to die is different from what any one supposed, and luckier"[37]—is based not so much on a notion of continuous progress toward some goal but endless transformation, and this imagination requires a sense of "limitless time"[38]: "We have thus far exhausted trillions of winters and summers; / There are trillions ahead, and trillions ahead of them."[39] This is why the speaker is fundamentally patient: "And whether I come to my own today or in ten thousand or ten million years, / I can cheerfully take it now, or with equal cheerfulness I can wait."[40] In this system of "perpetual transfers and promotions,"[41] every human is "just as immortal and fathomless as myself,"[42] although their individual selves will vanish in the immense reconfiguration of atoms across deep time. Nevertheless, it is precisely this immense scope that makes "this minute that comes to me over the past decillions,"[43] the present moment with all its complex configurations in which the self is embedded, all the more astonishing, and it is worth noting that the poem mainly operates in the present tense despite its extension into past and future. This dialectic of the present moment within an infinity of past and future is best captured in the following paradoxical image that violates all spatial rules to make a temporal point:

> My feet strike an apex of the apices of the stairs,
> On every step bunches of ages, and larger bunches between the steps,
> All below duly traveled—and still I mount and mount.[44]

Yet this is not just a long, long poem because it really includes "the amplitude of time" of "a few quadrillions of eras,"[45] and in a way such references would be quite shallow without a second aspect: Whitman's conflation of present and future, so that this long, long poem is not just about the future in an abstract sense, but really about our present as the future of the poem. In other words, this temporality folds two presents onto each other, and it ensures that we see our present moment of reading as an extension of the present moment of enunciation in the poem. This has a variety of effects: For one, it diminishes the pastness of the past by making the poem a presence in the present, and the speaker is not addressing future generations from their historical perspective but insists on their copresence, their contemporaneity. Whitman's poetry does not aim to be timeless but is always timely, and it achieves this through a unique incorporation of the reader in two major ways.

The first of these is that the present of the reader is deliberately constructed not only as the future of the speaker but as a future constructed by the speaker, so that we cannot but understand our present in relation to this past. At the same time, the speaker ensures that readers cannot merely consider this as historical precedent on a linear time line, since the speaker's present connects not just to our present but also to our future. This can be read as a positive gesture of transtemporal connection and continuity, even of equality across time; it can also be read as a gesture of dominance and inescapability, especially when Whitman seems to posit himself as the one-man avant-garde from which all future poetic production springs:

> Eleves I salute you,
> I see the approach of your numberless gangs. . . . I see you understand
>   yourselves and me,
> And know that they who have eyes are divine, and the blind and lame
>   are equally divine,
> And that my steps drag behind yours yet go before them,
> And are aware how I am with you no more than I am with everybody.[46]

As with the curious image of an apex among apices, the speaker here both follows and leads his "eleves," historically preceding them but already preparing not only them but also what is ahead of them; in lines such as these, Whitman ensures that any future we imagine or inhabit will be a Whitmanian future. Notably, this includes even any future that seeks to disconnect itself from such a past, and he includes a nice temporal catch-22 to ensure that he will always remain a presence in any present:

> I am the teacher of athletes,
> He that by me spreads a wider breast than my own proves the width
>   of my own,
> He most honors my style who learns under it to destroy the teacher.
>
> . . . .

> I teach straying from me, yet who can stray from me?
> I follow you whoever you are from the present hour;
> My words itch at your ears till you understand them.[47]

This inescapability—which is vaguely threatening in tone—is reinforced in the final lines of "Song of Myself," which pretend to be the speaker's farewell but actually insist on his future presence:

> Failing to fetch me at first keep encouraged,
> Missing me one place search another,
> I stop some where waiting for you[48]

We are searching for this speaker not in our past but in our present, and he is always already waiting for us, ahead of us, part of a future we have yet to move into; this long, long poem ensures it will never be dated or invalidated, never historical, never an object of the past, but always an object of our present and, even more importantly, of any of our futures.

LINGUISTIC AND MATERIAL DEIXIS

The second major way in which this perpetual timeliness and continuity is ensured is built into these motifs of preparation and connection across time, but it is mainly a linguistic device and not a function of content. Whitman uses this device in "Song of Myself," but he uses it even more prominently and effectively in "Crossing Brooklyn Ferry" and "So Long!,"[49] which are all long, long poems in their own right because of it. This device is deixis, or pragmatic referential language whose meanings are determined entirely by context and use, so that deictic terms are both highly specific and highly general at the same time: "now," "here," "I," and, most importantly for Whitman, "you." It is this particular deictic address that makes his poems unavoidably timely, as it ensures that the future present they address from their own present must necessarily be the present of the reader in the process of reading. In other words, because that "you" can refer to any reader in the future but always refers to an actual, concrete reader in their present, the poems ensure that this present and the present of the speaker are and must be folded onto each other. Whitman communicates "the similitudes of the past and those of the future" by assuring "I am with you, you men and women of a generation, or ever so many generations hence,"[50] and he ensures that they must think of their present as his future, and a future he prepared in his present: "What thought you have of me now, I had as much of you—I laid in my stores in advance, / I consider'd long and seriously of you before you were born."[51] This direct address of any particular "you" makes the long, long poem theoretically open to any future reading but practically recognizes the specificity of any reading in the present. Similarly, the "you" in "Song of Myself" that is first mentioned in the second line and actually concludes the poem as its final word achieves precisely this effect with its "shifting referent"[52]: This is not a lazy poetic trope of addressing "the reader" but really addressing *the* reader, and this achieves the desired temporal conflation. Kerry C. Larson's observation about "Crossing Brooklyn Ferry"—probably the long, long poem that is the fullest and most consistent example of Whitman's deictic method—applies to "Song of Myself" as well: "The addressee is hardly an implied reader, but neither is he an utterly accessible presence."[53]

There is one more aspect about this deictic poetics of conflating present and future that cannot be found in "Song of Myself" or "Crossing Brooklyn Ferry," but which is so important for a more rounded consideration of the Whitmanian long, long poem that it needs to be mentioned at least briefly in conclusion. This is best exemplified by "So Long!" among a number of other poems, which all use what could be called material, medial, or haptic deixis: Instead of using the personal pronoun "you" to keep the poem both general and highly specific with regard to any future reading, these poems use the material quality of the book to establish that the reader's present is the future of the poem's present. These references presuppose the material presence of the book as much as "Song of Myself" and "Crossing Brooklyn Ferry" presuppose the material presence of the reader. Of course, the latter are never wrong in this presupposition, as the absence of any reader also means they are not being read; references based on the bookishness[54] of *Leaves of Grass*, however, are actually lost once the text is read in a different medium and deprived of what makes it medium-specific poetry. "Crossing Brooklyn Ferry" still works even though there is no more Brooklyn ferry, and it does not even need one for its transtemporal imaginary work; "So Long!," however, needs that book, and it ceases to be a long, long poem as soon as the decisive material link between book text and reader is changed and thus broken.

In "So Long!," this link is created by the book object itself, and this is again tied to a transtemporal extension where two presents meet, this time in loving, tender caresses:

> My songs cease, I abandon them,
> From behind the screen where I hid I advance personally solely to you.
>
> Camerado, this is no book,
> Who touches this touches a man,
> (Is it night? are we here together alone?)
> It is I you hold and who holds you,
> I spring from the pages into your arms—decease calls me forth.
>
> O how your fingers drowse me,
> Your breath falls around me like dew, your pulse lulls the tympans of my ears,
> I feel immerged from head to foot,
> Delicious, enough.[55]

The speaker here not only points out the materiality of the book medium and thus points to the here and now of the reader, but he even attempts to break through any mediality itself by saying that what the reader is touching at this very moment of reading is not a book but a man. The deictic "this" denotes the concrete book but mainly means its author, and the material presence of the book is supposed to evoke his presence as it denies its material existence as a book. This is no longer just about reading a text but about touching an artifact, and the book and not just writing or text becomes the connecting element that establishes presence and presents.

Whitman uses this tactile image in several poems, and it combines with referential deixis most concisely in "Whoever You Are Holding Me Now in Hand" (1860),[56] whose title perfectly captures the oscillation between vague meaning and precise reference mentioned above. All these poems emphasize that this touch is mutual, connecting two presents as such with each other instead of simply presenting one present as the future of another. Touch is the only sense that allows for this mutual quality: Seeing and being seen, hearing and being heard all imply a separation of subject and object, while touching and being touched are one and the same. Thus only these haptic metaphors genuinely allow Whitman to construct the simultaneity of two presents in his long, long poetry. For example, Whitman insists on this duality in a single line in "A Song for Occupations" (1855), which ascribes to the book the quality of a touchable body: "When I can touch the body of books by night or by day, and when they touch my body back again."[57] The programmatic poem "Small the Theme of My Chant" (1867) includes a similar image: "(O friend, whoe'er you are, at last arriving hither to commence, I feel through every leaf the pressure of your hand, which I return. / And thus upon our journey, footing the road, and more than once, and link'd together let us go)."[58] Remarkably, it is the reader who arrives in order to begin, as if the speaker had only been waiting for them; the reader is making these beginnings but also finds them prepared for them, so that the genuine beginning is once more that of the speaker. This common beginning is enabled by the haptic and material connection that makes present the different times of speaker and reader: The page of the book becomes a medium of touch, and at the same time the reader, in touching the page, is also touched by it (and by implication also by the speaker). Perhaps this inevitable duality is what makes this deictic strategy the most effective one of the Whitmanian long, long poem: It opens itself up toward any indeterminate future but still ensures that it remains a concrete object of any present and never just a historical artifact or an empty future-oriented gesture that fails to find an addressee.

CONCLUSION: LONG, LONG POETRY AFTER WHITMAN

I said above that this perspective on Whitman's poetry challenges rather than affirms it as a model for the canonical long poem, as it openly and thoroughly rejects the historical focus of the latter's representative works, and I would describe their often nostalgic tone as the direct opposite of Whitman's future-founding poetics. Whitman only rarely takes a historical approach, such as in "Song of the Exposition,"[59] and it never ends well, poetically; Jed Rasula uses this poem for his justified verdict that "Whitman's increasing use in later years of the antiquarian 'thee' (forfeiting his arduous struggle to shed himself earlier of such poetic affectations) completes his mummification as resident national poet in the pornotopia of American kitsch culture, that bulwark of hyperbolic anachronism."[60] So if Whitman cannot serve as a model for the dominant temporal mode of the long poem in modernism, what is the later long, long poetry he actually did influence?

Sticking with the form of the long poem, I would pick Muriel Rukeyser's *The Book of the Dead* (1938) as a prominent example, and it also generally attests to an alternative modernism beyond the male-dominated canon. It is more historical and documentary than Whitman's poetry, and it is more explicit in its political agenda, but it also includes deictic gestures that open this community of resistance to futures that are not immediate, creating a continuity beyond contemporary generations:

> and you young, you who finishing the poem
> wish new perfection and begin to make;
> you men of fact, measure our times again.[61]

Yet the long, long poem does not have to be long at all, and the most concise example of one may well be Langston Hughes's undated "Promised Land," which also draws attention to the tacit normativity involved in imagining futures and that this is not an activity everyone gets to participate in:

> The Promised Land
> Is always just ahead.
> You will not reach it
> Ere you're dead.
>
> But your children's children
> By their children will be led
> To a spot from which the Land—
> Still lies ahead.[62]

Here, the poem imagines a future beyond the five-generational model to make a statement about its present; it is a variation of Hughes's major motif of the "dream deferred," of the postponement of social change for the better, of the recurring promise made to African Americans that they will eventually gain civil rights and equality, a promise made not with the intention to fulfill it but for the purpose of maintaining the status quo. The poem cleverly uses the linear, temporal reading process and its deferral of meaning to comment on the deferral of fulfillment, and each line break in the second stanza renews the promise just to qualify and disappoint it in the next.

These are just two examples of long, long poetry among many, but they illustrate a point that did not become evident in Whitman's model: Imagining the future and connecting it to the present is as much a political act as it is an aesthetic one, and there is as much normative power in imagining a common, unified future as in imagining alternative futures. Whitman's sweeping, collective gesture of his speaker's notoriously all-inclusive self does empower the individual to set themselves in relation to distant futures, with all the responsibility that comes with that, and its macrocosmic view tends to gloss over microscopic differences in problematic ways (as much as "Song of Myself" also acknowledges them). Rukeyser and Hughes remind us that imagining individual and collective futures is not a given for every subject position, and while Whitman would surely agree that doing so is hard work for anyone, it is clearly even harder for some. This is the most general implication of the long, long poem as an aesthetic and political text: In drawing attention to how we position ourselves toward our futures, it also draws attention to the conditions of these positions in our present.

NOTES

1. Edgar Allan Poe, "The Philosophy of Composition," in *Literary Theory and Criticism*, ed. Leonard Cassuto (Mineola, NY: Dover Publications, 1999), 103.
2. Edgar Allan Poe, "Review of *Twice-Told Tales*, by Nathaniel Hawthorne," in *Literary Theory and Criticism*, ed. Leonard Cassuto (Mineola, NY: Dover Publications, 1999), 59.
3. Dick Allen suspects that Poe's "The Poetic Principle," with its similar argument against the desirability of long poetry in favor of a poetry of effect, has had a lasting impact on how shorter, lyric forms were privileged in American poetic criticism. See Dick Allen, "The Forest for the Trees: Preliminary Thoughts on Evaluating the Long Poem," in *New Expansive Poetry: Theory, Criticism, History*, ed. R. S. Gwynn (Ashland, OR: Story Line Press, 1999), 199–203. Vincent B. Sherry goes as far as claiming that Poe's "objection to the long poem as a contradiction in terms—excitement is the proper effect of poetry and all excitements are by nature short-lived—has been cut into the consciousness of American critics with the gravity and finality of a Roman inscription." Vincent B. Sherry Jr., "Current Critical Models of the Long Poem and David Jones's *The Anathemata*," *ELH* 52, no. 1 (1985): 239.

4. Susan Stanford Friedman, "When a 'Long' Poem Is a 'Big' Poem: Self-Authorizing Strategies in Women's Twentieth-Century 'Long Poems,'" in *Dwelling in Possibility: Women Poets and Critics on Poetry*, ed. Yopie Prins and Maeera Shreiber (Ithaca, NY: Cornell University Press, 1997), 15.
5. Friedman, "When a 'Long' Poem Is a 'Big' Poem," 16.
6. Margaret Dickie, *On the Modernist Long Poem* (Iowa City: University of Iowa Press, 1986), 6.
7. Brian McHale, *The Obligation toward the Difficult Whole: Postmodernist Long Poems* (Tuscaloosa: University of Alabama Press, 2004), 101. In this context, see also Nathan Brown's take on incompleteness as a structural necessity of long-form poetry in his contribution to this volume.
8. Walt Whitman, *Leaves of Grass*, 1891–92, in *Poetry and Prose*, ed. Justin Kaplan (New York City: Library of America, 1996), 643.
9. Smaro Kamboureli, *On the Edge of Genre: The Contemporary Canadian Long Poem* (Toronto: University of Toronto Press, 1991), 101.
10. Lynn Keller, *Forms of Expansion: Recent Long Poems by Women* (Chicago: University of Chicago Press, 1997), 1–22.
11. Keller, *Forms of Expansion*, 13.
12. Matthew Carbery, *Phenomenology and the Late Twentieth-Century American Long Poem* (Basingstoke: Palgrave Macmillan, 2019), 3. Keller instructively outlines the history of the critical tradition of describing Whitman's long poetry as the model American epic, referring to Roy Harvey Pearce's *The Continuity of Poetry* (1961) and James E. Miller's *The American Quest for a Supreme Fiction: Whitman's Legacy in the Personal Lyric* (1979) as particularly formative sources. The latter also indicates that Whitman's poetry was constructed just as much as the beginning of a *non-epic* tradition "at the other end of the critical spectrum," the lyric "poetic sequence" as discussed by M. L. Rosenthal and Sally M. Gall. Finally, Keller points out that Thomas Gardner in *Discovering Ourselves in Whitman: The Contemporary American Long Poem* (Champaign: University of Illinois Press, 1989) discusses Whitman as a model of the American long poem without any concern "with Whitman's impact on the genres of epic and lyric," suggesting that, whatever you do, Whitman is somehow already there: "I stop some where waiting for you." Keller, *Forms of Expansion*, 7, 9, 11; Whitman, *Leaves of Grass*, 1855, in *Poetry and Prose*, ed. Justin Kaplan (New York City: Library of America, 1996), 88. For a recent consideration of what he terms the "false dichotomy" between epic and lyric in the case

of Whitman, see Thomas C. Austenfeld, "Questions of Epic and Lyric: The Challenge of Walt Whitman," *IdeAs* 14 (2019): 2.
13. My chapter thus contributes to an ongoing revisionist project that has a prominent beginning in Rachel Blau DuPlessis's *The Pink Guitar: Writing as Feminist Practice* (London: Routledge, 1990) and includes the aforementioned Friedman, Keller, and Kamboureli, as well as, for example, Oliver Tearle's *The Great War, "The Waste Land," and the Modernist Long Poem* (London: Bloomsbury, 2019) on "other" long poems after World War I that were obscured by the impact of *The Waste Land*.
14. "Für die anderen Dichter des 'long poem' mit Ausnahme Whitmans bedeutet die Errichtung einer Kontinuität die Vorbereitung zur Sinnbestimmung der modernen menschlichen Situation mit Hilfe der Vergangenheit." Klaus Heinrich Köhring, *Die Formen des „long poem" in der modernen amerikanischen Literatur* (Heidelberg: Winter, 1967), 96 (my translation).
15. William Carlos Williams's *Paterson* is the notable exception here as the major modernist long poem whose future-oriented scope parallels that of Whitman's poetry, and it is a harsh response to the reactionary historicism of *The Waste Land*: "Who is it spoke of April? Some / insane engineer. There is no recurrence. / The past is dead." William Carlos Williams, *Paterson* (New York: New Directions, 1992), 142. Of course, such neglect or rejection of the past also merits critique in terms of a deliberate ahistoricity that R. W. B. Lewis famously described as Adamism in American culture, and which especially ties in with dominant nineteenth-century notions of manifest destiny, imperialism, and progress.
16. My thoughts on the long, long poem are based on my theorization of "future-founding poetry" in *Future-Founding Poetry: Topographies of Beginnings from Whitman to the Twenty-First Century* (Rochester, NY: Camden House, 2015), which elaborates on the Whitmanian model of an American poetry that makes and marks beginnings. That study does not consider the long poem in particular, although it includes a chapter on *Paterson*, and so this chapter serves as a complementary discussion developed from a more extensive and complex argument there.
17. Keller, *Forms of Expansion*, 21.
18. McHale, *The Obligation toward the Difficult Whole*, 103.
19. Jan Assmann, *Das kulturelle Gedächtnis: Schrift, Erinnerung und politische Identität in frühen Hochkulturen* (München: C. H. Beck, 1997), 50 (my translation).

20. Assmann, *Das kulturelle Gedächtnis*, 52 (my translation).
21. T. S. Eliot, "The Waste Land," in *The Complete Poems and Plays 1909–1950* (New York: Harcourt, Brace, 1962), 37.
22. Ernst Bloch, *The Principle of Hope*, trans. Neville Plaice, Stephen Plaice, and Paul Knight (Cambridge, MA: MIT Press, 1986), 3.
23. Carbery, *Phenomenology and the Late Twentieth-Century American Long Poem*, 6.
24. The website Quote Investigator traces this much-quoted and much-adapted phrase back to Wendell Berry's 1971 book *The Unforeseen Wilderness: An Essay on Kentucky's Red River Gorge*, which reads: "I am speaking of the life of a man who knows that the world is not given by his fathers, but borrowed from his children."
25. Lee Edelman offers a vitriolic critique of what he calls the "Ponzi scheme of reproductive futurism" in *No Future: Queer Theory and the Death Drive* (Durham, NC: Duke University Press, 2004), 4.
26. Hans Jonas, *The Imperative of Responsibility: In Search of an Ethics for the Technological Age* (Chicago: University of Chicago Press, 1984), 11.
27. Malte-Christian Gruber discusses this issue from a legal perspective in his essay "What Is It Like to Be Unborn? Our Common Fate with Future Generations," in *Efficiency, Sustainability, and Justice to Future Generations*, ed. Klaus Mathis (Berlin: Springer, 2011), 113–37. With regard to the literary topic at hand, this kind of thinking adds a crucial aspect to Peter Baker's take on the Levinasian ethics of exteriority and intersubjectivity with regard to the long poem; if such poetry "turns deliberately outward in order to address the experience of others," are these others contemporaries or are they yet unborn? Peter Baker, *Obdurate Brilliance: Exteriority and the Modern Long Poem* (Gainesville: University of Florida Press, 1991), 3. For a Levinasian reading of long-form poetry, see also Carbery's contribution to this volume.
28. Allen Ginsberg, "Plutonian Ode," in *Collected Poems 1947–1997* (New York: Harper Perennial, 2007), 710–13.
29. See, for example, Christine Gerhardt, *A Place for Humility: Whitman, Dickinson, and the Natural World* (Iowa City: Iowa University Press, 2014), M. Jimmie Killingsworth, *Walt Whitman and the Earth: A Study in Ecopoetics* (Iowa City: Iowa University Press, 2004), and Jed Rasula, *This Compost: Ecological Imperatives in American Poetry* (Athens: University of Georgia Press, 2002), respectively.
30. McHale, *The Obligation toward the Difficult Whole*, 101.

31. Whitman, 1855, 27.
32. Whitman, 1855, 28.
33. Ed Folsom, "Counting from One to a Million: Whitman's Engagement with Large Numbers," *Walt Whitman Quarterly Review* 34 (2016): 151.
34. Whitman, 1855, 30.
35. Whitman, 1855, 55.
36. Whitman, 1855, 80.
37. Whitman, 1855, 32.
38. Whitman, 1855, 82. The second law of thermodynamics and theories about the heat death of the universe were formulated at around the same time as *Leaves of Grass* was first published; regardless of anachronism, Whitman's philosophy of compost may well be described as antientropic.
39. Whitman, 1855, 79.
40. Whitman, 1855, 46.
41. Whitman, 1855, 86.
42. Whitman, 1855, 33.
43. Whitman, 1855, 49.
44. Whitman, 1855, 79.
45. Whitman, 1855, 46, 81.
46. Whitman, 1855, 71.
47. Whitman, 1855, 83.
48. Whitman, 1855, 88.
49. Walt Whitman, *Leaves of Grass*, 1891–92, in *Poetry and Prose*, ed. Justin Kaplan (New York City: Library of America, 1996), 307–13; Whitman, 1892, 609–12.
50. Whitman, 1892, 308.
51. Whitman, 1892, 311.
52. William Chapman Sharpe, *Unreal Cities: Urban Figuration in Wordsworth, Baudelaire, Whitman, Eliot, and Williams* (Baltimore: Johns Hopkins University Press, 1990), 93.
53. Kerry C. Larson, *Whitman's Drama of Consensus* (Chicago: University of Chicago Press, 1988), 8.
54. On the notion of bookishness, see Jessica Pressman, *Bookishness: Loving Books in a Digital Age* (New York: Columbia University Press, 2020).
55. Whitman, 1892, 611.
56. Whitman, 1892, 270–71.
57. Whitman, 1892, 362.
58. Whitman, 1892, 628.

59. Whitman, 1892, 341–50.
60. Rasula, *This Compost*, 56.
61. Muriel Rukeyser, *The Collected Poems of Muriel Rukeyser*, ed. Janet E. Kaufman and Anne F. Herzog (Pittsburgh: University of Pittsburgh Press, 2005), 109.
62. Langston Hughes, *The Collected Poems of Langston Hughes*, ed. Arnold Rampersad and David Roessel (New York: Vintage, 1994), 592.

BIBLIOGRAPHY

Allen, Dick. "The Forest for the Trees: Preliminary Thoughts on Evaluating the Long Poem." In *New Expansive Poetry: Theory, Criticism, History*, edited by R. S. Gwynn, 199–203. Ashland, OR: Story Line Press, 1999.
Assmann, Jan. *Das kulturelle Gedächtnis: Schrift, Erinnerung und politische Identität in frühen Hochkulturen*. München: C. H. Beck, 1997.
Austenfeld, Thomas C. "Questions of Epic and Lyric: The Challenge of Walt Whitman." *IdeAs* 14 (2019): 1–7.
Baker, Peter. *Obdurate Brilliance: Exteriority and the Modern Long Poem*. Gainesville: University of Florida Press, 1991.
Bloch, Ernst. *The Principle of Hope*. Translated by Neville Plaice, Stephen Plaice, and Paul Knight. Cambridge, MA: MIT Press, 1986.
Carbery, Matthew. *Phenomenology and the Late Twentieth-Century American Long Poem*. Basingstoke: Palgrave Macmillan, 2019.
Dickie, Margaret. *On the Modernist Long Poem*. Iowa City: University of Iowa Press, 1986.
DuPlessis, Rachel Blau. *The Pink Guitar: Writing as Feminist Practice*. London: Routledge, 1990.
Edelman, Lee. *No Future: Queer Theory and the Death Drive*. Durham, NC: Duke University Press, 2004.
Eliot, T. S. "The Waste Land." In *The Complete Poems and Plays 1909–1950*, 37–55. New York: Harcourt, Brace, 1962.
Folsom, Ed. "Counting from One to a Million: Whitman's Engagement with Large Numbers." *Walt Whitman Quarterly Review* 34 (2016): 146–68.
Friedman, Susan Stanford. "When a 'Long' Poem Is a 'Big' Poem: Self-Authorizing Strategies in Women's Twentieth-Century 'Long Poems.'" In *Dwelling in Possibility: Women Poets and Critics on Poetry*, edited by Yopie Prins and Maeera Shreiber, 13–37. Ithaca, NY: Cornell University Press, 1997.

Gerhardt, Christine. *A Place for Humility: Whitman, Dickinson, and the Natural World*. Iowa City: Iowa University Press, 2014.

Ginsberg, Allen. "Plutonian Ode." In *Collected Poems 1947–1997*, 710–13. New York: Harper Perennial, 2007.

Gruber, Malte-Christian. "What Is It Like to Be Unborn? Our Common Fate with Future Generations." In *Efficiency, Sustainability, and Justice to Future Generations*, edited by Klaus Mathis, 113–37. Berlin: Springer, 2011.

Hughes, Langston. *The Collected Poems of Langston Hughes*. Edited by Arnold Rampersad and David Roessel. New York: Vintage, 1994.

Jonas, Hans. *The Imperative of Responsibility: In Search of an Ethics for the Technological Age*. Chicago: University of Chicago Press, 1984.

Kamboureli, Smaro. *On the Edge of Genre: The Contemporary Canadian Long Poem*. Toronto: University of Toronto Press, 1991.

Keller, Lynn. *Forms of Expansion: Recent Long Poems by Women*. Chicago: University of Chicago Press, 1997.

Killingsworth, M. Jimmie. *Walt Whitman and the Earth: A Study in Ecopoetics*. Iowa City: Iowa University Press, 2004.

Köhring, Klaus Heinrich. *Die Formen des „long poem" in der modernen amerikanischen Literatur*. Heidelberg: Winter, 1967.

Larson, Kerry C. *Whitman's Drama of Consensus*. Chicago: University of Chicago Press, 1988.

McHale, Brian. *The Obligation toward the Difficult Whole: Postmodernist Long Poems*. Tuscaloosa: University of Alabama Press, 2004.

Miller, James E. *The American Quest for a Supreme Fiction: Whitman's Legacy in the Personal Lyric*. Chicago: University of Chicago Press, 1979.

Pearce, Roy Harvey. *The Continuity of American Poetry*. Princeton, NJ: Princeton University Press, 1961.

Poe, Edgar Allan. "The Philosophy of Composition." In *Literary Theory and Criticism*, edited by Leonard Cassuto, 100–110. Mineola, NY: Dover Publications, 1999.

Poe, Edgar Allan. "Review of *Twice-Told Tales*, by Nathaniel Hawthorne." In *Literary Theory and Criticism*, edited by Leonard Cassuto, 57–63. Mineola, NY: Dover Publications, 1999.

Pöhlmann, Sascha. *Future-Founding Poetry: Topographies of Beginnings from Whitman to the Twenty-First Century*. Rochester, NY: Camden House, 2015.

Pressman, Jessica. *Bookishness: Loving Books in a Digital Age*. New York: Columbia University Press, 2020.
Rasula, Jed. *This Compost: Ecological Imperatives in American Poetry*. Athens: University of Georgia Press, 2002.
Rosenthal, M. L., and Sally M. Gall. *The Modern Poetic Sequence: The Genius of Modern Poetry*. Oxford: Oxford University Press, 1983.
Rukeyser, Muriel. *The Collected Poems of Muriel Rukeyser*. Edited by Janet E. Kaufman and Anne F. Herzog. Pittsburgh: University of Pittsburgh Press, 2005.
Sharpe, William Chapman. *Unreal Cities: Urban Figuration in Wordsworth, Baudelaire, Whitman, Eliot, and Williams*. Baltimore: Johns Hopkins University Press, 1990.
Sherry, Vincent B. Jr. "Current Critical Models of the Long Poem and David Jones's *The Anathemata*." *ELH* 52, no. 1 (1985): 239–55.
Tearle, Oliver. *The Great War, "The Waste Land," and the Modernist Long Poem*. London: Bloomsbury, 2019.
Whitman, Walt. *Leaves of Grass*. 1855. In *Poetry and Prose*, edited by Justin Kaplan, 5–145. New York: Library of America, 1996.
Whitman, Walt. *Leaves of Grass*. 1891–92. In *Poetry and Prose*, edited by Justin Kaplan, 147–672. New York: Library of America, 1996.
Williams, William Carlos. *Paterson*. New York: New Directions, 1992.

Rethinking the North American Long Poem

Contributors

Ridvan Askin is a senior teaching and research fellow in North American and general literature at the University of Basel and a senior SNSF researcher at the University of Geneva, Switzerland. He is the author of *Narrative and Becoming* (Edinburgh University Press, 2016) and the coeditor of several collections of essays, including, most recently, *New Directions in Philosophy and Literature* (Edinburgh University Press, 2019) and *The Aesthetics, Poetics, and Rhetoric of Soccer* (Routledge, 2018). He is currently completing his second book entitled *Transcendental Poetics and the Futures of American Romanticism*.

Nathan Brown is a professor of English and the Canada research chair in poetics at Concordia University, Montreal, where he directs the Centre for Expanded Poetics. He is the author of *Baudelaire's Shadow: An Essay on Poetic Determination* (MaMa, 2021), *Rationalist Empiricism: A Theory of Speculative Critique* (Fordham University Press, 2021), and *The Limits of Fabrication: Materials Science, Materialist Poetics* (Fordham University Press, 2017). His translation of Charles Baudelaire's *The Flowers of Evil* has just been published in a new edition by Verso (2024).

Matthew Carbery is a writer and independent researcher from Plymouth, UK. His book, *Phenomenology and the Late Twentieth-Century American Long Poem*, was published by Palgrave Macmillan in 2019. His research focuses on phenomenology, poetry, and politics.

Rachel Blau DuPlessis is a poet, scholar/critic, and collagist whose work includes the long poem *Drafts* (1986–2012), forthcoming from Coffee House Press in 2025. Her recent books are *Selected Poems 1980–2020* from CHAX Press (2022), *A Long Essay on the Long Poem* from the University of Alabama Press (2023), and a sociopoetic response to 2020, *Daykeeping* (Selva Oscura, 2023). In her career as a poet-critic, she has written extensively on gender, poetry, and both feminist and objectivist poetics.

Julius Greve is a postdoctoral research associate at the Institute for English and American Studies, University of Oldenburg, Germany. He is the author of *Shreds of Matter: Cormac McCarthy and the Concept of Nature* (Dartmouth College Press, 2018), and of numerous essays on contemporary American fiction and poetry, media studies, and critical theory. Recent work as a coeditor includes *The American Weird: Concept and Medium* (Bloomsbury, 2020) and "Poetic Voice and Materiality" (a cluster of *ASAP/J*, 2023). Currently he is working on a monograph that delineates the relation between modern poetics and ventriloquism.

Paul Jaussen is an associate professor of literature and the chair of the Department of Humanities, Social Sciences, and Communication at Lawrence Technological University in Southfield, Michigan. He is the author of *Writing in Real Time: Emergent Poetics from Whitman to the Digital* (Cambridge University Press, 2017) and, with Mary Balkun and Jeffrey Gray, an editor of *A Companion to American Poetry* (Wiley-Blackwell, 2022). His essays and reviews have appeared in *New Literary History*, *Comparative Literature*, *Contemporary Literature*, *Chicago Review*, and *ASAP/J*, among others. He is currently finishing a second book, tentatively titled *The Art of Breaking Worlds: On Contemporary Poetry and Public Language*.

Brian J. McAllister is an associate professor of English at the American University of Sharjah in the United Arab Emirates. His publications include studies on geological time in landscape poetry, visual poetry and narrative theory, inscription in postmodern art, the rhetoric of emergence in narrative, rhetoric and topography, disorienting narrative space, and science-fiction poetry. McAllister was the guest editor of a special issue of *Narrative* on poetry and narrative theory.

Peter Middleton is a professor emeritus at the University of Southampton and the author of several books including *Physics Envy: American Poetry and Science in the Cold War and After* (University of Chicago Press, 2015) and *Expanding Authorship: Transformations in American Poetry since 1950* (University of New Mexico Press, 2021). He is currently writing books on the genealogy of the concept of code and on neurodivergence in science fiction.

Josephine Nock-Hee Park is the School of Arts and Sciences President's Distinguished Professor of English at the University of Pennsylvania. She is the author of *Apparitions of Asia: Modernist Form and Asian American Poetics* (Oxford University Press, 2008) and *Cold War Friendships: Korea, Vietnam, and Asian American Literature* (Oxford University Press, 2016), as well as *Theresa Hak Kyung Cha in Black and White* (Cambridge Elements, 2023). She is the coeditor of *Ezra Pound in the Present: Essays on Pound's Contemporaneity* (Bloomsbury, 2016), with Paul Stasi, and *Asian American Literature in Transition, 1930–1965* (Cambridge University Press, 2021), with Victor Bascara.

Sascha Pöhlmann is a professor of American literature and culture at TU Dortmund University. He is the author of the monographs *Pynchon's Postnational Imagination* (2010), *Future-Founding Poetry: Topographies of Beginnings from Whitman to the Twenty-First Century* (2015), *Stadt und Straße: Anfangsorte in der amerikanischen Literatur* (2018), and *Vote with a Bullet: Assassination in American Fiction* (2021). He has edited and coedited essay collections on Thomas Pynchon, Mark Z. Danielewski, Percival Everett, foundational places in/of modernity, electoral cultures, American music, unpopular culture, video games, secrecy, and flyover fictions.

Kathy Lou Schultz is a professor of English at the University of Memphis. She is the author of the scholarly studies *Introduction to Claudia Rankine* (Lake Forest College Press, 2023) and *The Afro-Modernist Epic and Literary History: Tolson, Hughes, Baraka* (Palgrave, 2013), as well as four collections of poems. Her scholarship has been published in a wide variety of venues, including *Paideuma: Modern and Contemporary Poetry and Poetics*, *Journal of Modern Literature*, and *Contemporary Literature*. Recent creative works appear in *Bombay Gin*, *Marsh Hawk Review*, *Miracle Monocle*, *P Queue Literary Journal*, and *Touch the Donkey*.

Index

actors, 111–13
aesthetics, 8–9, 21–22, 25n32, 26n33, 109–11; *aesthesis*, 8–9
affect, 13, 22, 150–51, 154, 160
affordances, 10, 52, 64, 73, 109, 121
agency, 108, 110–14, 119, 123–24; agents, 69, 111–13
album, 40, 42, 45, 51–52; music, 109, 119, 154
alterity, 80–82, 96–100, 153
ambience, 16, 108–11, 114, 121, 124n5
analogy, 131, 134–35, 139–41, 143–44
apology, 203, 207–10
archive, 44, 113, 117–18, 131, 134, 151, 154–55, 185, 204
art, 9–10, 25n32, 26n33, 111, 164; criticism, 82–83, 85
assemblage, 39–48, 51–52, 54n23, 108, 110–11, 134, 172n37
attunement, 90–91, 107–8, 112–13, 121, 123
avant-garde, 13, 17, 125n31, 164, 211, 242. See also poetics

Bacigalupo, Massimo, 182–86, 188–89
Baker, Peter, 81, 99, 251n27
Baumgarten, Alexander Gottlieb, 9–10, 26n33
becoming, 7, 10, 12–13, 61, 75
Bennett, Jane, 108, 110–11
Brathwaite, Kamau, 40, 42, 47, 50–52, 54n22; *Ancestors*, 47, 50–51, 54n19; *ConVERSations*, 47, 50–51, 54n19

Carbery, Matthew, 12, 19, 237, 251n27
Caribbean, 49–51
Cecire, Natalia, 17, 21–22, 31n97
Celan, Paul, 152–53
Charlottesville, 184, 187
cognition, 9, 68, 111
collage, 43, 64, 156–57, 168
contingency, 45, 61–63, 65–66, 68, 71–73, 88–89, 91–92, 96, 131, 133–36, 139, 141, 143–44
creation, 6, 10, 13, 15, 19, 23, 83, 100, 109, 113, 131, 143
Cvetkovich, Ann, 154–55, 160

Dante, 39, 41–42, 190, 192–93, 218–19, 222, 227n57
death, 59, 61–62, 67, 69, 70, 74–75, 149, 155, 158; Black, 48, 165–66. See also finitude
deixis, 91, 99, 239, 243–47
Deleuze, Gilles, 1–3, 19, 22, 27n50, 164
dialectics, 2, 5, 64–65, 89, 116–17, 241
documentary, 150–52, 154, 157, 160, 163, 169–70
documentation, 121, 155
documents, 44, 49, 154–55, 203–4, 208–9, 215, 221–22, 240
DuPlessis, Rachel Blau, 3, 7, 12, 80, 156, 172n37; *Drafts*, 2, 60–61, 145n1, 157, 201
Dworkin, Craig, 4, 114, 116

ecology, 107–8, 110, 122, 203, 237–38; deep ecology, 238

[263]

Eliot, T. S., 3, 13, 15–18, 21, 28n66, 219; *The Waste Land*, 4, 14, 80, 95, 219, 236, 250n13, 250n15
emergence, 10–11, 13, 19, 108–9, 111, 113, 118–23, 124n5
Eno, Brian, 16, 109, 120, 124n7
environmentalism, 213–15, 237–38
epic, 3–6, 12, 39, 59, 62–63, 156–57, 181, 193–95, 249n12; Afro-Modernist, 157
epigenesis, 10–11
experience, 10, 18–22, 29n77, 62, 66, 68, 87, 89, 91, 94, 100, 130–31, 149, 151–53, 155, 160–62, 239–40; lived, 19, 30n85, 83, 134. *See also* life
experiment, 7, 16–23, 27n50, 29n77, 29n83, 89, 221; experimental literature, 6, 17–23, 28n71, 29n83, 30n90, 30n92, 31n97, 156–57; experimentation, 4, 7, 11, 17–23, 26n38, 27n50, 29n83
extension, 19–20, 39, 47, 53n5, 70–72, 74, 80–81, 83–84, 89–90, 98–99, 123, 151, 154, 158, 202, 205, 235, 237, 241, 245
exteriority, 69–70, 73–75, 81, 131, 251n27

fascism, 44, 182–84
film theory, 154, 159, 163–64
finitude, 5–6, 57, 61–62, 67–68, 70. *See also* death
form, 4, 6–14, 16, 21–22, 25n31, 52, 61–65, 70, 73, 75, 90, 96, 99, 108–9, 112–13, 116–19, 121–24, 130–31, 156, 167, 169–70, 211, 214, 216, 222. *See also* formalism; morphogenesis

formalism, 8–10, 156, 211, 214. *See also* form
fragment, 48–49, 58–59, 61–65, 67–68, 70–73, 75, 107, 116–18, 121–23
Friedman, Susan Stanford, 3, 15, 156, 233
future-founding poetry, 246, 250n16

gender, 4, 7, 15, 146n40; male domination, 233, 235, 247; masculinism, 3–4, 16, 62
genre, 2, 4, 6–7, 12, 16, 22, 39–42, 47, 63–64, 150–51, 169, 201, 233–35; book as genre term, 41–52; polysemy, 12, 39
Gesamtkunstwerk, 41–43, 45, 47–52, 54n23, 172n37
Gigante, Denise, 10–12, 19, 27n50
Grubbs, David, 16, 108, 119–21; *Frolic Architecture*, 120–21; *Souls of the Labadie Tract*, 120–21

H.D., 4, 15–16; *The Walls Do Not Fall*, 4; *Trilogy*, 4, 15
Hägler, Andreas, 17–19, 30n92
Harvey, David, 116–17
Hayles, N. Katherine, 108, 111–12
Heidegger, Martin, 67–69, 75, 80, 82, 86
Houen, Alex, 184–85, 187, 193
HOW(ever), 156, 223n2
Howe, Susan, 16, 107–8, 113–23, 125n31, 127n49; *Frolic Architecture*, 120–21; *Souls of the Labadie Tract*, 107–8, 113–15, 117–21; *Spontaneous Particulars*, 113, 122
Hughes, Langston, 40, 157, 247–48
Hui, Yuk, 131, 143

incompleteness, 1, 3, 5, 7, 12, 14, 45, 58–61, 70, 73, 75, 172–73n37, 249n7
infinity, 3–5, 80–81, 241. *See also* finitude; totality
internet, 21, 201–6, 209, 211–13, 215–16, 221, 224n14, 226n36
iteration, 130, 142, 212

Jaussen, Paul, 10–12, 16, 19, 123, 127n61

Kasper, John, 185–90, 192–94
Keller, Lynn, 4, 27n54, 156, 172n30, 234, 249n12
Kim-Cohen, Seth, 108, 110–11
Kindellan, Michael, 182, 188

language poets, 13, 17, 22
length, 2, 6–7, 12–13, 21–22, 52, 84, 157, 232–34
Levinas, Emmanuel, 80–82, 92, 96–100, 251n27
Levine, Caroline, 7–10, 12
life, 5–7, 70–72, 79, 82–88, 90–91, 93, 95–96, 149–50, 160, 163, 164, 170; literature and, 1, 3, 20, 22. *See also* experience
Long Soldier, Layli, 21, 201, 203–4, 207–11, 213, 222; "Whereas," 201, 203–5, 207–10
lyric, 3–6, 57, 62, 85, 167, 218, 249n12; sequence, 5–6, 156; speaker, 57, 63; subject, 151, 167

Mackey, Nathaniel, 42, 45–47, 54n19, 61, 158; *Double Trio*, 45–47; *School of Udhra*, 46; *Song of the Andoumboulou*, 45, 61, 158
Mallarmé, Stéphane, 41–43, 45, 47
Marsh, Alec, 185–90, 192–95
Martinelli, Sherri, 188–93, 195
Marx, Karl, 116, 237
matter, 2–3, 7, 13–16; material, 7–9, 13–17, 21–22, 29n73, 42, 44, 48, 120, 130, 132, 139, 146n24, 160, 168, 204, 214, 216, 221; materiality, 13–17, 20, 47, 108, 110–11, 113–15, 119, 121, 123, 137, 245
McHale, Brian, 17, 22, 116, 118, 121, 125n31, 127n59, 233, 236, 238
media, 16, 20, 22, 52, 150, 152, 154, 163, 168, 170, 203, 206, 212, 222; mediality, 16, 20, 245; social, 202, 204–6, 212, 215, 222
Merleau-Ponty, Maurice, 86, 89, 90, 92, 96, 98
modernism, 13, 15, 17, 27n59, 30n85, 59, 62–65, 235, 246–47; modernists, 4, 14, 17, 156, 235, 239
morphogenesis, 6, 10, 11, 15. *See also* form
Morton, Timothy, 108–11, 124, 124n5, 223n1
Mussolini, Benito, 44, 185, 191
myth, 45, 71–72, 143, 210, 228n67; mythography, 5, 15, 51; mythology, 2, 219

Nancy, Jean-Luc, 68–69, 75, 76n23
narrative, 4, 6, 10, 12, 40, 45, 52, 62–63, 107, 109, 118, 131, 141, 143, 216, 219, 220, 222
novel, 14, 26n38, 27n54, 63

Olson, Charles, 18, 58–75, 82, 136; *The Maximus Poems*, 58–65, 68, 136
Oppen, George, 39, 40, 60, 82
otherness. *See* alterity

parataxis, 17, 40, 94, 98, 114, 135, 150–51, 158, 169–70
perception, 8–9, 20, 25n30, 79, 85–86, 88–91, 97, 99–100, 169; apperception, 67–68
petitionary culture, 205–6, 213, 215, 224n13
phenomenology, 80–82, 89, 100
Philip, M. NourbeSe, 42, 47–49, 53n14, 54n22; *Zong!*, 14, 47–49, 53n14, 54n15
photographs, 151, 154–55, 159, 161, 164–70
Poe, Edgar Allan, 12–13, 27n56, 232, 234–35, 248n3
poem scripts, 152, 158–60, 162, 164
poetics, 3–4, 10–12, 14, 16, 19, 41–43, 45, 50–52, 54n19, 81–82, 84–86, 92, 98, 114, 124, 182, 191, 211, 216, 232–34, 244, 246; ambient, 16, 108–9, 122; avant-garde, 202–3; erasure, 204, 209, 221; materialist, 17–18. *See also* avant-garde
poiesis, 7, 11, 13, 27n50
polymorphous prolificity, 10–13, 21–22, 27n50
Pound, Ezra, 3, 5, 13, 16, 21, 27n59, 42–45, 59–60, 62, 65, 132, 135, 181–96; and the far right, 53n4, 181, 183, 185, 187, 193–94; *The Cantos*, 5, 14, 43–45, 59–60, 62–64, 181–96
process, 6–7, 9–13, 18–20, 61–62, 79, 83–84, 86, 89, 92–93, 100, 108, 113, 116–17, 121, 123, 130, 136, 204–6, 229n73, 233, 243, 247
project, 12–13, 16, 43, 46, 50, 52, 58–59, 61–65, 67–70, 72–73, 75, 82, 95, 117–19, 123, 149–50, 152–53, 155, 157–58, 164
prose, 6, 51, 114, 131, 150, 221, 232; poetry, 6, 21, 24n18, 213, 215–16
proximity, 73, 83, 92, 96–100, 221

racism, 15, 149, 162, 164, 166, 183, 185–86, 193–94
Rankine, Claudia, 4, 15–16, 149–71, 201, 210; *Citizen*, 4, 15, 149–52, 158–62, 165, 167, 169–70, 201, 210; *Don't Let Me Be Lonely*, 149–51, 153–55, 158, 162, 168, 170; *Just Us*, 168–70, 175n93
Rankine, Claudia and John Lucas, 152, 154, 157–60, 165–66, 168; "Situation" video poems, 152, 158–59; "Situation One," 159, 172n43; "Situation 5," 160, 162
Rasula, Jed, 63–64, 246
recursion, 130–32, 134–35, 137, 139–44
Reddy, Srikanth, 203–4, 209, 213, 215–22, 227n57, 228n67; *Voyager*, 203–4, 215–18, 220
Redman, Tim, 184, 194
rhetoric, 48, 54n14, 57, 108–9, 112–16, 119–21, 123–24, 142, 208–10, 215; ambient, 108, 113, 117, 123
Rickert, Thomas, 108, 112, 124, 124n5
romanticism, 10–12, 24n18, 25n30, 26n40, 59, 63–65, 67–68, 75, 76n23

Rukeyser, Muriel, 14, 150–51, 154, 156, 169–70, 195–96, 247–48; *The Book of the Dead*, 14, 150–51, 156, 170, 247; "Then I Saw What the Calling Was," 196

Schlegel, Friedrich, 63–65, 68
Schuyler, James, 12, 79–100; "A Few Days," 93–94; "Empathy and New Year," 97; "February," 79, 84–86; "Hymn to Life," 83–84, 87–91, 94–96; "The Morning of the Poem," 88, 98–99
segregation, 161, 169, 182, 185–87, 192
Shklovsky, Viktor, 9–10, 20
space: deep, 240; digital, 202; diegetic, 160; geographical, 122; institutional, 188; of existence, 72–73; page, 7, 18, 42, 47–52, 114; poetic, 134; semiotic, 139; social, 40; verbal, 220
Spahr, Juliana, 21, 203–4, 211, 213–15, 222; *That Winter the Wolf Came*, 203–4, 211–15
St. Elizabeths, 181, 183, 185, 188–89, 195
Stein, Gertrude, 6, 15, 17, 24n18, 134–35, 211
Stephens, Paul, 17–18
subjectivity, 45, 68, 81, 84–93, 96–100, 118, 139, 151–52, 159–61, 167, 218–19, 222; intersubjectivity, 79–81, 89, 96–100, 118, 222, 251n27

teleology, 39, 41–42
time, 7, 11, 71–73, 82, 84, 89, 92–94, 123, 130, 153, 232–33, 236, 243; deep, 240–42; temporality, 2, 7, 68, 73, 82, 91–93, 232–33, 237, 241
totality, 3, 12, 68, 80–81, 87, 96, 108, 116. *See also* infinity
touch, 153, 245–46
Twitter, 205–6, 215, 222

utopia, 30n92, 113–19

verse, 2, 14, 214; free, 2, 64, 66, 72–73, 75, 157; projective, 13, 66–67

Waldheim, Kurt, 204–5, 216–22, 227n48
Whitman, Walt, 2–3, 13, 16, 40, 42, 47, 157, 194, 209, 234–36, 238–48, 249n12, 250n16; *Leaves of Grass*, 2, 5, 13, 40, 238, 244; "Crossing Brooklyn Ferry," 243–44; "So Long!," 243–45; "Song of Myself," 13, 239–44, 248
Williams, William Carlos, 18, 59, 122, 131–44, 146n24, 218, 250n15; *Paterson*, 59, 122, 127n61, 131–44, 146n40, 250n15, 250n16

Zukofsky, Louis, 13, 40, 42–43, 60; *"A,"* 14, 42–43, 60

www.ingramcontent.com/pod-product-compliance
Lightning Source LLC
Chambersburg PA
CBHW020944230426
43666CB00005B/156